STOCK MARKET WINNERS

WHAT WORKS AND WHY

How to implement your own stock-picking strategy by looking at the proven techniques of investment "winners" ...

Maria Crawford Scott

Editor, AAII Journal

John Bajkowski

AAII Vice President, Financial Analysis
Editor, Computerized Investing

AAII

AMERICAN
ASSOCIATION OF
INDIVIDUAL
INVESTORS®

"The American Association of Individual Investors is an independent, not-for-profit corporation formed in 1978 for the purpose of assisting individuals in becoming effective managers of their own assets through programs of education, information, and research."

Chapter 6: It's Quality That Counts:

Chapter 7: The Peter Lynch Approach to Investing in "Understandable" Stocks . 91

Chapter 8: Diversifying Among Investing Styles:

INTRODUCTION

What are the winning stock market strategies and how can they be implemented? Those are the bottom-line questions every individual investor asks.

This book is designed to answer those questions. It provides a complete guide to the winning strategies and techniques of the investment legends and current-day investment professionals with proven records of long-term success. And it shows how these approaches can be translated into a series of practical rules or screens that individual investors can use as a starting point for building winning stock portfolios.

The Stock Market Winners we picked cover the full range of the investment spectrum, from the pure value players to the growth-only advocates and technology specialists, from those who focus on the smaller firms to those that stick with the large blue chips, and from relatively mechanical approaches to those that rely more on qualitative judgments. It includes such investment legends as Benjamin Graham, T. Rowe Price and Philip Fisher, as well as current-day legends such as Peter Lynch, Warren Buffett and David Dreman.

The chapters on the individual Stock Market Winners are divided into two parts. The first section provides a comprehensive discussion of each winning strategist's approach: their investment philosophy and universe of stocks; their primary criteria for selecting stocks; their secondary and conditioning criteria to narrow their lists of prospective stocks; their methods for valuing stocks; their rules for portfolio-building and monitoring; and their guidelines for when to sell. These sections are based on original works—books or articles written by each winning strategist—with the exception of Warren Buffett, who has not published any comprehensive materials concerning his method. The source for Buffett's approach is the book "Buffettology" by Mary Buffett and David Clark (for a complete list of reference sources, see page 201).

The second section of the individual winning strategist chapters describes how a series of specific screens can be used to generate a list of stocks that can serve as a starting point for implementing the strategy. In this section, we discuss many of the practical issues investors may face when trying to use stock screens as part of an investment strategy. To illustrate the process, we developed a series of primary screens to capture the major elements of each investment approach. For the screens, we used stock data and screening software from our own *Stock Investor Professional,* AAII's fundamental stock screening and data program [updates of these screens using current data, as well as current performance statistics are available from the AAII Web site at www.aaii.com]. However, the screens are generic, and can be used with other investment software [AAII's *Computerized Investing* publication provides reviews, comparisons and information on investment software and Web-based screening systems on a regular basis]. It should be emphasized that the screens are our own interpretations of the investment approaches advocated by these winning investment strategists. And, while we have attempted to illustrate a practical set of rules for each approach, the screens are only the first step—they will generate an initial list of potential investments, each of which merits further fundamental analysis and qualitative research before a final investment decision can be reached.

The last two chapters compare and contrast all of the investment approaches. Chapter 13 summarizes their individual investment characteristics, explaining the risk and return features of each, and how they would likely react under various market conditions. Chapter 14 discusses common traits among the approaches, such as the favored fundamental and technical criteria, and it outlines the factors that are critical for any investment approach to be successful over the long term.

The glossary at the end of the book defines the investment terms used throughout the book and in the stock screen tables.

Stock Market Winners: What Works and Why may not turn you into an investment legend. But learning from the legends can put you well on the way toward developing your own winning investment strategy.

Maria Crawford Scott
Editor, *AAII Journal*

John Bajkowski
AAII Vice President, Financial Analysis, & Editor, *Computerized Investing*

VALUE INVESTING: A LOOK AT THE BENJAMIN GRAHAM APPROACH

Value investing is an approach that is widely used today by individual investors and portfolio managers. But the approach was originally formulated some 60 years ago with the publishing of Graham and Dodd's college textbook "Security Analysis," and popularized in Benjamin Graham's book, "The Intelligent Investor." Benjamin Graham is properly credited as one of the "fathers" of value investing.

Graham's approach focuses on the concept of an intrinsic value that is justified by a firm's assets, earnings, dividends, and financial strength. Focusing on this value, he felt, would prevent an investor from being misled by the misjudgments often made by the market during periods of deep pessimism or euphoria.

Why Value Stocks: The Philosophy

Graham felt that it would be difficult for investors to "beat the market," that is, to find stocks that will do much better than the overall long-term market average. Stocks that will do better than average over the long term are those with greater growth, but the difficulty is finding those in advance.

The problem for investors, he reasoned, is twofold. First, even stocks with obvious growth prospects don't necessarily translate into extra profits for an investor because those prospects are incorporated into the price of the stock.

Second, there is the risk that the investor will be wrong about the firm's growth prospects. Graham felt that this risk is accentuated by the psychology of the stock market, where the "tides of pessimism and euphoria which sweep the market" could mislead investors into overvaluing or undervaluing a stock.

In short, over the long term most investors can only expect an average return, but there is the added risk of underperformance due to misjudgment.

Instead of seeking a way to produce above-average returns, Graham proposed a method to reduce the risk of misjudgment. He suggested that investors first determine an "intrinsic" value for a stock that is independent of the market. Graham never fully explained how to determine "intrinsic" value and admitted that it requires considerable investment judgment. However, he felt that a firm's tangible assets were a particularly important component; other factors included earnings, dividends, financial strength, and stability. Graham felt investors should limit their purchases to stocks selling not far above this value, while stocks selling below their intrinsic value would offer an even better margin of safety to investors.

Graham felt investors should view themselves as the owners of a business, with the goal of buying a sound and expanding business at a rational price, regardless of what the stock market might say. And a successful investment, he said, is a result of the dividends produced and the long-range trend of the average market value of the stock.

Types of Investors

Graham felt that individual investors fell into two camps: "defensive" investors and "aggressive" or "enterprising" investors. These two groups are distinguished not by the amount of risk they are willing to take, but rather by the amount of "intelligent effort" they are "willing and able to bring to bear on the task." Thus, for instance, he included in the defensive investor category professionals (his example—a doctor) unable to devote much time to the process and young investors (his example—a sharp young executive interested in finance) who are as-yet unfamiliar and inexperienced with investing.

Graham felt that the defensive investor should confine his holdings to the shares of important companies with a long record of profitable operations and that are in strong financial condition. By "important," he meant one of substantial size and with a leading position in the industry, ranking among the first quarter or first third in size within its industry group.

Aggressive investors, Graham felt, could expand their universe substantially, but purchases should be attractively priced as established by intelligent analysis. He also suggested that aggressive investors avoid new issues.

Value Stock Criteria for Defensive Investors

Graham suggested that conservative investors buy issues selling at prices that are reasonably close to their per share tangible asset (book) value (total assets excluding intangible assets such as goodwill and patents, less all liabilities), and no more than one-third above that figure. He cautioned, however, that this criterion alone does not indicate a sound investment. In addition, the company should be in a sufficiently strong financial position, with the prospect that its earnings will at least be maintained over the years, and its stock must be selling at a satisfactory ratio of earnings to price.

In "The Intelligent Investor," Graham laid out a specific set of rules for defensive investors:

- **Adequate size:** Exclude small companies with less than $100 million of annual sales for industrial companies and $50 million of total sales for public utilities. These levels were specified in 1972, over 25 years ago. Obviously, firms have grown; assuming a modest (around 5%) annual growth rate, these levels would roughly translate into sales today of $340 million for industrial companies and sales of $170 million for public utilities.
- **Strong financial condition:** For industrial companies, current assets (cash, accounts

receivable and inventory) should be at least twice current liabilities (short-term debt), and long-term debt should not exceed the net current assets (working capital, or current assets less current liabilities); for public utilities the debt should not exceed twice the stockholder's equity (total assets less total liabilities).

- **Earnings stability:** Positive earnings for at least the last 10 years.
- **Strong dividend record:** Uninterrupted dividend payments for at least the past 20 years.
- **Earnings growth:** Minimum increase of at least one-third in earnings per share in the past 10 years (a 2.9% average annual growth rate over 10 years).
- **Moderate price-to-earnings ratio:** The current price should not be more than 15 times average earnings for the past three years. His goal is a portfolio with an average price-earnings ratio that is reasonable compared to the inverse of the high-grade corporate bond yield. At the time the cut-off price-earnings ratio of 15 was stated, high-grade corporates yielded 7.5%, with an inverse of 13.3. However, cut-off price-earnings ratios should be adjusted based on prevailing interest rates; when rates go up, investors should require lower price-earnings ratios and when rates are lower, investors can accept higher price-earnings ratios as cut-offs.
- **Moderate price-to-book-value ratio:** The current price should not be more than 1½ times the last reported book value. Graham noted that a price-earnings ratio below the target level could justify a higher price-to-book-value ratio. As a rule of thumb, he proposed that the product of the two should not exceed 1½ times the cut-off price-earnings ratio. For instance, if the target price-earnings is 15, an issue selling at 2.25 times book value could be justified if it were selling at 10 times earnings (15 × 1.5 = 22.5; 10 × 2.25 = 22.5).

At the time he was writing, Graham viewed utilities as particularly attractive for defensive investors, which is why the criteria includes adjustments specifically for utilities. Graham felt these firms fulfilled his criteria well and were selling at particularly attractive prices at the time.

Graham certainly intended to skew a defensive investor's portfolio away from "growth" stocks, which he viewed as more likely to be overvalued and risky, and in today's environment, Graham's criteria will continue to exclude these kinds of firms. Investors should be aware of this tendency when employing this approach. In addition, because of the emphasis on book value, which excludes intangibles, the criteria will tend to exclude firms that have considerable assets in the form of goodwill, patents, software, franchises, etc., such as firms that are service-oriented, and those that are in the computer and technology sectors, areas of the market that have become much larger and more important than in Graham's day.

Enterprising Investors
Graham used the criteria for defensive investors as a base for "enterprising" investors to consider, but proposed that they could relax some of the rules. Among his suggested

possibilities:

- **Size:** Select from a wider universe of stocks.
- **Financial condition:** Current assets should be at least 1½ times current liabilities, and debt should not be more than 110% of net current assets for industrial firms.
- **Dividend record:** Some level of dividend payments.
- **Price-earnings ratio:** Among the lowest 10% of all stocks.
- **Price-to-book-value ratio:** The price should be less than 120% of net tangible assets.

He also suggested that the criteria be more flexible, allowing positive attributes in one rule (for instance, large average earnings) to compensate for small negatives (such as negative earnings in a bad environment) in another. Nonetheless, these criteria, like those for the defensive investor, will tend to exclude industries with large intangible assets.

Graham proposed several fertile areas for enterprising investors to investigate. One area was to look among large unpopular companies, indicated by a low price relative to current earnings. While small companies may also be undervalued, Graham felt that there was a much greater risk that they would not be able to sustain themselves through a period of adversity. In addition, he thought the market's neglect of these firms resulted in slow recognition of better earnings, extending the period of unpopularity. Graham did warn against being fooled by low price-earnings ratios among cyclicals in their good years, since the market recognizes that those high earnings will not be sustained. To avoid this, he suggested an additional requirement that the price be low in relation to past average earnings.

The second area Graham suggested was to look for "bargains," particularly among secondary stocks. Graham defined a "bargain" as a stock that is selling for 50% or less than its "indicated" value. The indicated value can be gleaned either by estimating future earnings or by valuing it as a private business, which includes a judgment concerning future earnings, but in addition pays attention to the value of realizable assets, with particular emphasis on working capital less all debt. The most obvious bargain, according to Graham, was one selling for less than its net working capital (current assets minus current liabilities) alone—in essence, the investor would be purchasing a company without paying for its plants and machinery, or any intangibles.

Of course, it is necessary for investors to distinguish between undervalued stocks and those that are properly selling at low prices relative to value. For that reason, Graham suggested that aggressive investors also look for reasonable stability of earnings over the past decade, with no years of negative earnings, and enough financial size and strength that would allow the firm to survive any future setbacks.

Graham thought enterprising investors could also find success investing in secondary companies if purchased as bargains. A secondary company is defined by Graham as one that is a smaller concern in an important industry, or a top firm in an unimportant industry; many mid-sized listed companies, Graham noted, would fit this definition.

Putting a Value on a Stock

How do you value a stock? That, of course, is the heart of any stock analysis.

Based on his observations of stocks over the years, Benjamin Graham developed one model that uses an earnings multiplier. This approach is to be distinguished from his notion of "intrinsic" value and simply provides another check on valuations:

$$\text{Value} = [EPS(8.5 + 2g)]\ \frac{4.4}{AAA}$$

where g is the expected annual earnings growth rate for the next seven to 10 years, EPS is the earnings per share for the most recent 12 months, AAA is the current interest rate on AAA-rated corporate bonds, and $(8.5 + 2g)$ is the earnings multiplier.

Graham's original formulation was based on AAA corporate bond interest rates prevailing at the time, about 4.4%. The formula above adjusts for current interest rates by dividing 4.4 by the current bond yield.

Clearly the expected annual growth rate over the next seven to 10 years is critical. Historical rates provide a starting point, although they may not be indicative of future rates. But using the proper historical rate requires considerable investment judgment.

As an example, assume the earnings growth rate for Company A is 7.8% over the past 10 years, and it has current earnings per share of $3.14. Also assume that the current AAA corporate bond rate is 7.6%. The equation would produce a value of:

$$\$3.14\ [8.5 + 2\ (7.8)]\ \frac{4.4}{7.6} = \$43.81$$

That value would then be compared to the stock's current price.

The Graham approach was developed for the average stock with average risk, and it does not adjust for stocks with greater than average risk. As risk increases, earnings multipliers should decline. Yet investors are often overly optimistic, assuming future earnings growth that cannot be maintained over the long run. If you are using the model, make sure you are conservative in your estimate of future earnings growth to reduce the tendency to estimate unrealistically high values. Here are some conservative guidelines:

- Very few firms can achieve a growth rate in earnings greater than 20% per year over long periods of time. In 10 years, a firm with a 20% annual earnings growth rate would have over a five-fold increase in earnings.
- Using an earnings growth rate that is higher than the firm's historical growth during normal circumstances may lead to an insupportably high valuation. Unless the firm is capable of selling new products, finding new customers, producing old products at reduced costs while maintaining or raising prices or some combination of these elements, future growth is unlikely to be higher than past growth.
- When unusually high growth rates are produced, they usually result from firms in fields of rapidly developing technology, new firms that started out with very small earnings per share figures or firms that had abnormally low earnings at some point in their history and the earnings growth rate was calculated from that low point.
- Without detailed knowledge of the firm, the industry the firm operates in and how the changing economic environment will influence the earnings of the industry and the firm, a rational, useful forecast of earnings is unlikely to be made.

In general, Graham felt the stock market tends to undervalue these firms. At the same time, he believed these firms were large enough to sustain themselves through various economic environments, with the ability to earn a fair return on invested capital; investors would thus profit both from earnings paid in dividends and those that were reinvested. And in bull markets, he noted, the price of these firms often advances to full valuation.

Secondary Factors

Clearly, any investor needs some understanding of business and economic conditions and will form some opinion concerning the prospects of a firm or industry. But Graham was distrustful of subjective factors and felt that they could mislead investors as much as help them. Thus, he preferred basing decisions on quantitative, rather than qualitative, factors.

He noted in his book that an investor's "operations for profit should be based not on optimism but on arithmetic."

Stock Monitoring and When to Sell

Graham was a strong believer in defensive investing and protecting a portfolio against errors in judgment. For that reason, he placed a heavy emphasis on diversification. He recommended that individuals purchase a minimum of 10 different issues and a maximum of 30.

Stock holdings should be reviewed at least annually, he said, paying attention to dividend returns and the operating results of the company, and ignoring share price fluctuations. However, if the holdings were properly valued originally, he felt there would be little need for changes.

Graham felt that as long as the earnings power of the holdings remained satisfactory, the investor should stick with the stock and ignore any market movements, particularly on the downside. On the other hand, investors should take advantage of market fluctuations on the upside, when a stock becomes overvalued (or fairly valued for stocks that were purchased at below their intrinsic value); at these times, investors should sell and replace their holding with one that is more fairly valued or undervalued.

Graham in Summary

Graham's emphasis on tangible assets may need modifications for current use in light of the many companies whose lines of business depend heavily on intangibles. But his concern with value relative to price maintains its relevance.

Graham summarized his own philosophy by stating that intelligent investing consists of analyzing potential purchases according to sound business principles. This includes: an understanding of what you are doing, making your own decisions, ensuring that you are not risking a substantial portion of your original investment, and sticking to your own judgments without regard to market opinion.

"You are neither right nor wrong because the crowd disagrees with you," he said. "You are right because your data and reasoning are right. In the world of securities, courage becomes the supreme virtue after adequate knowledge and a tested judgment are at hand."

The Benjamin Graham Approach in Brief

Philosophy and style

Investment in companies whose share prices are near their intrinsic value based on tangible assets, earnings, dividends, financial strength and stability, and quality of management. Buying at or below intrinsic value provides a margin of "protection" that can help absorb unfavorable developments, with subsequently less risk of a market overreaction on the downside.

Universe of stocks

For "defensive" investors: High-grade dividend-paying common stocks of leading companies; utilities viewed as particularly fertile ground. For "enterprising" investors: no restrictions; stocks of unpopular large companies and secondary companies (ones that are not leaders in a fairly important industry) considered particularly promising.

Criteria for initial consideration

- Exclude small companies with less than $100 million of annual sales for industrial companies and $50 million of total sales for public utilities in 1972 dollars. In today's market, this would roughly translate into sales of $340 million for industrial companies and total sales of $170 million for public utilities.
- Strong financial condition—for industrial companies, current assets (cash, accounts receivable and inventory) should be at least twice current liabilities (short-term debt) and long-term debt should not exceed the net current assets

(working capital, or current assets less current liabilities); for public utilities the debt should not exceed twice the stockholder's equity (total assets less total liabilities). For "enterprising" investors, he relaxed some of this criteria: current assets should be at least 1½ times current liabilities, and debt should not be more than 110% of net current assets.
- Positive earnings for at least the last 10 years.
- Uninterrupted dividend payments for at least the past 20 years; for "enterprising" investors, some current dividend.
- Minimum increase of at least one-third in per share earnings in the past 10 years (a 2.9% average annual growth rate).
- Current price should not be much more than 13.33 times average earnings for the past three years when high-grade corporates yield 7.5% (1 ÷ 0.75 = 13.33). However, adjust the price-earnings ratio based on current high-grade corporate yields, with the goal of having a portfolio average price-earnings ratio that is reasonable compared to the inverse of current yields:

$$\text{Cut-off P/E} = \left[\frac{1}{CY} \right]$$

where CY is the current yield on high-grade corporates in decimal form.
- Current price should not be more than 1½ times book value last reported, but price-earnings ratio below the cut-off level could justify higher multiplier of assets. [Rule of thumb: the product of the stock's multiplier times its price-to-book-value

(cont'd on next page)

The Benjamin Graham Approach in Brief *(cont'd)*

ratio should not exceed 1½ times the cut-off multiplier determined in the previous rule.] For "enterprising" investors, he suggested trying to find firms selling at two-thirds or less of book value.

Secondary factors
Skeptical as to accuracy of subjective judgments concerning growth prospects and management; good management indicated by a good long-term track record.

In terms of financial strength, surplus cash and no outstanding issues ahead of the common stock is preferable to firms with large bank loans and senior securities, but modest amount of bonds or preferred stock is not necessarily a disadvantage, nor is moderate use of seasonal bank credit.

Stock monitoring and when to sell
Emphasized diversification—minimum of 10 different issues and maximum of 30.

Buy and hold for the long term and try to ignore market vagaries.

Review holdings at least annually in light of intrinsic value and if no shrinkage, continue to hold. Sell if issues rise "excessively" above their intrinsic value and can be replaced by issues much more reasonably priced.

Earnings Growth

Graham recommends a minimum increase of at least one-third in per share earnings in the past 10 years, which translates into about a 3% annual growth rate—a rate that roughly keeps pace with inflation over the long term. Without such a criterion, a screen looking for companies with low price-earnings ratios may list companies with poor prospects. While Graham feels that even companies in a state of "retrogression" could be of interest if purchased at a low enough price, this is not the domain of the defensive investor. Our screen specified a seven-year annual growth rate in earnings greater than 3%. When used as a single screening criterion, this requirement turns out to be one of the more restrictive filters for both market groups—less than half of the companies passed.

Moderate Price-Earnings Ratio

Graham expresses frustration with the impact of special charges on the earnings per share calculation in corporate financial statements. He feels that management's discretion in establishing reserve accounts makes it difficult for the investor to determine whether earnings per share truly reflect the operation of the firm for a specific time period. To help circumvent this problem and smooth the impact of the business cycle, Graham often averages earnings over a period of several years. When defining the price-earnings screen, Graham requires that the price relative to average earnings over the last three years be no more than 15, with the goal of producing a stock portfolio with an average price-earnings ratio of 12 to 13. Graham's ultimate goal is to establish a portfolio that is priced reasonably compared to the yield available for AA bonds. At the time he wrote the book, investment-grade bonds were yielding 7.5%. The inverse of this yield, 1 divided by 0.075 = 13.3, determines the overall portfolio price-earnings ratio objective. However, long-term high-grade corporate bond yields were at 7.0% at the time of our screen, so the price-earnings cut-off was raised. When bond yields go up, an investor should require a lower price-earnings ratio to consider a stock purchase. Conversely, lower bond yields mean that an investor could accept a higher price-earnings cut-off, which makes more stocks available for consideration. The inverse of the current yield is 14.3 (1 divided by 0.07), a point higher than the original screen. Therefore in our screen the original cut-off of 15 is boosted by one point to 16.

Moderate Ratio of Price to Assets

Graham is a believer in using low price-to-book-value ratios to select stocks and normally requires a ratio below 1.5 for the defensive investor. However, he also feels that a low price-earnings ratio could justify a higher price-to-book-value ratio. Therefore, he recommends that investors multiply the price-earnings ratio by the price-to-book value ratio and not let

Graham Defensive Investor, Non-Utilities
Screening Criteria
Definitions for screens and terms can be found in the glossary starting on page 191.

Screening Criteria:
- Exclude: Utility sector
- Sales (last 12 months) greater than or equal to $340 million
- Current ratio (latest fiscal quarter) greater than or equal to 2.0
- Long-term debt relative to working capital (latest fiscal quarter) less than 100%*
- Long-term debt relative to working capital (latest fiscal quarter) greater than 0%*
- EPS for last 12 months and each of the last 7 fiscal years greater than $0*
- 7-year EPS growth rate greater than 3%
- Indicated dividend greater than $0
- Dividends for last 12 months and for each of the last 7 fiscal years greater than $0*
- P/E (using 3-year average EPS) less than or equal to 16
- P/E times price/book less than or equal to 24*

*Data not shown in table. Also note that the table shows additional data columns that may be of interest to those using this approach.

the resulting value exceed the product of the current price-earnings ratio cut-off [16 in our screen] and a price-to-book value ratio of 1.5. For our non-utility segment this screen, a figure of less than 24 (16 × 1.5), turned out to be the most restrictive individual criterion.

Results for the Defensive Investor

The stocks passing our screens based on a Benjamin Graham approach are presented in Tables 1 (non-utilities) and 2 (utilities), and are based on data as of February 25, 2000. Screening tips for using this approach on your own are at the end of the chapter.

SCREENING: THE ENTERPRISING INVESTOR

Graham has a number of recommendations for how the enterprising investor can hope to profit in the market. His procedure for developing a list of candidates among the secondary issues is of particular interest to the investor using a screening program. Graham believed secondary issues are areas of interest for the aggressive investor with the time to carefully study the market and buy these securities at a significant discount.

Table 1.
Graham Defensive Investor, Non-Utilities Screening Results*

Company (Exch: Ticker)	P/E (x)	P/E (3-yr Avg EPS) (x)	5-yr Avg P/E (x)	Sales Last 12 mos. ($ mil)	Curr Ratio (x)	LT Debt/ Equity (%)	5-yr EPS Grth Rate (%)	Div Yield (%)	5-yr Avg Div Yield (%)	P/Bk (x)	5-yr Avg P/Bk (x)
Oxford Industries, Inc. (N: OXM)	5.5	6.0	25.2	836.9	2.4	26.1	7.2	5.2	3.4	0.80	1.49
Standard Register Company (N: SR)	7.0	6.3	13.9	1,367.0	4.0	36.8	7.4	6.3	2.9	0.70	1.73
Coachmen Industries (N: COA)	6.0	6.4	13.1	817.0	2.9	4.0	17.3	1.8	0.9	0.83	2.18
A.M. Castle & Co. (A: CAS)	19.0	7.2	12.2	721.1	2.6	109.5	20.9	6.6	2.9	1.15	2.35
Cooper Tire & Rubber Co. (N: CTB)	6.0	7.2	15.3	1,994.7	3.0	21.6	6.1	3.9	1.4	0.86	2.39
Hughes Supply, Inc. (N: HUG)	6.3	7.4	12.2	2,873.2	3.0	103.3	20.1	2.0	1.0	0.78	1.55
Tidewater, Inc. (N: TDW)	13.2	7.9	21.0	632.1	5.6	0.0	47.4	2.3	1.6	1.31	2.68
Standex Int'l Corp. (N: SXI)	6.7	8.2	13.9	633.7	2.9	86.6	6.3	5.0	2.5	1.21	2.76
Tecumseh Products Co. (M: TECUA)	6.0	8.3	10.7	1,814.3	3.4	1.5	4.9	3.1	2.6	0.82	1.16
Bowne & Co., Inc. (N: BNE)	15.0	8.4	13.7	940.0	2.1	28.7	−6.4	2.0	1.4	1.03	1.61
Skyline Corporation (N: SKY)	8.7	8.9	12.6	644.2	3.8	0.0	15.9	3.5	2.3	0.95	1.38
A. Schulman, Inc. (M: SHLM)	8.8	9.1	15.9	1,004.6	3.2	21.4	4.9	4.1	2.0	1.16	1.99
Pitt–Des Moines, Inc. (A: PDM)	6.9	9.7	10.1	608.0	2.3	12.2	80.2	3.8	2.3	0.93	1.18
Noland Company (M: NOLD)	10.4	10.9	14.5	482.5	2.0	22.1	12.3	1.9	1.3	0.49	0.70
Kimball International (M: KBALB)	11.1	11.0	14.2	1,135.0	2.3	0.3	11.6	4.2	3.1	1.30	1.74
Genuine Parts Company (N: GPC)	10.3	11.5	16.8	7,707.9	3.1	31.6	7.5	5.1	3.0	1.82	3.10
Pier 1 Imports, Inc. (N: PIR)	11.2	11.9	25.9	1,183.0	3.0	19.8	63.6	1.5	0.9	1.76	2.66
Lubrizol Corporation (N: LZ)	11.2	12.2	14.8	1,747.9	2.5	46.2	−3.4	4.1	3.3	1.74	2.25
Watsco, Incorporated (N: WSO)	8.9	12.5	26.6	1,159.7	4.3	57.0	19.6	1.1	0.7	0.81	2.39
Superior Industries Int'l (N: SUP)	9.0	13.0	14.7	576.0	2.9	0.1	5.2	1.5	0.9	1.87	3.13
Thor Industries, Inc. (N: THO)	8.5	13.4	13.0	837.6	2.7	0.0	16.1	0.3	0.4	1.68	1.85
Park Electrochemical Corp (N: PKE)	11.3	13.5	15.7	418.5	3.8	55.7	6.7	1.4	1.1	1.34	2.06
Applied Industrial Tech. (N: APZ)	13.6	13.6	16.3	1,530.6	2.8	32.9	4.4	2.8	2.2	1.18	1.70
Carlisle Companies, Inc. (N: CSL)	10.3	13.8	17.9	1,597.5	2.1	60.7	25.0	2.3	1.5	2.05	3.14
Teleflex Inc. (N: TFX)	11.0	14.6	18.4	1,576.5	2.0	47.8	17.4	1.9	1.2	1.76	2.59

na = not available

Exchange Key: N = New York Stock Exchange
A = American Stock Exchange
M = Nasdaq

*Screening criteria used to produce table results can be found on opposite page.

Source: AAII's Stock Investor/Market Guide, Inc. Data as of February 25, 2000.

Graham Defensive Investor, Utilities
Screening Criteria
Definitions for screens and terms can be found in the glossary starting on page 191.

Screening Criteria:

- Utilities sector only
- Total assets (latest fiscal quarter) greater than or equal to $170 million*
- Long-term debt relative to equity (latest fiscal quarter) less than or equal to 200%
- EPS for last 12 months and for each of the last 7 fiscal years greater than $0*
- 7-year EPS growth rate greater than 3%
- Indicated dividend greater than $0
- Dividends for last 12 months and for each of the last 7 fiscal years greater than $0*
- P/E (using 3-year average EPS) less than or equal to 16
- P/E times price/book less than or equal to 24*

*Data not shown in table. Also note that the table shows additional data columns that may be of interest to those using this approach.

Low Price-Earnings Ratio

One of the keys to selecting secondary issues is to purchase them at a significant discount—Graham feels these stocks tend to trade below their intrinsic value. It is only during a bull market, when little distinction is made between primary and secondary issues, that the prices of these secondary issues approach or exceed their intrinsic value.

Graham's first screen for the enterprising investor is to look for companies trading with price-earnings ratios in the lower 10% of all stocks.

One warning that Graham gives of the low price-earnings screen concerns cyclical firms with widely fluctuating earnings. These firms often trade at high prices and low price-earnings ratios in good years when they should be sold and low prices and high or non-existent price-earnings ratios in bad years when they should be considered for purchase. For these firms, Graham recommends a test of low price relative to past average earnings as suggested for the defensive investor.

Financial Condition

For the enterprising investor, Graham relaxes his tests of the firm's financial position. For the current ratio (current assets divided by current liabilities), a minimum of 1.5 is specified, while long-term debt is not to be higher than 110% of net current assets.

Table 2.
Graham Defensive Investor, Utilities Screening Results*

Company (Exch: Ticker)	P/E (x)	P/E (3-yr Avg EPS) (x)	5-yr Avg P/E (x)	Sales Last 12 mos. ($ mil)	Curr Ratio (x)	LT Debt/ Equity (%)	5-yr EPS Grth Rate (%)	Div Yield (%)	5-yr Avg Div Yield (%)	P/Bk (x)	5-yr Avg P/Bk (x)
Sierra Pacific Resources (N: SRP)	9.4	7.7	13.7	1,080.8	0.4	109.5	−1.4	8.0	7.0	0.57	1.34
RGS Energy Group, Inc. (N: RGS)	8.8	8.2	12.1	1,169.2	0.9	93.3	3.0	9.5	7.3	0.90	1.24
Consolidated Edison, Inc. (N: ED)	8.3	8.8	12.4	7,219.2	0.9	78.4	2.7	8.3	5.8	1.04	1.51
OGE Energy Corp. (N: OGE)	9.1	10.1	13.9	1,956.3	0.5	101.9	8.1	7.5	5.9	1.33	1.90
NiSource, Inc. (N: NI)	12.3	10.2	15.3	3,013.4	0.5	135.0	6.8	6.9	4.0	1.43	2.38
FPL Group, Inc. (N: FPL)	9.0	10.3	15.0	6,550.0	0.7	57.7	10.9	5.9	3.8	1.18	1.90
SIGCORP, Inc. (N: SIG)	10.0	10.3	14.2	588.8	0.7	73.1	5.6	6.3	4.5	1.23	1.86
Peoples Energy Corp. (N: PGL)	9.9	10.8	13.9	1,296.6	0.9	66.7	4.1	7.3	5.6	1.25	1.67
SCANA Corporation (N: SCG)	13.8	11.5	15.5	1,616.0	0.6	83.8	2.7	9.6	5.4	1.29	1.73
Energen Corporation (N: EGN)	9.6	12.0	13.9	512.5	0.5	99.3	4.9	4.4	4.0	1.22	1.50
NICOR Inc. (N: GAS)	11.4	12.1	14.8	1,503.8	0.6	56.4	3.8	5.2	4.0	1.83	2.35
Northwest Natural Gas (M: NWNG)	11.4	12.2	16.0	472.4	0.6	91.4	−10.1	6.4	5.0	1.14	1.58
Piedmont Natural Gas Co. (N: PNY)	13.1	13.1	15.8	686.4	0.9	86.0	6.8	5.6	4.5	1.56	1.94
IdaCorp, Inc. (N: IDA)	12.4	13.2	14.4	1,055.0	0.8	99.0	2.1	6.1	6.0	1.52	1.68
Indiana Energy, Inc. (N: IEI)	11.7	13.3	18.4	432.8	0.6	67.4	4.0	6.4	4.3	1.42	2.03
American Water Works Co. (N: AWK)	14.3	13.8	17.2	1,203.3	0.7	149.8	6.6	4.5	3.0	1.21	1.73
Cascade Natural Gas Corp. (N: CGC)	10.5	14.0	25.4	208.6	1.0	109.3	15.4	6.9	5.6	1.34	1.56
NSTAR (N: NST)	15.2	14.7	13.0	1,631.6	0.8	97.3	3.9	5.1	5.9	1.20	1.53

na = not available

Exchange Key: N = New York Stock Exchange
A = American Stock Exchange
M = Nasdaq

*Screening criteria used to produce table results can be found on opposite page.

Source: AAII's Stock Investor/Market Guide, Inc. Data as of February 25, 2000.

Graham Enterprising Investor
Screening Criteria
Definitions for screens and terms can be found in the glossary starting on page 191.

Screening Criteria:
- P/E among the lowest 10% in database*
- Current ratio (latest fiscal quarter) greater than or equal to 1.5
- Long-term debt relative to working capital (lastest fiscal quarter) less than 110%*
- Long-term debt relative to working capital (latest fiscal quarter) greater than 0%*
- EPS for last 12 months and each of the last five fiscal years greater than $0*
- Indicated dividend greater than $0
- Dividends for last 12 months greater than $0*
- EPS (last 12 months) greater than EPS five years ago*
- EPS (last fiscal year) greater than EPS five years ago*
- Price-to-book ratio less than or equal to 1.2

*Data not shown in table. Also note that the table shows additional data columns that may be of interest to those using this approach.

Earnings Stability

Graham also loosens the requirement of earnings stability. Here we require that earnings be positive for each of the last five years.

Dividend Record

For the enterprising investor, Graham only specifies that firms pay some level of current dividends—a simple filter that in our screening process screened out nearly two-thirds of the firms when used as a stand-alone criterion. As a rule, only more mature companies past their stage of strong, capital-intensive growth can afford to pay a cash dividend. This filter will also cut out some low price-earnings stocks that are troubled and under financial duress.

Earnings Growth

When it comes to earnings growth, Graham again is less restrictive for the enterprising investor. We require only that earnings for the latest year be higher than earnings five years ago for our screen.

Table 3.
Graham Enterprising Investor Screening Results*

Company (Exch: Ticker)	P/E (x)	P/E (3-yr Avg EPS) (x)	5-yr Avg P/E (x)	Sales Last 12 mos. ($ mil)	Curr Ratio (x)	LT Debt/ Equity (%)	5-yr EPS Grth Rate (%)	Div Yield (%)	5-yr Avg Div Yield (%)	P/Bk (x)	5-yr Avg P/Bk (x)
K–Swiss Inc. (M: KSWS)	3.5	20.7	46.7	275.9	6.8	0.0	3.7	0.6	0.4	1.02	1.94
Allegheny Technologies (N: ATI)	4.5	6.1	84.0	3,683.4	2.0	18.1	46.0	4.8	3.0	1.12	4.40
Atlantic Tele–Network,Inc (A: ANK)	4.9	4.7	10.2	79.0	2.5	12.5	52.8	6.5	na	0.61	1.21
Friedman's Inc. (M: FRDM)	5.0	6.0	16.2	334.7	2.4	4.2	12.4	0.8	na	0.44	1.61
Fleetwood Enterprises (N: FLE)	5.5	5.6	14.0	3,719.0	1.5	9.7	17.2	4.9	2.2	0.89	2.36
Oxford Industries, Inc. (N: OXM)	5.5	6.0	25.2	836.9	2.4	26.1	7.2	5.2	3.4	0.80	1.49
Federal Screw Works (M: FSCR)	5.6	5.9	6.5	120.2	2.2	6.9	24.8	0.9	3.8	0.89	1.01
Coachmen Industries (N: COA)	6.0	6.4	13.1	817.0	2.9	4.0	17.3	1.8	0.9	0.83	2.18
Cooper Tire & Rubber Co. (N: CTB)	6.0	7.2	15.3	1,994.7	3.0	21.6	6.1	3.9	1.4	0.86	2.39
Tecumseh Products Co. (M: TECUA)	6.0	8.3	10.7	1,814.3	3.4	1.5	4.9	3.1	2.6	0.82	1.16
Ameron International Corp (N: AMN)	6.3	7.7	11.9	568.1	2.1	82.1	23.1	3.7	2.9	0.81	1.24
Hughes Supply, Inc. (N: HUG)	6.3	7.4	12.2	2,873.2	3.0	103.3	20.1	2.0	1.0	0.78	1.55
Steel Technologies, Inc. (M: STTX)	6.6	9.9	13.0	411.3	2.5	72.5	10.3	1.3	0.9	0.86	1.20

na = not available

Exchange Key: N = New York Stock Exchange
A = American Stock Exchange
M = Nasdaq

Screening criteria used to produce table results can be found on opposite page.

Source: AAII's Stock Investor/Market Guide, Inc. Data as of February 25, 2000.

Price-to-Book-Value Ratio

The final criterion specifies that the current price be less than or equal to 120% of tangible book value. This requirement is more restrictive than for the defensive investor and makes no adjustment for the level of the price-earnings ratio. Since Graham feels that secondary firms normally trade at a discount to their intrinsic value it is not surprising that a tougher filter is specified.

Results for the Enterprising Investor Screen

The companies that passed the enterprising investor screen are presented in Table 3 based on data as of February 25, 2000, using AAII's *Stock Investor Professional*. As is always the case with screening, this represents only a starting point fur further analysis. Screening tips for the Benjamin Graham approach are on page 21.

Screening Tips: The Benjamin Graham Approach

THE DEFENSIVE INVESTOR
Primary Factors
Market Sector
Companies in the various market sectors have different operating and financing characteristics. Ratio analysis is typically more meaningful when examined within industry groups. Graham analyzed utilities separately from other sectors.

Adequate Size of the Enterprise
Exclude smaller firms, which carry additional risks and tend to trade at a central value below their intrinsic value. Graham specified that industrials should have sales above $100 million back in the early 1970s. A rough inflation adjustment brings this level up to a minimum level of $340 million. Graham specified utilities should have sales above $50 million in the early 1970s; a rough inflation adjustment brings this level to $170 million.

Financial Condition
For Non-Utilities:
• Current assets should be at least twice current liabilities—a 2-to-1 current ratio.
• Long-term debt should not exceed working capital (current assets less current liabilities). This type of ratio is unique to Graham and will not typically be found in a screening program. If the program allows for custom fields, it should be easy to create. If you must work with a fixed set of fields, then look for a good measure of financial leverage, such as total debt to total assets or debt-to-equity.

For Utilities:
• Debt should not exceed twice the stock equity at book value.

Earnings Stability
Graham specified some earnings for the common stock for the past 10 years. Most screening programs will not have data going back that far. Use the greatest number of years available and check your final list of candidates against a printed publication that goes back 10 years, such as Value Line.

Dividend Record
Uninterrupted payments for at least the past 20 years. Most screening programs will not have data going back that far. S&P Stock Guide is a printed source that indicates how long the dividends have been paid. At a minimum, screen for positive dividends in each of the last five years, along with a positive indicated dividend (most recent dividend multiplied by four).

Earnings Growth
Graham specified a 3% annual growth rate over a 10-year period using a three-year average at the beginning and ending years. This type of growth rate calculation will not be found in most screening programs. A reasonable substitution would be to specify a minimum annual growth rate of 3% over 10 years using a more standard growth rate calculation that only looks at the beginning and ending years' earnings.

Moderate Price-Earnings Ratio
Graham specified that the current price to the average of the last three years' earnings per share should not exceed

(cont'd on next page)

Screening Tips: The Benjamin Graham Approach (cont'd)

15, with the goal of having a portfolio with an average price-earnings ratio that does not exceed the inverse of the high-grade corporate bond yield. You should be able to calculate this field with a screening program that allows you to create custom fields. At the time your P/E of 15 was determined, AA bonds were yielding 7.5%, or an inverse of 13.3; the higher P/E cut-off of 15 was used to help build a portfolio with an overall average P/E ratio of around 13.3. To determine the average P/E goal for your portfolio, use this formula:

$$\text{Cut-off P/E} = \left(\frac{1}{\text{current yield}} \right)$$

Moderate Ratio of Price to Assets

Graham felt that the stock's current price should be less than or equal to 1½ times the stock's book value. However, a low price-earnings ratio could justify a higher price-to-book-value ratio. As a rule of thumb, multiplying the stock's price-earnings ratio by its price-to-book value should produce a figure that does not exceed 1½ times the cut-off price-earnings ratio determined in the previous rule. Most screening programs will not have the product of the price-earnings ratio and price-to-book ratio calculated, but will allow you to calculate it.

THE ENTERPRISING INVESTOR

Low Price-Earnings Ratio

A primary factor to indicate that a stock is cheap on a relative basis is to look only at firms whose price-earnings ratios are among the lowest 10% of the overall market.

Financial Condition

- Current assets should be at least 1½ times current liabilities—current ratio greater than or equal to 1.5.
- Long-term debt no more than 110% of net working capital (current assets less current liabilities). This type of ratio is unique to Graham and will not typically be found in a screening program. If the program allows for custom fields, it should be easy to create. If you must work with a fixed set of fields, look for a good measure of financial leverage such as total-debt-to-total-assets or debt-to-equity.

Earnings Stability

Graham specified some earnings for the common stock for the past five years.

Dividend Record

Graham specified some current dividend payout.

Earnings Growth

Graham specified that last year's earnings should be higher than that of five years ago.

Moderate Ratio of Price to Assets

Graham felt that current price should be less than or equal to 120% of tangible book value. Not all screening programs will provide a tangible book value measure and may provide book value that includes intangibles such as purchased goodwill.

Going Against the Crowd: David Dreman's Contrarian Investment Strategy

Men are from Mars; women are from Venus. But according to efficient market academics, stock investors are from Vulcan, home planet of Star Trek's totally rational and unemotional Mr. Spock.

The theorists, of course, are referring to the market as a whole. But anyone who has put their own money into the market knows that investment judgments can be affected by emotions.

One approach that seeks to understand and profit from such investor misjudgments is the contrarian strategy—going against the crowd by seeking stocks that are out-of-favor with the market, and avoiding the high-flying fashionable stocks that have been swept up in market euphoria. Eventually, of course, the market rediscovers out-of-favor stocks and lets the high-fliers fall back to earth. Contrarian investors have a chance to profit from the rediscoveries.

The person most associated with the term "contrarian" is David Dreman, chairman of Dreman Value Advisors and also a regular columnist in Forbes magazine.

Dreman feels that institutional investors and research analysts are particularly prone to psychological biases and "running with the crowd," so his contrarian approach is well-suited for individual investors.

Why Contrarian Stocks: The Philosophy

Dreman contends that psychological biases tend to interfere with sound investment decisions. Investors who understand these biases can prevent them from overwhelming their own decisions, and they can profit from the biases in others.

Many psychological biases occur because of information-processing short-cuts that everyone uses in daily life. For example, when driving a car, attention is focused on information that directly affects driving, while other distracting information is screened out. Individuals also use probabilities to judge everyday events—they are "intuitive statisticians."

But these mental short-cuts can lead to bad investment decisions when they are carried over to stock market decisions. For instance:

- Investors tend to base decisions on information that is insufficient, drawn from a sample that is too small. The best example Dreman points to is investors who flock to mutual funds with the hottest record over the past year—the record upon which they are judging the fund is too brief.

- Investors tend to immerse themselves in the unique details of a particular situation, and at the same time, they ignore the probabilities based on prior situations that are similar. And the more "certain" an individual is of the particular, the less weight that is given to the prior probabilities. An example is the popularity of hot new issues, which investors tend to view as unique opportunities without examining the high probability of loss that frequently exists in the new issue area.
- Investors tend to be drawn to situations that are currently performing above the average and assume that the high level of performance will continue, even though most stocks do not deviate from the long-term averages for very long.
- Investors' inclinations are reinforced when others interpret information in the same way, so market confirmations and agreement can lock in an individual's position. Similarly, investors tend to demand immediate feedback—if they view a stock as promising, they want this to be immediately confirmed by a quick price rise.
- Investors tend to misread probabilities, putting great emphasis on recent or emotional events, whether positive or negative.
- Investors tend to have hindsight blindness—they look at their past errors and feel that the mistake made would have been "obvious" if they hadn't been blinded by an overly optimistic or overly pessimistic view. The problem with hindsight blindness, Dreman points out, is that it interferes with a proper assessment of past errors, and prevents the investor from learning from his mistakes.

Investment fads and market overreactions tend to occur when many of these factors are combined: A fashionable investment is "proven" by recent statistics that are easy to recall and is further confirmed by the market in the form of rising prices. All of these biases are used to project the current short-term trend far into the future, even though such a performance would not be representative of most stocks over long time periods. And once the mistake is discovered, the investor in hindsight sees the errors as obvious and can't figure out why he went along with the fad.

The trick for investors, according to Dreman, is to get the biases working for you, rather than against you.

How?

First, observe four rules to avoid falling prey to the biases yourself:
- Rule 1: Don't be influenced by a hot performance record.
- Rule 2: Don't rely solely on the specific situation, but take into account prior probabilities of similar situations. The greater the uncertainty, the less emphasis you should place on your own unique appraisal.
- Rule 3: Don't be seduced by recent rates of investment return for individual stocks when they deviate sharply from past norms. For investors, longer-term characteristics of stocks are far more likely to be established again.
- Rule 4: Don't expect the strategy you adopt to be a quick success.

Second, favor stocks that are out-of-favor with the market as indicated by measures such as

your assessment, you haven't paid for your error. If you are right and earnings grow faster than the market, the stock will do very well. The risk-reward level, in Dreman's view, is highly favorable—not much downside, but a good deal of upside if you are right.

- When making an assessment of the general direction of earnings, use conservative earnings estimates, to provide a margin of safety.

For "high-rollers," Dreman suggests buying stocks of companies that show a loss. This strategy takes advantage of market overreactions to bad news. Investors always shun stocks reporting losses, and Dreman points to several studies indicating excess returns over one-year and five-year periods from stocks purchased one year after reporting losses. Dreman says investors using this approach should be very sure of a company's financial strength. They should also make sure the company's assessment of the reason for the loss is sound and that it is taking steps to fix the problem. The investor should be seeking companies that have stumbled temporarily. The risk, of course, is that it won't be temporary, but this risk is lower for larger corporations. However, Dreman cautions that investors should devote only a small portion of their portfolio to this strategy.

More Mechanical

Dreman also believes that more mechanical approaches are feasible using his basic low price-earnings ratio approach. Such portfolios would consist of 15 to 20 medium- to large-sized companies diversified among 10 to 12 industries. He suggests three primarily mechanical approaches:

- Buy and hold for a long period of time (three to nine years) the lowest 20% price-earnings ratio stocks. Alternatively, an investor could pick a large company paying good dividends that is priced at a 20% discount or more from the S&P 500.
- Buy low price-earnings stocks and weed the holdings periodically as the ratios improve or if a stock fails to perform as well as the market over a given time period. He suggests, however, that investors keep the number of trades per year low.
- Purchase the lowest 20% price-earnings ratio stocks, and re-apply the screen annually. Dreman says the approach may appear to be high turnover at first glance, but notes that usually less than half low price-earnings ratio stocks move up in less than a year.

When to Sell

A positive side benefit of the approach, according to Dreman, is a low portfolio turnover. He notes that low price-earnings ratio stocks can move much higher in price and still be good holdings if earnings are moving up rapidly enough so that the ratio remains low.

Dreman recommends a portfolio size of roughly 12 to 15 stocks for adequate diversification.

But he also suggests that investors keep their portfolios to a manageable size.

Stocks should be sold when their price-earnings ratios approach that of the overall market, regardless of how favorable prospects look. The stock should then be replaced with another low price-earnings ratio stock. On the other hand, a stock that attains a high price-earnings ratio solely because of an earnings decline should not be sold, since the price drop is likely an overreaction to the earnings decline.

While Dreman warns against overtrading, he also suggests a strategy of substituting a better stock for one you already own.

What about stocks that simply don't seem to be going anywhere? He suggests a two-year holding period as a test. If a stock has not done as well as the overall market over the two-year time period, sell it and replace it.

Lastly, Dreman says you should part with a stock if you see management behaving badly or acting only in its own self-interest.

Dreman in Summary

Dreman's contrarian investment strategy provides a disciplined approach that seeks to take emotions out of the decision-making process. It is also a classical value approach that offers a somewhat different slant on the underlying philosophy. The reasoning, though, provides investors with useful insights on how underlying behavioral traits can lead to investment mistakes.

The important point is that investors can only profit when making intelligent decisions that are contrary to the consensus thinking reflected in the market prices of many companies. And that is difficult to do, unless you understand where the common mistakes are made. On the other hand, it is an approach that is easier for individuals to implement than for institutions.

Writing in 1982, Dreman summed up:

"When I was a student reading the newspapers of the 1930s, 1940s and 1950s, I was amazed by the value so abundant in the stock markets of those days and felt a little cheated because I thought the great days of investment coups all lay in the past.

Today, nothing seems further from the truth. Institutional concentration, conformity pressures on professionals, and overreactions to the current economic problems seem to me to present the investor with some of the greatest stock market opportunities in decades."

The David Dreman "Contrarian" Approach in Brief

Philosophy and style

Psychological biases tend to interfere with sound investment decisions, but investors who understand these biases can prevent them from affecting their own judgment and can profit from the biases in others.

To prevent the biases from affecting your own decisions:

- Don't be influenced by a hot performance record.
- Don't rely solely on the specific situation, but take into account prior probabilities of similar situations.
- Don't be seduced by recent rates of investment return for individual stocks when they deviate sharply from past norms; use long-term stock characteristics.
- Don't expect the strategy you adopt to be a quick success.

To profit from the biases of others:

- Favor stocks that are out-of-favor with the market as indicated by low price-earnings ratios.

Universe of stocks

Large and medium-sized companies, which offer a level of stability and staying power.

Criteria for initial consideration

- Buy low price-earnings ratio stocks: those that are among the bottom 40% of stocks ranked by price-earnings ratio and have ratios below that of the S&P 500.

Secondary factors

- The stock should provide a high dividend yield that can be maintained or, preferably, raised; stock should also have low payout ratios (dividends per share divided by earnings per share).
- The company should have a strong financial position: high ratios of current assets relative to current liabilities; and low debt as a percentage of equity.
- The company should have favorable operating conditions, such as high returns on equity and high pretax profit margins relative to others in the industry.
- The company should have a higher rate of earnings growth than the S&P 500 both in the recent past and projected one year down the road. In assessing earnings growth, make sure to understand a company's main line of business, its components, and which components add the most to earnings.
- When making an assessment of the general direction of earnings, use conservative earnings estimates.
- For "high-rollers": Buy stocks that show a loss, but be sure of a company's financial strength, and that the company's assessment of the reason for the loss is sound, and it is taking steps to fix the problem. In addition, use only a small portion of your portfolio for this strategy.

Stock monitoring and when to sell

- Portfolios should contain at least 12 to 15 stocks that are in 10 to 12 different industries for adequate diversification, but portfolios should be kept to a manageable size.
- Stocks should be sold when their price-earnings ratios approach that of the overall market, regardless of how favorable prospects look. However, stocks that reach high ratios solely because of an earnings decline should not be sold, since the price drop is likely an overreaction to the earnings decline. When stocks are sold, they should be replaced with low price-earnings ratio stocks.
- You can substitute better stocks for ones you already own, but do so selectively and avoid overtrading.
- Use a two-year holding period as a test to weed out stocks that aren't going anywhere: If a stock has not done as well as the overall market over the two-year time period, sell it and replace it.
- Sell a stock if you see management behaving badly or acting only in its own self-interest.

STOCK SCREENS: APPLYING THE DREMAN APPROACH

David Dreman believes that for an investment approach to be of value, it must take into account both the behavioral and interpretational obstacles of investing. While the price of a stock will ultimately move toward its actual intrinsic value, mistakes in estimating that value (interpretational obstacles) and market emotions and preferences (behavioral obstacles) may lead to periods of undervaluation or overvaluation. For that reason, he favors techniques that are not overly complex.

Dreman prefers to start the analysis among the bottom 40% of stocks according to their price-earnings ratio. Most investor software programs should be able to perform this screen.

Dividend Yield

Dreman seeks companies with a high dividend yield that the company can sustain and possibly raise. The yield helps to provide protection against a significant price drop and contributes to the total return of the investment. There are many ways to screen for dividend yield: You can simply establish a minimum level, or perform a relative screen that compares the current yield to the market level or to the company's historical norm. Yield screens typically result in the exclusion of small, high-growth companies because they need all cash generated through operations to expand and therefore tend not to pay dividends.

If an absolute level of yield is specified in a screen, it cannot be too high or only companies from industries that traditionally pay a high dividend will pass. Now that utilities are relatively stable and mature with limited potential for capital appreciation, they trade at yields two to three times the average for the S&P 500. At the time we set up our screens, the S&P 500 dividend yield was approximately 1.2%, so we specified a minimum yield of 1.5%—high enough to be significant, yet low enough not to exclude too many industries.

Dividends in danger of being reduced by the company are no bargain, so it is a good idea to also examine payout ratios. The payout ratio is computed by dividing the dividend by earnings and indicates what portion of the earnings is being paid out to shareholders. Companies cannot sustain very high payouts without harming the long-term growth potential of the firm. Positive payout ratios of 50% or less for industrials and 80% or less for utilities are rule-of-thumb benchmarks for dividend safety. The dividend growth rate over the last three years also helps gauge the recent dividend policy of the firms.

Company Size

Dreman favors large- and medium-sized companies for three primary reasons—first, there is a greater chance for a rebound if the company missteps; second, there is greater market visibility with the rebound, and third, there is a reduced chance of "accounting gimmickry."

Table 1.
Stocks Passing the Contrarian Screening

Company (Exchange: Ticker)	P/E (x)	P/E Rank (%)	5-yr Avg. P/E (x)	Div. Yield (%)	5-Yr Avg Div Yield (%)	Div Grth Rate (3-yr) (%)	Market Cap ($ mil)	Mkt Cap Rank (%)	Total Liab. to Assets (%)	EPS Cont. Grth (5-yr) (%)	Long-Term EPS Grth Est. (%)
Lafarge Corporation (N: LAF)	5.3	5	13.0	3.0	1.5	10.3	1,449.2	84	50.0	100.9	10.3
Cooper Tire & Rubber Co. (N: CTB)	6.0	7	15.3	3.9	1.4	13.0	815.4	78	42.7	6.1	9.5
Heller Financial, Inc. (N: HF)	6.5	9	na	2.2	na	na	1,735.5	86	87.2	8.6	14.9
Finova Group Inc. (N: FNV)	8.0	15	17.5	2.6	1.3	12.6	1,676.1	86	86.6	27.5	15.7
Albemarle Corporation (N: ALB)	8.1	16	14.5	2.6	1.3	20.8	715.9	76	48.6	34.7	9.5
Cooper Industries, Inc. (N: CBE)	8.8	20	18.1	4.6	3.0	0.0	2,889.6	90	55.7	6.7	10.7
United Dominion Ind. (N: UDI)	8.8	20	14.6	1.8	1.0	21.6	768.7	77	58.9	30.1	12.2
Energen Corporation (N: EGN)	9.6	26	13.9	4.4	4.0	3.3	452	70	64.5	4.9	7.2
Puget Sound Energy, Inc. (N: PSD)	9.6	26	16.4	9.3	7.5	0.0	1,675.4	86	69.3	-1.5	3.8
Wisconsin Energy Corp. (N: WEC)	9.8	27	23.1	8.9	5.4	2.2	2,062.9	87	65.9	-1.7	3.7
Peoples Energy Corp. (N: PGL)	9.9	28	13.9	7.3	5.6	2.1	977.4	80	65.5	4.1	5.1
La-Z-Boy Incorporated (N: LZB)	10.1	29	15.9	2.1	2.0	7.4	811.2	78	37.8	14.7	12.6
Carlisle Companies, Inc. (N: CSL)	10.3	30	17.9	2.3	1.5	12.6	951	80	56.8	25	14.7
Energy East Corporation (N: NEG)	10.3	30	13.0	4.2	5.2	3.7	2,339.2	88	62.0	7.7	8.8
Longs Drug Stores Corp. (N: LDG)	10.4	30	19.4	3.0	2.1	0.0	723	76	45.6	6.4	10.7
Mercantile Bankshares (M: MRBK)	10.5	31	16.0	4.0	2.6	14.7	1,643.5	85	87.5	12.1	9.7
Cedar Fair, L.P. (N: FUN)	10.8	32	14.0	8.3	5.8	4.2	912.9	79	45.0	3.3	na
Leggett & Platt, Inc. (N: LEG)	11.1	34	19.7	2.5	1.3	19	3,152.9	90	45.4	19.4	14.1
Lubrizol Corporation (N: LZ)	11.2	35	14.8	4.1	3.3	2.3	1,374.7	84	53.0	-3.4	7.4
Staten Island Bancorp Inc (N: SIB)	11.3	36	na	3.0	na	na	628.9	75	86.1	20.6	10.0
Corn Products Intl., Inc. (N: CPO)	11.4	36	na	1.7	na	na	889.1	79	49.3	na	12.0
Lee Enterprises, Inc. (N: LEE)	11.5	37	19.3	3.2	2.1	7.7	894.9	79	47.3	9.9	10.8
John Nuveen Company (N: JNC)	11.8	39	15.8	3.4	2.5	13	1,053.4	81	24.0	7.9	10.0

na = not available

Exchange Key: N = New York Stock Exchange
A = American Stock Exchange
M = Nasdaq

*Screening criteria used to produce table results can be found on opposite page.

Source: AAII's Stock Investor/Market Guide, Inc. and I/B/E/S.
Statistics are based on figures as of February 25, 2000.

Screening Tips: The David Dreman Approach

Price-Earnings Ratio
Price-earnings ratios should be among the lowest 40% of all firms. Better screening programs allow you to specify the percentile rank for figures such as price-earnings ratios, growth rates, and price strength. If your screening system does not provide percentile ranks, start with a low maximum price-earnings requirement and keep raising the figure until only 40% of the stocks pass the screen.

Dividend Yield
Dreman seeks out companies with high, but sustainable dividend yields. Because Dreman's contrarian analysis is limited to mid- and large-cap stocks, we are screening for stocks with a dividend yield above the dividend yield for the S&P 500. Financial newspapers such as the Wall Street Journal or Investor's Business Daily report the S&P 500 dividend yield. We did not "test" for sustainability. But you may wish to add a screen that looks for factors such as company payout ratios (dividends per share divided by earnings per share) below industry norm. (Additional information on dividend yield screening is contained in Chapter 3, which covers Geraldine Weiss' approach.)

Market Capitalization
Dreman limits his analysis to large- and mid-cap companies because of their resources and visibility. Our screen looks for companies that are at least among the largest 30% of all firms when measured by market capitalization. For our screen we specified a market capitalization greater than 70% of all stocks. If your screening system does not provide percentile ranks, start with a low minimum market cap requirement and keep raising the figure until only 30% of the stocks pass the screen.

Strong Financial Position
Dreman looks for favorable financial strength to allow the company to work through any operating difficulties. You can make use of any current financial strength and financial leverage factors your screening program supports. Optimally your screen should cover both short- and long-term liabilities. We looked for companies with total liabilities to total assets below the industry median.

Reasonable Growth
Dreman looks for higher than average growth for the recent past and into the next year or two. Most programs supply historical growth rates, but fewer provided screening for consensus growth expectations. You may have to simply screen for above average short-term historical growth and then study the near-term growth prospects for the firms passing all of your screening criteria. Our screen first required historical one-year growth above the median for all firms. We then also required that expected earnings per share show year-over-year increases for the current and next fiscal year.

Blue-Chip Value Investing:
The Geraldine Weiss Approach

"A bird in the hand is worth two in the bush."

It's an old saying, but it's a sentiment felt by many conservative stock investors who prefer the stocks of stable and established companies that provide part of their return sooner, in the form of dividends, rather than later, in the form of capital gains.

How does one choose among these kinds of stocks?

One approach is followed by Geraldine Weiss, editor of the highly regarded Investment Quality Trends, a La Jolla, California-based newsletter that tracks and recommends stocks based on her approach.

Weiss melds a conservative, blue-chip investment style with a value approach, using dividend yield as a guide to value. A high dividend yield signals out-of-favor stocks, but many such stocks are out-of-favor for good reason—they are financially troubled. Weiss' strategy attempts to weed out truly financially troubled firms by seeking out-of-favor stocks within a relatively safe sector of high-quality stocks.

The Philosophy

Weiss can best be described as a blue-chip value investor—buying quality stocks at a good value.

Quality is Weiss' first concern—investing in companies that have withstood the test of time by surviving numerous economic cycles without lowering or canceling a dividend. These stocks tend to be more stable and are usually the last to fall when the economy is declining, making them less risky than lower-quality or unproven stocks.

Weiss also notes that quality companies provide, through their dividend payments, a reliable source for steady and increasing income. These payments significantly contribute to an investor's bottom line return, and in particular provide support during bear markets by supplying a source of income.

Of course, significant profits come from price appreciation. Weiss maintains that all stocks go through cycles of undervaluation and overvaluation, and that investor profits can be achieved by taking advantage of these cycles—buying stocks when they are undervalued and subsequently selling them when they are overvalued.

But dividends are the star players in the approach. In Weiss' view, dividends offer the best indication of both quality and value, besides providing a source of return.

The quality of corporate management can be judged by examining a firm's dividend payments and policies. Companies that provide steady dividend payments over the long term are generating sufficient earnings to first cover all expenses and debt payments; companies that increase cash dividends year-after-year are able to do so through increased earnings and thus are particularly well-managed.

For Weiss, the most important measure of investment value is the dividend yield—a company's current annual dividend per share divided by share price.

Why? In the long run, the underlying value of the stream of dividend payments determines the price of a stock. As Weiss points out, the impact of dividends on price is reflected when changes occur—if a dividend is increased, the stock becomes more valuable and more highly rated; if a dividend is decreased, stock values decrease.

The dividend yield ratio relates dividends per share to share price, similar to other popular valuation measures such as price-earnings ratios (price divided by earnings per share) and price-to-book-value ratios (price divided by book value per share). Weiss does not discount these other ratios, but notes that they can be more misleading due to distortions in reported earnings and book value. Dividend payments, in contrast, tend to be more predictable and not subject to differing accounting interpretations; they are real, measurable dollars paid out to shareholders, and offer a more stable measure to relate to share price.

On the other side of the equation, Weiss believes that over the short term, prices can go to extremes. This causes a company's dividend yield to fluctuate within a range that is unique to each company. When dividend yields are relatively high, the share price is low relative to dividends per share paid out, indicating that the stock may be undervalued; when dividend yields are relatively low, the share price is high relative to dividends per share, indicating that the stock may be overvalued. Weiss suggests buying and selling blue-chip stocks when they reach the extremes of their historical dividend yield range.

The philosophy combines a high-quality strategy with a value approach, and has a goal of minimizing downside risk, maximizing the potential for capital gains, and maximizing the growth of dividend income.

The Blue-Chip Universe

Because the safety of dividend payments and their ability to rise are central to her approach, Weiss suggests that investors begin their selection process by narrowing their initial list down to a universe of blue-chip stocks. In this sense, the pre-selection of the "universe" of stocks is particularly important.

Weiss seeks companies that are well-known, with good managers, good research and development efforts, good marketing skills, well-known products and services, and that are reluctant to cut a dividend even in times of cyclical stress. In particular, she lays out six criteria, of which a firm must pass at least five:

1) **Dividend increases in five of the last 12 years:** A measure of good long-term performance of the company's ability to increase net earnings, reflected by a trend of increasing dividends. Weiss terms this the most reliable measure of good management.

2) **Improved earnings in at least seven of the last 12 years:** Another sign of a well-managed company, indicating that a company can survive the tough years and prosper in the good ones. Weiss notes that she also looks for sales increases and profit margins that are under control.

3) **It must have paid dividends, with no interruptions, for roughly the past 25 years:** Consistent dividend payments are a sign of a profitable, well-managed company; a long record also provides the historical data necessary to evaluate the range of dividend yields indicating valuation extremes. Weiss suggests that if an investor wants to relax the number of years, dividends should have been paid long enough for several cycles of overvaluation and undervaluation to be established.

4) **The stock must carry a Standard & Poor's quality ranking no lower than A–:** S&P ranks the quality of stocks on a scale of A+ to C (a D indicates reorganization) based on past growth and stability of earnings and dividends; Weiss finds the rankings a useful guide to investment quality. Although stocks must have a quality ranking of A– to make the initial list, Weiss allows stocks to drop to B+ once on the list; however, if they drop to B, the stock is deleted from her blue-chip list.

5) **A minimum of five million shares outstanding:** An assurance of liquidity, which in turn prevents manipulation of share price. Firms smaller than this may have trouble attracting institutional investors, which leads to illiquidity.

6) **Shares must be held by at least 80 institutions:** Another assurance of liquidity, but Weiss views this rule as the least rigid of her criteria.

How many should be included in the universe? Weiss herself follows around 350, a number she says is somewhat arbitrary but is a manageable size, while including a wide variety of industry groups.

Dividend Yield Criteria

Once a pre-selected list of blue-chip stocks is developed, Weiss recommends the purchase of these stocks based on a value approach, using historical dividend yields as a guide. Specifically, Weiss charts a firm's dividend yield and its price over a decade or more, and looks for historical high and low dividend yield "turning points," when stock prices change direction. Weiss maintains that most stocks turn at roughly the same dividend yield each cycle; averaging these dividend yields defines the boundaries.

"If a major rising price trend has ended in a 2% yield area many times, and a major declining price trend repeatedly has ended in a 5% yield area, a profile of value has been established for that stock—a 2% dividend yield identifies a historically overvalued price where the stock should be sold to preserve capital and protect profits. Conversely, when that stock is priced to yield 5%, it is historically undervalued and a good buying opportunity is at hand."

Weiss suggests that investors buy from their blue-chip stock list when the prices cause dividend yields to be within 10% of their historical high dividend yield. On the other hand, she does not suggest investors purchase an undervalued stock without first examining the reasons why a stock's price has fallen—in particular, checking for the possibility of a dividend decrease, which would eliminate it from consideration.

Other Factors

Weiss does not discount the use of other value measures when analyzing stocks, and in fact suggests several that are useful in confirming valuations derived from the dividend yield approach. In addition, these valuations can help an investor more fully understand how the market perceives a stock.

In particular, she suggests:

- **A price-earnings ratio that is historically low for that particular stock and other similar stocks, and that is below the market multiple.** A low price-earnings ratio reflects the market's low growth-in-earnings outlook for the firm.
- **A price-to-book-value ratio that is no higher than 1.3, and the closer to 1.0, the better.** This is a Benjamin Graham rule-of-thumb that seeks to buy stocks as close to the bare-bones worth of a company as possible.

Weiss' investment approach demands that the cash dividend be safe. A change in the dividend payment causes the dividend yield to change, so that a share price that was once regarded as undervalued may become fairly valued or overvalued, and vice versa.

How can investors judge the safety of dividend payments for both prospective stocks and stocks that they own? Of course, stocks on a blue-chip list should have relatively safe dividends. But Weiss also provides some other guidelines:

- Seek stocks with a ratio of current assets to current liabilities of at least 2.0, and a debt-to-equity ratio of no more than 50% debt to equity (utility stocks are excluded because of their unique regulatory status); conservative investors should look for a debt-to-equity ratio of no more than 20%. Companies with high levels of debt can run into financial problems more quickly during a slowdown, putting the dividend in jeopardy.
- Payout ratios approaching 100% are a danger signal. Dividends are paid out of earnings, and are relatively safe and can even be safely increased if the payout ratio (dividend as a percent of earnings) is 50% or less. The closer the payout ratio is to 100%, the more endangered the dividend and the less likely it is to be increased. A rising earnings trend, however, can support rising dividends.

- Similarly, an indicated dividend higher than reported annual earnings is a danger sign. Since firms pay dividends primarily from earnings, a company cannot sustain dividend payments above annual earnings. Although strong cash flow can help cover a dividend payment when earnings temporarily drop, an "unprotected dividend is in greater danger than a protected dividend."

Lastly, Weiss states that investors should examine all fundamental factors to fully understand the company before purchasing it, and when judging the merits of one prospective blue chip relative to another. She does not go into detail concerning what to look for, but she does provide a generalized guide of what to look at when judging the quality of a firm:

- The company's financial performance, including its record of earnings, dividends, debt-to-equity ratio, dividend payout ratio, book value, and cash flow.
- The company's product performance, whether it is manufacturing goods or services that are in demand, its research and development efforts, and its ability to market its products or services.
- The company's investment performance in the form of capital gains and dividend growth.

Portfolio Monitoring and When to Sell

Weiss suggests that individuals aim for a portfolio of about 20 stocks, enough to assure that the portfolio is diversified but small enough to be manageable. In addition, selected stocks should be in a variety of industry groups.

On the other hand, Weiss does not believe that an investor should always be fully invested—if, for example, few stocks are undervalued, or if the overall market appears to be overvalued (based on historical market dividend yields). Keeping money in cash during these times, she believes, allows an investor to take advantage when the opportunities eventually arise at the end of a bear market or during a major correction in a bull market. Weiss notes that these times offer investors the best opportunities to diversify their holdings because of the large selection of undervalued stocks.

Portfolios must be continually monitored to weed out stocks that no longer satisfy the requirements of good value or quality.

Within an investor's portfolio, Weiss believes stocks should be sold when changes in share prices cause their dividend yields to be within 10% of their overvalued extreme range. She views historically low dividend yields as "alarm bells," and although the stock price may continue to rise, the upside potential is outweighed by the downside risk. Of course, dividend yields tend to fall when prices are rising—and Weiss notes that investors are often reluctant to sell these shares, particularly if they have held on to them for some time. Her suggestion: Place a stop-loss order 12% to 15% below the overvalued price; the market will then dictate the sale.

What happens when dividend yields rise—indicating undervaluation—for stocks held within a portfolio? Dividend yields will rise if the price drops, and Weiss notes that investors should try to determine the cause of the price drop. In general, however, she views this as a buying opportunity to add shares.

"When bad things happen to good companies, it must be viewed as a buying opportunity rather than a bailout. As long as a stock's dividend is maintained, even an extremely undervalued stock merits investment consideration."

Dividend yields may also rise, and prices drop, if the company omits a dividend. In this instance, she suggests that investors wait temporarily, since stock prices may move up shortly after, once the uncertainty has been eliminated. After the "rebound" however, the stock should be sold because it no longer meets the blue-chip criteria.

Conclusion

Weiss' strategy is an interesting derivative of a classic value approach that reverses the process: Rather than finding undervalued companies first, and then analyzing for quality, Weiss first focuses on developing an initial list of quality companies in which you would be comfortable investing, and then purchasing them when they become undervalued and selling them as they become overvalued.

The approach is particularly useful for investors who seek stocks that pay a steady dividend and are likely to continue paying a steady dividend; it is less useful for investors primarily seeking growth and who are trying to limit annual taxable income.

Weiss summarizes her own approach this way:

"Successful investing in the stock market is not brain surgery. Anyone can be a successful investor. The secret is no secret. It is simply that you confine your selections to blue-chip stocks, you buy them when they are undervalued, and you sell them when they become overvalued. This is the well-lit path of the enlightened investor."

The Geraldine Weiss Approach in Brief

Universe of stocks

High-quality 'blue-chip' stocks. To get on this initial list, stocks should have at least five of the following characteristics:

- The dividend must have increased a minimum of five times in the past 12 years.
- In at least seven of the last 12 years, corporate earnings should have improved.
- It must have paid dividends, with no interruptions, for the past 25 years.
- The stock must carry an S&P quality ranking no lower than A–.
- Shares outstanding should number at least five million.
- Shares must be held by at least 80 institutions.

Stocks are removed from the blue chip universe when they no longer pass at least four of the rules.

Criteria for initial consideration

Buy from the blue-chip stock list when changing share prices cause dividend yields to be within 10% of their historical levels of high dividend yield, indicating the stock is historically undervalued.

Other factors

- A price-earnings ratio that is historically low for that particular stock and other similar stocks, and that is below the market multiple.

- A price-to-book-value ratio that is no higher than 1.3, and the closer to 1.0, the better.

- A ratio of current assets to current liabilities of at least 2.0, and a debt-to-equity ratio of no more than 50% debt to equity (utility stocks are excluded because of their unique regulatory status). Conservative investors should look for a debt-to-equity ratio of no more than 20%.

- Also be wary of other signs that dividend payments may be in jeopardy: Payout ratios approaching 100%, although a rising earnings trend can support rising dividends; and an indicated dividend higher than reported annual earnings, although strong cash flow can help cover a dividend payment when earnings temporarily drop.

- In general, when evaluating a stock for potential purchase, examine:
  - The company's financial performance, including its record of earnings, dividends, debt-to-equity ratio, dividend payout ratio, book value, and cash flow.
  - The company's product performance, whether it is manufacturing goods or services that are in demand, its research and development efforts, and its ability to market its products or services.
  - The company's investment performance in the form of capital gains and dividend growth.

Stock monitoring and when to sell

Aim for a portfolio of about 20 stocks selected from a variety of industry groups.

Continually monitor the portfolio to weed out stocks that no longer satisfy the requirements of good value or quality.

Sell stocks when they are within 10% of their historical low dividend yield, indicating overvaluation. If you tend to be reluctant to sell when prices are rising, consider placing a stop-loss order 12% to 15% below the overvalued price.

If dividend yields rise among stocks you own, make sure you understand why, but in general view it as an opportunity to buy more. However, if the rise occurs because a company omits a dividend, wait temporarily for prices to shore up and then sell, since it no longer meets the blue-chip criteria.

STOCK SCREENS: APPLYING THE WEISS APPROACH

Weiss uses six criteria to help identify "high-quality" companies suitable for valuation. She requires that a company pass at least five of the criteria to be included for further analysis in her blue-chip list, and removes companies from her list when they no longer meet four of the criteria. However, it is difficult to fully apply these criteria in the computerized stock screening programs available to most individual investors. Our screens are based on the data available through AAII's *Stock Investor Professional*.

History of Dividend Increases

The first criterion specifies that dividends must have increased a minimum of five times in the past 12 years—a difficult screen to implement electronically with the current batch of screening programs sold to individuals. The screen is trying to capture companies with a strong record of dividend increases, but does not eliminate companies that skip a dividend increase during a year or two. Increasing dividends have a corresponding increase effect on valuation levels. The software we used (AAII's *Stock Investor Professional*) provides seven years of income statement data. We required passing firms to have an increase in dividends in at least three of the past seven years.

Earnings Strength

Earnings growth helps to fuel dividend growth, so Weiss specifies that corporate earnings should have increased in at least seven of the last 12 years. As with dividends, most screening programs do not supply 12 years of data. We changed the screen to require an earnings per share increase in at least four of the past seven years tracked by *Stock Investor Professional*. We also required earnings over the last 12 months to be greater than or equal to earnings for the last fiscal year.

Record of Uninterrupted Dividends

Weiss requires her blue-chip companies to have a minimum of 20 to 25 years of uninterrupted cash dividends to help ensure that companies used for her relative yield analysis have a high resistance to cutting dividends. While not a variable we could screen for completely, we are screening for dividend payments for each of the last seven years.

Quality Rankings

Weiss requires that firms have Standard & Poor's earnings and dividends quality rankings of

A- or better. The ranking, which can be found in the S&P Stock Guide, examines the growth, stability and cyclicality of earnings and dividends over the last 10 years. The rankings are further adjusted based upon corporate size, with minimum size limits placed for various rankings. B+ is considered average, so Weiss requires above-average rankings for her blue-chip universe. This is one variable that we cannot screen for.

Minimum Liquidity

It is important to be able to have a sufficient number of outstanding shares to help ensure that investors can purchase and sell shares at appropriate times. Weiss specifies that the initial universe of stocks should have at least five million outstanding shares, which is relatively easy to incorporate using the typical software.

Institutional Sponsorship

Weiss states that 95% of the trading volume in today's market involves institutional investors. It is therefore important for a company to have sufficient interest in the powerful institutional market to prevent the stock price of even a quality company from languishing. Weiss requires that a company's shares be held by at least 80 institutions. Most stock screening programs track both the number of institutions and the percentage of outstanding shares held by institutional investors. We followed Weiss' recommendation and required at least 80 institutional shareholders.

These six variables were used to establish the blue-chip universe. In the next section we will further screen this blue-chip universe to see which stocks are potentially trading at undervalued levels.

The Blue-Chip Yield Comparison

Once the list of blue chip stocks is established, Weiss proposes that purchase and sell decisions be based on dividend yields. For our analysis, we calculated the average high and low dividend yield for each blue-chip stock over the last seven years. We then screened our list of blue chips for stocks whose current yield was within 10% of the high dividend yield average. The comparison of current yield to the firm's own past record of dividend yields allows firms with low absolute dividend yields to pass the screen.

Safety of the Dividend

A high relative current yield by itself does not indicate that a stock is undervalued. It may indicate that the dividend is in jeopardy. For a high relative yield to be considered a sign of

Geraldine Weiss' Blue Chip
Screening Criteria

Definitions for screens and terms can be found in the glossary starting on page 191.

Screening Criteria:
- Exclude REITs (real estate investment trusts)
- Dividend increases in at least 3 of the last 7 years
- EPS increases in at least 4 of the last 7 years
- EPS (last 12 months) greater than or equal to last fiscal year*
- Dividends equal to (or greater than) the prior year for each of the last 7 years*
- Shares outstanding numbering at least 5 million*
- Institutional shareholders numbering at least 80*
- Dividend yield within 10% of the seven-year average high dividend yield
- Current ratio (latest quarter) greater than or equal to 2.0
- Non-utility sector stocks: Long-term debt to equity (latest quarter) less than or equal to 50%
- Non-utility sector stocks: Payout ratio (last 12 months) less than or equal to 50%
- Utility sector stocks: Payout ratio (last 12 months) less than or equal to 85%

*Data not shown in table. Also note that the table shows additional data columns that may be of interest to those using this approach.

an undervalued stock, the company must be expected to continue to pay and expand the dividend over time. While the blue-chip screen helps to reveal strong firms, Weiss also relies on many traditional ratios as indications of the safety of the dividend and the attractiveness of the yield.

Weiss uses the current ratio as a measure of cash liquidity. Current ratios are determined by dividing current assets by current liabilities; ratios above 2.0 are generally considered desirable. We screened for a current ratio of 2.0 or higher. However, it is important to keep some of the weaknesses of the current ratio in mind. For example, it includes inventory as an asset, but in a cash squeeze inventory may be very illiquid. The current ratio is also meaningless for financial firms because of their unique balance sheets.

Weiss also suggests using the debt-to-equity ratio, which compares long-term debt to book equity. Weiss likes to see a ratio of no more than 50%, but excludes this measure for utilities because of their unique regulatory status. For non-utility stocks we required a debt-to-equity ratio less than 50%. More conservative investors should look for a debt-to-equity ratio of no more than 20%. Companies with high levels of debt can run into financial problems more quickly during a slowdown, putting the dividend in jeopardy.

The final filter uses the payout ratio, which is a common measure of the safety of the

Table 1.
Stocks Passing the Weiss Screening*

Company (Exchange: Ticker)	Price ($)	Div Grth (7-Yr) (%)	No. of Div Increases in Last 7 yrs.	Curr. Div Yield (%)	7-Yr Avg Div Yield High (%)	7-Yr Avg Div Yield Low (%)	No. of EPS Increases in Last 7 yrs.	EPS Grth (7-Yr) (%)	EPS Grth Est (%)	Curr Ratio (%)	Debt-Equity Ratio (%)	Payout Ratio (12 Mos.) (%)
Standard Register Company (N: SR)	13.88	6.0	6	6.3	3.80	2.46	5	9.1	10.0	4.0	36.8	31.4
Genuine Parts Company (N: GPC)	21.75	6.3	6	5.1	3.37	2.64	6	7.4	7.9	3.1	31.6	49.3
Cooper Tire & Rubber Co. (N: CTB)	10.75	17.0	6	3.9	1.61	0.96	4	8.0	9.5	3.0	21.6	23.5
J.M. Smucker Company (N: SJM.A)	17.00	5.6	5	3.5	2.79	1.91	4	1.6	9.8	3.1	22.8	44.0
Lafarge Corporation (N: LAF)	19.88	5.5	4	3.0	1.94	1.27	6	28.0	10.3	2.0	45.1	16.4
Applied Industrial Tech. (N: APZ)	16.94	8.0	5	2.8	2.94	1.74	4	39.8	14.1	2.8	32.9	38.4
ABM Industries, Inc. (N: ABM)	24.13	12.2	6	2.6	2.70	1.79	6	13.9	15.0	2.0	10.4	31.5
Brady Corporation (N: BRC)	24.75	18.9	6	2.6	2.39	1.45	4	33.6	15.0	3.1	0.4	34.7
Diebold Incorporated (N: DBD)	24.13	8.3	6	2.6	2.41	1.31	5	11.0	12.8	2.2	2.7	31.9
Lawson Products, Inc. (N: LAWS)	23.00	4.9	6	2.6	2.30	1.66	4	5.3	na	3.8	0.0	27.7
Leggett & Platt, Inc. (N: LEG)	16.06	16.5	6	2.5	1.66	1.06	6	24.6	14.1	2.8	47.1	25.0
Lancaster Colony Corp. (N: LANC)	29.19	15.1	6	2.2	1.96	1.30	6	18.1	12.7	2.7	0.7	24.1
Wynn's International Inc. (N: WN)	12.50	10.4	5	2.2	1.44	0.88	6	23.3	na	2.2	0.0	17.6
LSI Industries (N: LYTS)	16.25	40.9	5	2.0	1.72	0.89	6	24.6	20.5	2.8	1.6	22.6
Teleflex Inc. (N: TFX)	27.19	12.3	6	1.9	1.49	1.02	6	13.7	16.0	2.0	47.8	20.2
Coachmen Industries (N: COA)	10.94	25.8	5	1.8	1.39	0.71	5	22.1	na	2.9	4.0	9.9
Alberto-Culver Co. (N: ACV)	21.50	11.7	5	1.4	1.20	0.84	5	12.3	11.0	2.0	40.2	16.7
Donaldson Co., Inc. (N: DCI)	21.25	12.6	6	1.3	1.27	0.86	6	16.4	12.6	2.0	33.4	16.8
Sigma-Aldrich Corp. (N: SIAL)	24.00	14.3	6	1.3	0.92	0.60	5	11.0	11.7	6.2	0.0	16.4
Barrick Gold Corp. (N: ABX)	16.69	17.0	6	1.2	0.74	0.44	4	13.0	12.7	3.7	12.8	21.8
Wabash National Corp. (N: WNC)	13.56	na	6	1.2	0.72	0.33	5	9.8	19.5	2.5	44.0	14.5
Claire's Stores, Inc. (N: CLE)	16.63	21.9	4	1.0	0.87	0.41	5	35.7	17.5	3.7	0.0	10.7
Franklin Resources (N: BEN)	27.69	13.6	6	0.9	0.91	0.51	5	18.0	14.7	4.0	13.9	12.1
Tootsie Roll Industries (N: TR)	28.94	21.9	6	0.9	0.65	0.44	6	15.6	na	3.0	1.8	14.7
Molex, Inc. (N: MOLX)	53.81	29.2	4	0.2	0.19	0.11	5	14.7	16.6	2.6	1.4	5.6

na = not available

Exchange Key: N = New York Stock Exchange
A = American Stock Exchange
M = Nasdaq

*Screening criteria used to produce table results can be found on opposite page.

Source: AAII's Stock Investor/ Market Guide Inc. and I/B/E/S.
Statistics are based on figures as of February 25, 2000.

dividend. It is calculated by dividing dividends by earnings. In general, the lower the payout ratio, the more secure the dividend. Weiss considers any ratio above 50% as a warning sign, but she points out that for some industries, such as utilities, levels as high as 85% are considered normal. Figures above 100% indicate that the payout is greater than earnings. The company can sustain this in the short run, but too high a payout destroys liquidity and growth opportunities in the long run. Strong cash flow can help cover a dividend payment when earnings temporarily drop, but an "unprotected dividend is in greater danger than a protected dividend." Weiss likes to see low payout ratios coupled with high earnings growth as signs of strong opportunities for continued dividend growth.

Table 1 is a list of stocks passing the screens we used to illustrate how Geraldine Weiss' blue chip value approach can be implemented. It is based on data as of February 25, 2000, using AAII's *Stock Investor Professional*. Screening tips for the Weiss approach are on page 47.

Screening Tips: Geraldine Weiss' Blue-Chip Value Approach

Universe: Blue-Chip Stocks

- The dividend must have increased a minimum of five times in the past 12 years. Most screening programs do not supply more than five years of data for screening; use maximum number of years available.
- Corporate earnings should have improved in at least seven of the past 12 years. Most screening programs do not supply more than five years of data for screening; use maximum number of years available.
- Company must have paid dividends, with no interruptions, for the past 25 years. This is not a variable generally found in screening programs, but it is easy to check by hand using the S&P Stock Guide.
- The stock must carry a Standard & Poor's quality ranking no lower than A–. Proprietary S&P rankings are found only in programs using S&P data. However, the information can be looked up manually in the S&P Stock Guide.
- Shares outstanding should number at least five million. This screen for adequate float should be easy to replicate in most programs.
- Shares must be held by at least 80 institutions. This screen for adequate institutional following and liquidity should be easy to replicate in most screening programs.

Primary Criteria for Selection

Buy from the blue-chip stock list when price changes cause the dividend yields to be within the 10% of their historical levels of high dividend yield, indicating it is historically undervalued. Screen for stocks with a current dividend yield within 10% of their high dividend yield for the period you have available.

Secondary Factors to Ensure Safety of Dividend

- A ratio of current assets to current liabilities (current ratio) of at least 2.0, and debt-to-equity ratio of no more than 50% debt to equity. Conservative investors should look for a debt-to-equity ratio of no more than 20%. These are common screens for liquidity (current ratio) and leverage (debt to equity) that could be easily applied in most screening programs. Industry factors can come into play, so investors may wish to screen for ratios better than industry norms. Also, utilities should be excluded because of their unique regulatory status.
- Be wary of other signs that dividend payments may be in jeopardy: payout ratios approaching 100%, although a rising earnings trend can support rising dividends; and an indicated dividend higher than reported annual earnings, although strong cash flow can help cover a dividend payment when earnings temporarily drop. The payout ratio is a common screening element found in many dividend yield screens.

THE DOGS OF THE DOW: A MECHANICAL APPROACH TO VALUE

Can a stock selection process that is simple and mechanical actually beat the market?

That's the appealing belief underlying the Dogs of the Dow approach.

The "dogs" are the stocks within the 30 Dow industrial average stocks that have the highest dividend yields (individual dividends per share divided by share price). The approach calls for equal investment in the highest-yielding stocks, with a total revamping of the portfolio once a year.

In theory, the approach takes advantage of the long-term positive returns associated with the market as defined by the Dow Jones industrial average, and adds a bonus by its selection of only the highest-yielding stocks. Higher-yielding stocks are often temporarily out-of-favor issues that are possibly underpriced. In addition to greater price appreciation potential, investors should benefit from higher dividend payments.

The purely mechanical nature of the approach also forces strict investor discipline, and requires no investment decision-making expertise—a highly appealing strategy to many individual investors, particularly market newcomers.

Although the appeal is to individuals managing their own stock portfolios, the popularity of the approach prompted development of a series of unit investment trusts offered by Merrill Lynch, Smith Barney, PaineWebber, and other brokerage firms; sales charges, however, are steep. In addition, a handful of mutual funds employ the strategy, although only with a part of their assets due to IRS diversification requirements.

The Philosophy

The approach limits its universe to a highly select group of stocks—the 30 stocks that comprise the Dow Jones industrial average. These are large, well-known companies with immense financial resources and solid long-term track records that have weathered many economic storms. Their size and history provide these companies with a resilience that makes them relatively conservative investments.

On the other hand, Dow theory proponents maintain that the investing public, particularly institutions, tends to overreact to unfavorable short-term developments and business cycles, driving prices down to bargain levels. The Dow Dogs approach proposes that investors emphasize Dow stocks that have been driven down by overreaction, since they will quickly regain a value that reflects the actual underlying risk.

What if a stock is cheap because the company has real problems? The Dow Theory holds that the Dow stocks are so visible and widely analyzed that surprises with major adverse financial implications rarely occur. Surprises with big financial implications that have occurred in the past—Union Carbide's Bhopal and Exxon's Valdez oil spill, for example—have been weathered in stride by the companies, although stocks dropped temporarily, providing a buying opportunity for contrarians. Even in the few worst-case instances of near-bankruptcies, Dow stocks historically have become turnaround situations, with one exception: Manville Corp., a Dow stock until 1982 when it was forced into bankruptcy in the face of massive asbestos-related lawsuits.

According to the Dow Dogs approach, identifying undervalued Dow stocks is most effectively done by examining dividend yield—a company's indicated annual dividend (expected quarterly dividend multiplied by four) per share divided by share price. It is similar to other popular valuation measures such as price-earnings ratios (price divided by earnings per share) and book value per share. However, price-earnings ratios and book value are subject to more distortion due to short-term earnings fluctuations, as well as different accounting interpretations in book value and reported earnings. Dividend payments, in contrast, tend to be more predictable and not subject to differing accounting treatments, offering a more stable measure to relate to share price.

Over the short term, the prices of Dow stocks fluctuate with short-term earnings expectations. This causes a company's dividend yield to fluctuate—when the dividend yield is relatively high, the share price has dropped relative to the dividend, usually because the market has doubts about the company's immediate earnings prospects. However, over the long term, prices for Dow stocks tend to be driven by dividends, since they are stable and have provided a considerable portion of an investor's long-term total return. Thus, dividend yields are brought back into line, and owners of the stocks benefit from both the price appreciation and the higher dividend yields they received when they owned the stock.

The philosophy combines a strategy of investing in high-quality stocks with a contrarian approach.

The Mechanics

The Dogs of the Dow strategy is straightforward:

- Select any starting day (the first trading day of the year is most common) and determine the 10 stocks of the 30 Dow Jones industrials that have the highest current dividend yield. The stocks that make up the Dow industrial average are listed in The Wall Street Journal in the Dow Jones Averages summary graph. All are listed either on the New York Stock Exchange or Nasdaq National Market, and dividend yields (as well as closing prices) for stocks are listed in the financial

Table 1.
Dogs of the Dow vs. the Dow 30 & S&P 500
(excludes taxes and transaction costs)

	Average Annual Returns*(%)		
	Dow Dogs	**Dow 30**	**S&P 500**
1930s	−1.04	2.23	−0.05
1940s	12.62	9.73	9.17
1950s	20.38	19.24	19.35
1960s	9.18	6.66	7.81
1970s	13.32	6.79	5.86
1980s	21.78	18.59	17.55
1990–97	19.45	16.83	16.57

*Returns exclude taxes and transaction costs, which would have a greater impact on the returns of the Dow Dogs approach.

Source: "Stocks for the Long Run," 2nd edition by Jeremy Siegel, McGraw Hill, 1998.

sections of most major newspapers, including The Wall Street Journal. Alternatively, you can calculate dividend yields by using the indicated annual dividend for each of the 30 Dow stocks reported weekly in Barron's Market Laboratory section and the closing prices for the 30 stocks on the chosen starting day.

- Invest an equal dollar amount in each of those 10 stocks.
- One year later, determine the total value of the portfolio, including all dividends and other cash distributions, along with the closing values of the stocks. Rebalance the portfolio by again investing an equal dollar amount in each of the 10 highest-yielding Dow Jones industrial stocks at this time. This means that stocks that have dropped off the top-10 yields list should be sold and replaced with additions to the list. At the same time, the amount invested in stocks remaining on the list should be only 10% of the value of the portfolio at this time, which may mean adding shares or selling shares from existing holdings.
- Repeat the process on each one-year anniversary date, and ignore the portfolio at all other times.

Portfolio Turnover

The downside to the Dogs of the Dow approach is portfolio turnover, which will be higher than a strict buy-and-hold investment approach due to the annual rebalancing requirement. Portfolio turnover generates two major costs to an investor: transaction costs from the sale and purchase of stocks, and capital gains taxes if the portfolio is in a taxable account.

Transaction costs would vary based on the total amount being invested and the size of the trades that might be required to rebalance. Low-cost discount brokers can be used to help hold down these costs.

Does it Work?

Numerous studies in the mid-'90s appeared from both the academic and the investment community providing data on the superior performance of the 10 top-yielding Dow Jones stocks over long time periods, although actual results from various studies differ depending on starting dates used and how dividend yields are defined.

More recent studies suggest that the phenomenon may be playing out, perhaps a victim of its own success. Since high dividend yields reflect unpopularity, the more popular the Dogs of the Dow strategy becomes, the more likely it is that the stocks selected by the strategy will become overvalued.

The strategy has fared poorly relative to the Dow average in recent years. A contributing factor has been record-low dividend yields, greatly reducing the contribution that dividends make to total return.

On the other hand, the strategy has beaten the Dow 30, as well as the S&P 500, much of the '90s (through 1997), as well as in every decade since the 1930s, according to Jeremy Siegel in his most recent edition of "Stocks for the Long Run." Table 1 summarizes his findings.

Whether the phenomenon will continue appears to be an open question. However, it is important to note that none of the studies take into consideration taxes and transaction costs, which would substantially reduce the returns from the approach to an individual investor relative to a buy-and-hold approach.

A Summary K.I.S.

Keep It Simple (KIS) aptly summarizes the Dogs of the Dow approach. It offers a purely mechanical approach that focuses exclusively on high-quality, well-known companies, purchasing them when they become undervalued relative to each other.

The approach is particularly useful for individuals who prefer strict guidelines for buying and selling, who want a steady source of dividend income, and who lack the financial expertise required for more in-depth stock analysis. It is less useful for investors seeking primarily growth and who are trying to limit annual taxable income.

The Dogs of the Dow Approach

Philosophy and style

Dow Jones industrial average stocks are a select group of high-quality firms with strong financial positions and a long-term history of positive returns. These returns can be enhanced by picking the Dow stocks that are temporarily out-of-favor and possibly underpriced relative to the others, as indicated by high dividend yields. In addition to greater price appreciation potential, investors should benefit from higher dividend payments. The purely mechanical nature of the approach also forces strict investor discipline.

Universe of stocks

The 30 Dow Jones industrial average stocks.

Criteria for purchase

• Select any starting day (the first trading day of the year is most common) and determine the 10 stocks of the 30 Dow Jones industrials that have the highest current dividend yield.

• Invest an equal dollar amount in each of those 10 stocks.

Portfolio monitoring and when to sell

• Annually determine the total value of the portfolio, including all dividends and other cash distributions, along with the closing values of the stocks. Also determine the 10 stocks of the 30 Dow industrials with the highest current dividend yield. Sell all current holdings that have dropped off the list and replace them with new additions to the list. Rebalance the portfolio so that there is an equal dollar amount invested in each of the 10 holdings (each stock represents 10% of the value of the portfolio).

Other factors

Taxes and transaction costs will substantially lower an investor's bottom-line return. Keep transaction costs low by using a low-cost discount broker.

Stock Screens: Applying the Dogs of the Dow Approach

Few investment strategies have attracted the attention of such a diverse group of investors as that of the Dogs of the Dow approach. The "dogs" are the stocks within the 30 Dow Jones industrial average that have the highest dividend yields. The approach calls for equal investment in the 10 highest-yielding stocks, with a total revamping of the portfolio once a year.

A stock's dividend yield is computed by taking the indicated dividend—the most recent quarterly dividend multiplied by four—and dividing it by the share price. Both the indicated dividend and the dividend yield can be found in publications such as the Wall Street Journal, Investor's Business Daily, Barron's, S&P's Stock Guide, and the Value Line Investment Survey.

This is a simple screen that doesn't require a sophisticated software program to apply. Table 1 lists the 10 stocks that met the screen requirements on February 25, 2000. AAII's *Stock Investor Professional* was used to perform the screen.

Dogs of the Dow Screen

The first step was to create a screen that included only the 30 stocks in the Dow Jones industrial average. Then we ranked the companies by dividend yield and selected the top 10 yielding firms.

If you are doing the filter by hand, you could obtain a list of the stocks that make up the Dow Jones industrial average from the Dow Jones Averages summary graph within the Money and Investing Section of the Wall Street Journal. You can easily locate the closing price, dividend per share, and dividend yield for these stocks in the financial section of most major newspapers, including the Wall Street Journal.

When using the Dogs of the Dow approach it is important to understand that the Dow Jones industrial average is actually a diverse group of companies. Rather than a homogenous set of blue-chip companies, you will find companies of varying financial strength that compete in a wide range of industries, not all of which are industrial. Table 1 provides other investment characteristics of the selected stocks.

Historical Norm

While these stocks passed the Dogs of the Dow screen because of their high current dividend yield compared with other Dow stocks, a study of the company's own dividend yield history can be equally revealing. A current dividend yield higher than its historical average would be a sign that a stock is potentially undervalued. Models that examine historical averages assume that the growth prospects of the firm have not changed fundamentally over time and, based on historical relationships of dividends to price, the market is not correctly discounting the future potential of the firm. The dividend yield one year ago along with the average dividend yield over the last seven years is provided to help judge the normal dividend level for these stocks. It is important to keep in mind that dividend yields for cyclical firms often creep up late in an economic cycle as investors start to fear the potential of an economic slowdown.

Industry Norm

The diverse range of the Dow stocks exposes a potential weakness of the Dogs of the Dow screen. While all of the stocks are industry leaders, they operate in a wide range of industries with varying normal levels for dividend yields. Financials and established natural resource firms, for example, typically have higher dividends.

Dividend History

For stocks to succeed, the companies must perform well financially, and the market must take notice. Contrarian "bets" on widely followed stocks such as those that make up the Dow benefit from tremendous visibility. Increases in dividends and earnings will quickly translate into stock price increases.

A strong record of dividend increases is one sign of a company's commitment to supporting the stock price. Another simple statistic that has some meaning in judging the continuity of dividends is the number of consecutive years a cash dividend has been paid— a figure reported in the S&P Stock Guide.

Safety of the Dividend

Before a company can be considered a buy, the security of the dividend must also be examined. A high dividend yield may be a signal that the market expects the dividend to be cut shortly and has pushed down the price accordingly. Dividend payments are set by the board of directors, who go to great lengths to avoid lowering the indicated dividend. Decreasing or eliminating a dividend is tantamount to an announcement that the firm is financially distressed. While all of the Dow stocks are market-leading companies, a number of the cyclical firms have a history of reduced dividend levels during economic slowdowns.

Earnings of companies in cyclical industries can vary greatly. To avoid constantly increasing and lowering the indicated dividend, some of these companies set a very low base dividend that they will have no trouble paying during the worst of times, and they pay "special" dividends during economic upturns.

Measures exist that help to identify the safety of the dividend. The payout ratio is perhaps the most common of these and is calculated by dividing the dividend per share by earnings per share. Generally the lower the number, the more secure the dividend. Any ratio above 50% is considered a warning flag. However, for some industries, such as utilities, ratios around 80% are common. A 100% payout ratio indicates that a company is paying out all of its earnings in the form of dividends. Firms cannot afford to pay out more than they earn in the long term. Both the recent and long-term average payout ratio is listed for stocks making up the Dogs of the Dow.

Earnings Strength

Profitability ultimately determines the ability of a firm to reward shareholders through both dividend payments and capital appreciation. The historical earnings growth rate provides an indication of past company performance, while the analyst consensus earnings growth rate estimates indicate future expectations for these companies. Some software programs do provide consensus earnings estimates, but thier usefulness depends on how frequently the data is updated.

Conclusion

The Dogs of the Dow approach takes advantage of the long-term positive returns associated with the market as defined by the Dow Jones industrial average, and adds a bonus through its selection of only the highest-yielding stocks. Higher-yielding stocks are often temporarily out-of-favor issues that are possibly underpriced. The Dow stocks are large firms that in the long term possess both the depth of management and the strength of resources to recover from any short-term stumbles.

Table 2.
Dogs of the Dow Screening Results*

Company (Exchange: Ticker)	Price ($)	52-Wk Price High ($)	52-Wk Price Low ($)	Div Yield (%)	Div Yield 1 yr Ago (%)	Avg. Div Yield (7-Yr) (%)	Div Grth (5-Yr) (%)	EPS Grth (5-Yr) (%)	Long-Term EPS Grth Est. (%)	Payout Ratio 12 Mos. (%)	Payout Ratio 7-Yr Avg. (%)
Philip Morris Companies (N: MO)	19.63	43.00	18.69	9.8	4.5	3.9	14.1	13.6	12.0	71.1	60.5
J.P. Morgan & Co. Inc. (N: JPM)	107.88	147.81	104.69	3.7	3.4	3.4	9.1	−8.2	9.9	45.1	45.0
Caterpillar, Inc. (N: CAT)	36.00	66.44	34.88	3.6	2.6	1.4	49.0	21.0	9.8	43.3	na
Eastman Kodak Company (N: EK)	57.88	79.81	56.31	3.0	2.7	2.8	−2.5	24.0	10.1	47.4	na
International Paper Co. (N: IP)	36.00	60.00	35.81	2.8	2.5	2.2	3.5	−8.0	4.4	234.9	na
SBC Communications Inc. (N: SBC)	35.44	59.88	34.81	2.8	1.7	2.9	4.3	37.4	12.2	43.0	na
E.I. DuPont de Nemours (N: DD)	51.50	75.19	49.50	2.7	2.7	2.6	9.3	58.2	9.9	12.2	na
Minn. Mining & Mfg. (N: MMM)	85.75	103.81	69.31	2.7	3.0	2.8	4.9	7.0	10.9	51.0	59.2
General Motors Corp. (N: GM)	77.06	94.88	59.75	2.6	2.4	2.4	20.1	14.9	7.7	19.9	na
Exxon Mobil Corp. (N: XOM)	71.06	86.56	70.00	2.5	na	na	3.0	2.4	9.7	82.7	67.6

na = not available

Exchange Key: N = New York Stock Exchange
A = American Stock Exchange
M = Nasdaq

*Screening criteria used to produce table results can be found on opposite page.

Source: AAII's Stock Investor/Market Guide Inc. and I/B/E/S.
Statistics are based on figures as of February 25, 2000.

THE WARREN BUFFETT WAY: INVESTING FROM A BUSINESS PERSPECTIVE

One of the best-known investment "winners" still playing the game is Warren Buffett. Through his publicly traded holding company, Berkshire Hathaway, Buffett has built an impressive investment track record, as well as a personal fortune that places him consistently on the Forbes list of the wealthiest Americans.

Buffett is often identified with Benjamin Graham, with whom he studied, worked under, and maintained a long friendship (see Chapter 1). However, his own investment experience has led him to adopt the approaches of other investment pioneers, in particular Philip Fisher's focus on the importance of a business's growth prospects and management (see Chapter 6). Buffett has not published any comprehensive materials concerning his own method. The source for this chapter is the book "Buffetology" by Mary Buffett and David Clark [see References on page 201 for more details].

Investing in a Business: The Philosophy

Warren Buffett believes that a successful stock investment is a result first and foremost of the underlying business. Its value to the owner comes primarily from the company's ability to generate earnings at an increasing rate each year. Buffett, in fact, views stocks as bonds with variable yields, and their yields equate to the firm's underlying earnings. If the business is good, earnings will be more predictable and will consistently grow. That, in turn, makes the stock more valuable than a credit-risk-free government bond, which has an unchanging yield.

The price at which Buffett will buy a stock is, of course, a consideration, but it is not as critical as it was for Benjamin Graham. Graham proposed that investors buy stock below their "intrinsic value"; this would provide investors with a margin of protection that could help absorb unfavorable developments, with subsequently less risk of a market overreaction on the downside.

Buffett, in contrast, views the underlying business as the investor's "margin of protection." If a business is mediocre, the stock will do poorly even if purchased cheaply because any gain will be limited to the difference between the purchase price and the company's intrinsic value, assuming the stock price eventually reaches that level—which, Buffett points out, does not always occur.

Consequently, Buffett targets successful businesses—those with expanding intrinsic values, which he seeks to buy at a price that makes economic sense.

What makes economic sense? First, he compares the price against what it can reasonably earn based on the kind of business it is in, and based on the quality of the management running the company. Then, he purchases the stock if he believes he can earn an annual rate of return of at least 15% for at least five or 10 years. However, his goal is not to sell—as long as a business continues to have earnings growth greater than alternative investments, Buffett believes it makes more sense to hold indefinitely, putting off capital gains taxes, and enjoying the fruits of compounding intrinsic value.

Stock Criteria

Buffett pays close attention to the kinds of businesses he wishes to invest in. He seeks businesses whose product or service will be in constant and growing demand; he also seeks businesses that are in areas that are relatively easy to understand.

In his view, businesses can be divided into two basic types:

- Commodity-based firms, selling products in highly competitive markets in which price plays the key role in a consumer's purchase decision. Examples include textile manufacturers, producers of raw food items such as corn and rice, oil and gas companies, the lumber industry, and even car manufacturers.
- Consumer monopolies, selling products in which there is no effective competitor, either due to a patent or brand name or similar intangible that makes the product unique. Examples include brand-name companies such as Coca-Cola, media and communications companies, and certain financial services firms.

Buffett does not purchase the stocks of commodity-based businesses. These industries are highly competitive and dominated by the lowest-cost producer. To compete effectively, companies must spend heavily on manufacturing improvements, which leaves less that can be spent on new product development or new enterprises. In addition, these companies must have top-notch management to survive, but profits are kept low by price competition.

How do you spot a commodity-based company? Buffett looks for these characteristics:

- The firm has low profit margins (net income divided by revenues);
- The firm has low returns on equity (net income divided by shareholder's equity);
- There is little brand-name loyalty for its products;
- The industry has multiple producers;
- The industry tends to have substantial excess production capacity;
- Profits tend to be erratic; and
- The firm's profitability depends on management's abilities to efficiently use tangible assets.

The kinds of businesses Buffett seeks are those that have a consumer monopoly. These are companies that have managed to create a product or service that is somehow unique and difficult to reproduce by competitors, either due to brand-name loyalty, a particular market niche that only a limited number of companies can enter, or an unregulated but legal monopoly such as a patent. The exceptions to the consumer monopoly rule are utilities and similar industries that have a legal monopoly but are heavily regulated.

In Buffett's view, the real value of consumer monopolies is in their intangibles—for instance, brand-name loyalty, regulatory licenses, and patents. They do not have to rely heavily on investments in land, plant, and equipment, and typically the products are low-tech. As a result of all of these factors, they tend to have large cash flows and low debt.

Consumer monopolies can also typically adjust their prices quickly to inflation since there is little price competition to keep prices in check. This inflation-adjusting ability is another key factor Buffett favors in a firm.

In determining whether a company has a consumer monopoly, Buffett poses the question: If he had access to billions of dollars and the top 50 managers in the country, could he start his own business and compete with the business in question? If the answer is no, the company is most likely protected from competition by some kind of strong consumer monopoly.

Consumer monopolies can be businesses that sell products or services. They include:

- Businesses that make products that wear out or are used up quickly and have brand-name appeal that merchants must carry to attract customers. The best example is Coca-Cola, a favorite Buffett holding for more than 20 years. The product is an item that grocery stores, restaurants, and other retailers simply must carry. In addition, the brand name loyalty exists worldwide, not just in the U.S. Other examples include leading newspapers, drug companies with patents and brand-name prescription drugs, and popular brand-name restaurants such as McDonald's.
- Communications firms that provide services businesses must use to reach consumers. All businesses must advertise their wares to potential consumers, and many of the available media face little competition. These include worldwide advertising agencies, magazine publishers, newspapers, and telecommunications networks.
- Businesses that provide consumer services that are always in demand. Most of these services require little in the way of plants and equipment, so the company does not require heavy capital expenditures, and they do not tend to require highly paid workforces. Examples include tax preparers H&R Block; ServiceMaster, which provides professional cleaning, maid service and lawn care; and credit card companies such as American Express.

Other Characteristics

While Buffett believes that a consumer monopoly is a key ingredient of an excellent company, another key ingredient is a capable management that can exploit the company's unique advantage.

How do you judge management's ability? Buffett looks for the following characteristics:

- ***A strong upward trend in earnings:*** Buffett seeks not only a strong upward trend in earnings over a long-term time period, but he seeks year-by-year increases as well, providing an indication that management is able to turn the company's consumer monopoly advantage into shareholder value.

- **Conservative financing:** Consumer monopolies tend to have strong cash flows, with little need for long-term debt. Buffett does not object to the use of debt for a good purpose—for example, if a company adds debt to purchase another consumer monopoly. However, he does object if the added debt is used in a way that will produce mediocre results—such as purchasing a commodity-type business.

- **A consistently high return on shareholder's equity:** Since the average return on equity for U.S. firms over the last 40 years has been about 12%, Buffett seeks firms with returns on equity of 15% or higher, providing a good indication that management can make money from its existing business and can profitably employ retained earnings.

- **A high level of retained earnings:** Buffett believes that the real growth in stock value comes from reinvesting earnings to expand operations or purchase new ventures. Thus, he prefers companies that tend to reinvest retained earnings rather than those that are committed to paying out a high percentage of profits in dividends.

- **Low level of spending needed to maintain current operations:** Retained earnings must first go to maintain current operations at competitive levels, so the lower the amount required to maintain current operations, the more retained earnings can be used to finance expansions or new ventures.

- **Profitable use of retained earnings:** Buffett considers this one of the most important questions in analyzing a company's management. The nature of the business will tend to dictate a company's ability to retain earnings and the need to spend those earnings to maintain current operations; putting those retained earnings to profitable use, however, requires managerial talent. Retained earnings can be used to buy profitable business ventures, to expand existing operations, or to repurchase existing shares from shareholders; it is management's responsibility to determine which alternative offers the greater investment return to shareholders. Buffett views share repurchases favorably, since they cause per share earnings increases for those who don't sell, resulting in an increase in the stock's market price. Thus, Buffett examines management's use of retained earnings, looking for managements that have proven they are able to employ retained earnings in new moneymaking ventures, or for stock buybacks when they would offer a greater return.

Valuing a Share

Identifying a company that he wants to own is only the first step in Buffett's investment approach. The next step is to determine whether the purchase price makes economic sense.

Buffett uses a number of different methods to evaluate share price, including sophisticated and detailed analyses of a company's various operations.

One approach is to examine a prospective firm's earnings yield (earnings per share divided by share price) relative to government bonds. The earnings yield represents a rate of return that can be quickly compared to other investments. Buffett views stocks as bonds with variable yields, and their yields equate to the firm's underlying earnings. The analysis is dependent upon the predictability and stability of the earnings, which is why he emphasizes earnings strength. Buffett likes to compare the company's earnings yield to the long-term government bond yield. An earnings yield near the government bond yield is considered attractive: The bond interest is cash in hand but it is static, while the earnings of the company should grow over time and push the stock price up.

Another approach Buffett uses is to project a 10-year annual rate of return based on historical earnings per share growth. For example, if earnings per share at a firm had increased at a compound average annual rate of return of 18.9% for the prior 10 years, and current earnings per share were $2.77, earnings per share in 10 years would be $15.64, assuming the firm continued to grow at the 18.9% historical rate [$2.77 \times (1 + 0.189)^{10}$]. This estimated earnings per share figure can then be multiplied by the average price-earnings ratio for the stock over the past 10 years to provide an estimated price in year 10. For instance, if the average price-earnings ratio were 14.0, the estimated price in year 10 would be $218.96 ($15.64 \times 14.0$). If dividends are paid, an estimate of the amount of dividends paid over the 10-year period should also be added to the year 10 price.

Once future prices are estimated, estimated rates of return can be determined over the 10-year period based on the current selling price for the stock. For example, if the stock was currently selling for $48.25, and its estimated future price is $218.96, the average annual return over 10 years would be 16.3% [$($218.96 \div $48.25)^{1/10} - 1$]. Buffett requires a return of at least 15%.

A third valuation approach is based upon the sustainable growth rate model. Buffett uses the average rate of return on equity and average retention ratio (1 − average payout ratio) to calculate a sustainable growth rate [ROE × retention ratio]. The sustainable growth rate is used to calculate the book value per share in year 10 (the current book value per share compounding for 10 years at the sustainable growth rate). Earnings per share can be estimated in year 10 by multiplying the average return on equity by the projected book value per share. To estimate the future price, you multiply the earnings by the average price-earnings ratio. If dividends are paid, they can be added to the projected price to compute the total gain.

For example, if a company's average return on equity was 22.8%, and its average payout ratio was 15.9%, its sustainable growth rate would be 19.2% [$22.8\% \times (1 − 0.159)$]. If its current book value per share was $11.38, it would grow to roughly $65.90 in 10 years [$11.38 \times (1 + 0.192)^{10}$]. If return on equity remains 22.8% in the 10th year, earnings per share that year would be $15.03 ($0.228 \times \$65.90$). The estimated earnings per share can then be multiplied by the average price-earnings ratio to project the price; assuming a 14.0 price-earnings ratio, the projected price would be $210.42 [$15.03 \times 14.0$]. That would imply a 10-year annual return of 15.9%, assuming a current price of $48.25 [($210.42 ÷ 48.25)$^{1/10}$ – 1].

Buffett will certainly take advantage of "bargains"—for instance, if a bear market drives all prices down or if an unfavorable short-term outlook by the market causes a particular stock that Buffett has identified as an "excellent" business to drop in price. However, his valuation methods focus on earnings growth, and he is not adverse to buying stocks at somewhat higher valuations if he is confident of earnings expansion.

Stock Monitoring and When to Sell

Buffett does not favor extensive diversification, since it is difficult to sufficiently analyze and understand a large number of companies. In addition, he does not diversify based on industry sectors; his avoidance of commodity-type businesses, in fact, leads to the exclusion of certain groups. Instead, Buffett's method of controlling risk within a portfolio is to seriously address the major factors of his approach: to make sure he is investing in expanding businesses, to thoroughly understand and analyze the nature of the businesses in which he invests, and to make sure he does not pay too much for the shares.

Buffett is also a long-term investor—some of his holdings have been in his portfolio for over 20 years. While his mentor, Benjamin Graham, favored a sale when a company's share price reached its intrinsic value, Buffett will continue to hold as long as the company's growth prospects are better than alternative investments. The time to sell, in Buffett's view, is never, if he has bought an excellent company that is consistently growing and has quality management that operates for the benefit of shareholders. If those circumstances change—the nature of the business changes or management changes, for example—then Buffett would sell. He would also consider selling if an alternative investment offered a better return.

Buffett in Summary

Warren Buffett's approach identifies "excellent" businesses based on the prospects for the industry and the ability of management to exploit opportunities for the ultimate benefit of shareholders. He then waits for the share price to reach a level that would provide him with a desired long-term rate of return.

Sound easy? For individual investors who want to duplicate the process, it requires a considerable amount of time, effort, and judgment in perusing a firm's financial statements, annual reports, and other information sources to thoroughly analyze the business and quality of management. It also requires patience, waiting for the right price once a prospective business has been identified, and the ability to stick to the approach during times of market volatility.

The Warren Buffett Approach

Philosophy and style

Investment in stocks based on their intrinsic value, where value is measured by the ability to generate earnings and dividends over the years. Buffett targets successful businesses—those with expanding intrinsic values, which he seeks to buy at a price that makes economic sense, defined as earning an annual rate of return of at least 15% for at least five or 10 years.

Universe of stocks

No limitation on stock size, but analysis requires that the company have been in existence for a considerable period of time.

Criteria for initial consideration

Consumer monopolies, selling products in which there is no effective competitor, either due to a patent or brand name or similar intangible that makes the product unique. In addition, he prefers companies that are in businesses that are relatively easy to understand and analyze, and that have the ability to adjust their prices for inflation.

Other factors

- A strong upward trend in earnings
- Conservative financing
- A consistently high return on shareholder's equity
- A high level of retained earnings
- Low level of spending needed to maintain current operations
- Profitable use of retained earnings

Valuing a Stock

Buffett uses several approaches, including:

- *Comparing a firm's earnings yield relative to government bonds*: An earnings yield (earnings per share divided by share price) near the long-term government bond yield is attractive, since bond interest is static while earnings should grow over time.

- *Projecting an annual rate of return based on historical earnings per share increases*: Current earnings per share are compounded by the average growth in earnings per share over the past 10 years to determine the projected earnings per share in year 10; this figure is then multiplied by the average high and low price-earnings ratios for the stock over the past 10 years to provide an estimated price range in year 10. If dividends are paid, an estimate of the amount of dividends paid over the 10-year period should also be added to the year 10 prices. The projected price in year 10 is compared to the current price to determine the projected average rate of return.

- *Projecting an annual rate of return based on the sustainable growth rate*: The current return on equity is multiplied by the average retention ratio to calculated sustainable growth rate. The current book value per share is compounded for 10 years at the sustainable growth rate to book value per share in year 10. Multiplying the book value in year 10 by the average return on equity provides an estimate of earnings per share in year 10; multiplying projected earnings per share by the average price-earnings rate provides an estimate of price in year 10. If dividends are paid, an estimate of the amount of dividends paid over the 10-year period should be added to the year 10 price estimate. The year 10 price estimate can be compared to current prices to estimate an average annual rate of return.

Stock monitoring and when to sell

Does not favor diversification; prefers investment in a small number of companies that an investor can know and understand extensively.

Favors holding for the long term as long as the company remains "excellent"—it is consistently growing and has quality management that operates for the benefit of shareholders. Sell if those circumstances change, or if an alternative investment offers a better return.

STOCK SCREENS: APPLYING THE WARREN BUFFETT APPROACH

Consumer Monopoly or Commodity?

Buffett seeks consumer monopolies selling products in which there is no effective competitor, either due to a patent or brand name or similar intangible that makes the product unique. How can investors screen for these companies? Consumer monopolies typically have high profit margins because of their unique niche. However, simple screens for high margins may only highlight firms in industries with traditionally high margins. Our screens look for companies with operating margins and net profit margins above their industry norms. Operating margin measures the costs directly associated with the production of the goods and services, while the net margin takes all of the company's activities and actions into account. Follow-up examinations should include a detailed study of the firm's position in the industry and how it might change over time.

Is the Company Conservatively Financed?

Consumer monopolies tend to have strong cash flows, with little need for long-term debt. Buffett does not object to the use of debt for a good purpose—for example, if a company uses debt to finance the purchase of another consumer monopoly. However, he does object if the added debt is used in a way that will produce mediocre results—such as expanding into a commodity line of business.

The conservative financing screen here seeks companies with total liabilities relative to assets below the median for their industry. Appropriate levels of debt vary from industry to industry, so it is best to construct a screen relative to industry norms. The ratio of total liabilities to total assets is more encompassing than using ratios based on long-term debt, such as the debt-equity ratio.

Are Earnings Strong and Do They Show an Upward Trend?

Buffett invests only in businesses whose future earnings are predictable to a high degree of certainty. Companies with predictable earnings have good business economics and produce cash that can be reinvested or paid out to shareholders. Earnings levels are critical in valuation. As earnings increase, the stock price will eventually reflect this growth.

Buffett looks for strong long-term growth as well as an indication of an upward trend. The software used here, AAII's *Stock Investor Professional*, contains seven years of data, so we examine the seven-year growth rate as the long-term growth rate and the three-year growth rate for the intermediate-term growth rate. The screen requires that a company's seven-year earnings growth rate be higher than that of 75% of the stocks in the overall database.

It is best if the earnings also show an upward trend. Buffett compares the intermediate-term growth rate to the long-term growth rate and looks for an expanding level. For that reason, we also require that the three-year growth rate in earnings be greater than the seven-year growth rate.

Consumer monopolies should show both strong and consistent earnings; wild swings in earnings are characteristic of commodity businesses. An examination of year-by-year earnings should be performed as part of the evaluation. A screen requiring an increase in earnings for each of the last seven years would be too stringent and not in keeping with the Buffett philosophy. However, a screen requiring positive earnings for each of the last seven years should help to eliminate some of the commodity-based businesses with wild earnings swings.

Has the Company Been Buying Back Its Shares?

Buffett prefers that firms reinvest their earnings within the company, provided that profitable opportunities exist. When companies have excess cash flow, Buffett favors shareholder-enhancing maneuvers such as share buybacks. Buffett views share repurchases favorably since they cause per share earnings increases for those who don't sell, resulting in an increase in the stock's market price. Share repurchases are difficult to screen for, since most data services do not provide this variable. You can screen for a decreasing number of outstanding shares, but this factor is best analyzed during the valuation process. While we did not screen for this factor, a follow-up examination of a company should reveal if it has a share buyback plan in place.

Have Retained Earnings Been Invested Well?

Buffett examines management's use of retained earnings, looking for a management that has proven it is able to employ retained earnings in the new moneymaking ventures, or for stock buybacks when they offer a greater return. A company should retain its earnings if its rate of return on its investment is higher than the investor could earn on his own. Dividends should only be paid if they would be better employed in other companies. If the earnings are properly reinvested in the company, earnings should rise over time and stock price valuations will also rise to reflect the increasing value of the business. The screens for strong and consistent earnings and strong return on equity help to capture this factor.

Warren Buffett's Historical Earnings Growth
Screening Criteria
Definitions for screens and terms can be found in the glossary starting on page 191.

Screening Criteria:
- Operating profit margin (last 12 months) greater than or equal to industry median*
- Net profit margin (last 12 months) greater than or equal to industry median*
- Total liabilities relative to total assets (latest fiscal quarter) less than or equal to industry median*
- 7-year EPS (from continuing operations) growth rate greater than 75% of stocks in database
- 3-year EPS (from continuing operations) growth greater than or equal to 7-year EPS growth
- Positive EPS (from continuing operations) each year for last 7 years*
- 7-year return on equity (last 12 months) greater than 12%
- Return on equity (last 12 months) greater than 12%
- Projected return (using historical earnings growth model) greater than 15%

Data not shown in table. Also note that the table shows additional data columns that may be of interest to those using this approach.

Is the Company's Return On Equity Above Average?

Buffett considers it a positive sign when a company is able to earn above-average returns on equity. The average return on equity over the last 40 years is roughly 12%. For our screens, we created a field that calculated the average return on equity over the last seven years, and then filtered for companies with an average return on equity above 12%. An average return on equity for the last seven years should provide a better indication of the normal profitability for the company than a current return on equity. However, we also included a screen requiring that the current return on equity be above 12% to help assure that the past is still indicative of the future direction of the company.

Does the Company Need to Constantly Reinvest in Capital?

In Buffett's view, the real value of consumer monopolies is in their intangibles—for instance, brand-name loyalty, regulatory licenses, and patents. They do not have to rely heavily on investments in land, plant, and equipment, and they often produce products that are low tech. Therefore they tend to have large free cash flows (operating cash flow less dividends and capital expenditures) and low debt. Retained earnings must first go to maintaining current operations at competitive levels. This is a factor that is best examined once a

Table 1.
Stocks Passing Warren Buffett's
Historical Earnings Growth Model Screening*

Company (Exchange: Ticker)	2/25/00 Price ($)	EPS 3-yr Grth Rate (%)	EPS 7-yr Grth Rate (%)	EPS Grth (Est) (%)	ROE (12-mo) (%)	7-yr Avg. ROE (%)	Earn'gs Yield (12-mo) (%)	P/E (x)	7-yr Avg. P/E (x)	Sustain. Grth Rate (%)	Estimated Ret. Based on: Hist. EPS Grth (%)	Sustain. Grth (%)
Williams-Sonoma, Inc. (N: WSM)	27.19	172.3	65.3	25.1	19.7	12.5	4.30	24.9	86.5	12.54	88.5	22.3
Theragenics Corporation (N: TGX)	13.13	81.7	57.5	30.0	15.4	16.7	3.81	23.9	85.7	16.67	77.3	32.4
Synopsys, Inc. (M: SNPS)	40.25	101.8	50.7	21.7	18.6	14.3	5.71	17.9	56.5	14.29	69.4	25.1
Astec Industries, Inc. (M: ASTE)	26.13	78.1	64.4	20.3	20.6	14.7	6.70	16.3	19.6	14.67	68.9	13.9
TSR, Inc. (M: TSRI)	6.56	71.7	45.0	na	30.5	13.6	13.10	7.5	33.4	12.39	68.1	21.4
Analytical Surveys, Inc. (M: ANLT)	8.00	49.1	45.2	22.0	16.3	16.1	17.00	6.2	24.2	16.09	67.3	33.5
M.D.C. Holdings, Inc. (N: MDC)	14.44	53.1	51.4	13.0	23.0	12.5	27.77	3.7	8.2	11.57	64.6	14.8
Birmingham Utilities Inc (M: BIRM)	17.50	93.9	43.9	na	42.0	19.8	12.51	8.3	17.4	6.03	55.9	7.8
Monaco Coach Corporation (N: MNC)	16.50	54.6	37.7	14.4	30.6	20.7	13.03	7.3	21.0	20.71	52.3	28.3
Keane, Inc. (A: KEA)	22.88	65.5	38.4	23.3	23.5	15.6	6.30	22.4	38.2	15.57	51.1	21.1
National RV Holdings, Inc (N: NVH)	13.38	103.2	33.3	20.0	26.0	20.7	22.13	4.5	15.7	20.74	51.0	33.9
Mohawk Industries, Inc. (N: MHK)	21.63	143.6	29.4	15.0	20.3	16.1	11.33	8.9	31.5	16.07	47.0	28.6
Chico's FAS, Inc. (M: CHCS)	12.00	72.0	32.0	25.0	28.7	26.3	6.83	15.2	30.5	26.33	42.1	34.8
Buckle, Inc. (N: BKE)	13.25	47.8	29.1	15.7	22.9	18.4	12.68	8.3	19.0	18.40	41.0	26.7
Bed Bath & Beyond Inc. (M: BBBY)	23.94	34.1	34.0	25.8	23.0	26.5	3.55	29.6	44.2	26.47	40.2	33.9
Jabil Circuit, Inc. (N: JBL)	71.50	49.5	49.5	30.2	16.2	17.5	1.69	61.6	30.2	17.50	39.8	9.9
Crossmann Communities (M: CROS)	15.38	29.2	28.7	12.5	21.3	30.7	21.20	4.5	10.1	30.70	38.9	46.2
Technitrol, Inc. (N: TNL)	46.63	54.0	37.0	15.0	19.4	15.7	5.28	17.1	20.7	10.38	38.4	9.4
Microsoft Corporation (M: MSFT)	91.31	49.6	39.5	24.7	25.2	29.4	1.87	57.4	42.6	29.44	36.4	28.4
United Capital Corp. (A: AFP)	15.13	44.7	26.1	na	20.9	14.4	15.40	5.7	13.8	na	36.0	na
Micros Systems, Inc. (M: MCRS)	52.81	124.2	30.7	25.0	22.1	19.1	3.65	29.2	40.0	19.09	35.8	21.6
Herbalife International (M: HERBA)	15.00	36.5	25.6	na	26.7	41.7	11.87	8.1	15.7	22.23	34.6	36.7
Craftmade International (M: CRFT)	7.38	44.9	27.3	30.0	24.6	21.7	9.36	11.3	17.4	20.21	34.0	25.2
Pacific Sunwear of CA (M: PSUN)	21.88	95.7	29.7	27.0	21.1	15.0	4.57	22.3	29.7	15.04	33.7	14.6
Burlington Nrth./Santa Fe (N: BNI)	20.06	62.8	21.3	9.8	13.9	14.6	11.96	8.2	20.4	7.53	33.1	18.9
Kohl's Corporation (N: KSS)	69.56	35.5	34.9	22.3	14.8	17.5	2.08	49.3	40.8	17.51	32.7	17.3
Ducommun Incorporated (N: DCO)	9.50	41.6	23.7	8.5	17.0	37.9	14.95	7.4	13.1	37.89	32.3	60.2
T. Rowe Price Associates (M: TROW)	34.19	29.6	28.0	15.3	30.5	27.2	5.18	18.5	25.4	20.04	32.0	22.6
Robert Half Int'l Inc. (N: RHI)	41.50	45.2	28.4	20.2	24.3	18.7	3.69	26.9	34.1	18.67	31.4	18.3
Virco Manufacturing Corp. (A: VIR)	12.50	50.3	26.2	18.8	14.7	12.5	10.88	9.5	12.4	11.87	30.3	13.7
Home Depot, Inc. (N: HD)	53.00	29.0	28.0	23.5	18.3	16.4	1.85	53.0	46.5	14.55	26.2	11.7
Federal Screw Works (M: FSCR)	42.25	23.2	22.5	na	16.1	13.5	17.96	5.6	6.8	10.03	25.4	11.0
Fossil, Inc. (M: FOSL)	22.25	36.4	21.2	21.1	26.7	27.9	6.56	14.3	20.3	27.86	24.7	32.0
JONES PHARMA, Inc. (M: JMED)	71.00	54.2	25.8	26.3	16.5	16.6	1.42	64.5	56.5	14.63	23.2	12.3
Brookstone, Inc. (M: BKST)	16.75	24.9	21.5	19.0	15.0	26.6	7.16	14.8	15.2	26.63	22.5	35.0
Washington Post Co. (N: WPO)	478.75	34.0	22.4	10.0	13.6	18.0	4.71	21.5	18.9	13.45	21.6	16.0
Expeditors Int'l of WA (M: EXPD)	33.97	38.7	23.4	21.1	20.3	16.5	3.21	30.9	26.5	15.18	21.6	11.1

*Screening criteria used to produce table results can be found on opposite page.

Source: AAII's Stock Investor/Market Guide Inc. and I/B/E/S. Statistics are based on figures as of February 25, 2000.

company has passed all screenable factors, although a screen for relative levels of free cash flow might help to confirm a company's status.

The Price is Right

The price that you pay for a stock determines the rate of return—the higher the initial price, the lower the overall return; the lower the initial price paid, the higher the return. Buffett first picks the business, and then lets the price of the company determine when to purchase the firm.

Buffett uses a number of different methods to value share price, including:
- **Earnings Yield (earnings per share divided by share price):** Buffett considers an earnings yield near the government bond yield to be attractive.
- **Historical Earnings Growth:** Buffett projects earnings per share 10 years from now based on their annual growth rate over the last 10 years. This estimated earnings per share figure is then multiplied by the company's historical average price-earnings ratio to provide an estimate of the price in year 10. If dividends are paid, an estimate of the amount of dividends paid over the 10-year period should also be added to the year 10 price. Most software programs do not provide 10 years of historical data, so you may have to use historical growth rates and average price-earnings ratios that cover shorter time periods. Once this future price is estimated,

Table 2.
Stocks Passing Warren Buffett's
Sustainable Growth Model Screening*

Company (Exchange: Ticker)	2/25/00 Price ($)	EPS 3-yr Grth Rate (%)	EPS 7-yr Grth Rate (%)	EPS Grth (Est) (%)	ROE (12-mo) (%)	7-yr Avg. ROE (%)	Earn'gs Yield (12-mo) (%)	P/E (x)	7-yr Avg. P/E (x)	Sustain. Grth Rate (%)	Estimated Ret. Based on: Hist. EPS Grth (%)	Estimated Ret. Based on: Sustain. Grth (%)
Ducommun Incorporated (N: DCO)	9.50	41.6	23.7	8.5	17.0	37.9	14.95	7.4	13.1	37.89	32.3	60.2
Crossmann Communities (M: CROS)	15.38	29.2	28.7	12.5	21.3	30.7	21.20	4.5	10.1	30.70	38.9	46.2
Herbalife International (M: HERBA)	15.00	36.5	25.6	na	26.7	41.7	11.87	8.1	15.7	22.23	34.6	36.7
Brookstone, Inc. (M: BKST)	16.75	24.9	21.5	19.0	15.0	26.6	7.16	14.8	15.2	26.63	22.5	35.0
Chico's FAS, Inc. (M: CHCS)	12.00	72.0	32.0	25.0	28.7	26.3	6.83	15.2	30.5	26.33	42.1	34.8
Bed Bath & Beyond Inc. (M: BBBY)	23.94	34.1	34.0	25.8	23.0	26.5	3.55	29.6	44.2	26.47	40.2	33.9
National RV Holdings, Inc (N: NVH)	13.38	103.2	33.3	20.0	26.0	20.7	22.13	4.5	15.7	20.74	51.0	33.9
Analytical Surveys, Inc. (M: ANLT)	8.00	49.1	45.2	22.0	16.3	16.1	17.00	6.2	24.2	16.09	67.3	33.5
Theragenics Corporation (N: TGX)	13.13	81.7	57.5	30.0	15.4	16.7	3.81	23.9	85.7	16.67	77.3	32.4
Fossil, Inc. (M: FOSL)	22.25	36.4	21.2	21.1	26.7	27.9	6.56	14.3	20.3	27.86	24.7	32.0
Mohawk Industries, Inc. (N: MHK)	21.63	143.6	29.4	15.0	20.3	16.1	11.33	8.9	31.5	16.07	47.0	28.6
Microsoft Corporation (M: MSFT)	91.31	49.6	39.5	24.7	25.2	29.4	1.87	57.4	42.6	29.44	36.4	28.4
Monaco Coach Corporation (N: MNC)	16.50	54.6	37.7	14.4	30.6	20.7	13.03	7.3	21.0	20.71	52.3	28.3
Buckle, Inc. (N: BKE)	13.25	47.8	29.1	15.7	22.9	18.4	12.68	8.3	19.0	18.40	41.0	26.7
Craftmade International (M: CRFT)	7.38	44.9	27.3	30.0	24.6	21.7	9.36	11.3	17.4	20.21	34.0	25.2
Synopsys, Inc. (M: SNPS)	40.25	101.8	50.7	21.7	18.6	14.3	5.71	17.9	56.5	14.29	69.4	25.1
T. Rowe Price Associates (M: TROW)	34.19	29.6	28.0	15.3	30.5	27.2	5.18	18.5	25.4	20.04	32.0	22.6
Williams-Sonoma, Inc. (N: WSM)	27.19	172.3	65.3	25.1	19.7	12.5	4.30	24.9	86.5	12.54	88.5	22.3
Micros Systems, Inc. (M: MCRS)	52.81	124.2	30.7	25.0	22.1	19.1	3.65	29.2	40.0	19.09	35.8	21.6
TSR, Inc. (M: TSRI)	6.56	71.7	45.0	na	30.5	13.6	13.10	7.5	33.4	12.39	68.1	21.4
Keane, Inc. (A: KEA)	22.88	65.5	38.4	23.3	23.5	15.6	6.30	22.4	38.2	15.57	51.1	21.1
Burlington Nrth./Santa Fe (N: BNI)	20.06	62.8	21.3	9.8	13.9	14.6	11.96	8.2	20.4	7.53	33.1	18.9
Robert Half Int'l Inc. (N: RHI)	41.50	45.2	28.4	20.2	24.3	18.7	3.69	26.9	34.1	18.67	31.4	18.3
Kohl's Corporation (N: KSS)	69.56	35.5	34.9	22.3	14.8	17.5	2.08	49.3	40.8	17.51	32.7	17.3
Washington Post Co. (N: WPO)	478.75	34.0	22.4	10.0	13.6	18.0	4.71	21.5	18.9	13.45	21.6	16.0

na = not available

Exchange Key: N = New York Stock Exchange
A = American Stock Exchange
M = Nasdaq

*Screening criteria used to produce table results can be found on opposite page.

Source: AAII's Stock Investor/Market Guide Inc. and I/B/E/S. Statistics are based on figures as of February 25, 2000.

projected rates of return can be determined over the 10-year period based on the current price of the stock. Buffett requires a return of at least 15%, so screen for stocks that have a projected rate of return of 15% based on historical earnings growth.

- **Sustainable Growth:** Buffett uses the average rate of return on equity and average retention ratio (1 – average payout ratio) to calculate a sustainable growth rate [ROE × retention ratio]. The sustainable growth rate is used to calculate the book value per share in year 10 (the current book value per share compounding for 10 years at the sustainable growth rate). Earnings per share can be estimated in year 10 by multiplying the average return on equity by the projected book value per share. To estimate the future price, you multiply the earnings by the average price-earnings ratio. If dividends are paid, they can be added to the projected price to compute the total gain 10-year annual return based on current prices. Buffett requires a return of at least 15%, so screen for stocks that have a projected return of 15% based on the sustainable growth model.

Tables 1 and 2 provide a list of stocks passing the screens we used to illustrate how the Warren Buffett approach could be implemented, based on data as of February 25, 2000, using AAII's *Stock Investor Professional*. Screening tips for the Buffett approach are on page 73.

Screening Tips: The Warren Buffett Approach

Consumer monopoly or commodity?

Buffett seeks consumer monopolies selling products in which there is no effective competitor, either due to a patent or brand name or similar intangible that makes the product unique. Consumer monopolies typically have high profit margins because of their unique niche. However, simple screens for high margins may only highlight firms in industries with traditionally high margins. Look for companies with operating margins and net profit margins above their industry norms. Additional screens for strong earnings and high return on equity will also help to identify consumer monopolies. Follow-up examinations should include a detailed study of the firm's position in the industry and how it might change over time.

Do you understand how it works?

Buffett only invests in industries he can grasp. While you cannot screen for this factor, you should only analyze the companies passing all screening criteria that operate in areas you understand.

Is the company conservatively financed?

Buffett seeks companies with conservative financing. Consumer monopolies tend to have strong cash flows, with little need for long-term debt. Look for companies with total liabilities below the median for their respective industry. Alternative screens might look for low debt relative to capitalization or to equity.

Are earnings strong and do they show an upward trend?

Buffett looks for companies with strong, consistent, and expanding earnings. We screened for companies with long-term (greater than five years) earnings per share growth greater than 75% of all firms. To help indicate that earnings growth remains strong, you should also require that the intermediate term (such as three years) earnings growth rate be higher than the long-term growth rate. Buffett also seeks firms with consistent earnings. Follow-up examinations should include a careful examination of the year-by-year earnings per share figures. As a simple screen to exclude companies with more volatile earnings, look for companies with positive earnings for each of the last few years (preferably longer than five years) and the latest 12 months.

Has the company been buying back its shares?

Buffett prefers that firms reinvest their earnings within the company, provided that profitable opportunities exist. When companies have excess cash flow, Buffett favors shareholder-enhancing maneuvers such as share buybacks. This is difficult to screen for, but a follow-up examination of a company would reveal if it has a share buyback plan in place.

Have retained earnings been invested well?

Earnings should rise as the level of retained earnings increase from profitable operations. Screens for strong and consistent earnings and strong return on equity will help capture this factor.

Is the company's return on equity above average?

Buffett considers it a positive sign when a company is able to earn above-average returns on equity. The average return on equity for the last 40 years is roughly 12%. Look for companies with a long-term (preferably five years or longer) average return on equity above 12%.

(cont'd on next page)

Screening Tips: The Warren Buffett Approach *(cont'd)*

Does the company need to constantly reinvest in capital?
Retained earnings must first go toward maintaining current operations at competitive levels, so the lower the amount needed to maintain current operations, the better. This factor is best applied through a qualitative examination of the company and its industry. However, a screen for high relative levels of free cash flow may also help to capture this factor.

IT'S QUALITY THAT COUNTS: THE PHILIP FISHER APPROACH TO STOCK INVESTING

Successful investing is often called a mix between science and art. Despite many attempts to find winning combinations of measurable factors that can be used to predict stock market winners, investment decisions often boil down to judgment calls that take qualitative factors into consideration.

One of the first investment "philosophers" to focus almost exclusively on qualitative factors was Philip A. Fisher, who began as a securities analyst in 1928 and three years later founded the investment counseling firm Fisher & Co.

At a time when many investment professionals attempted to make money in stocks by betting on the business cycle, Fisher instead favored buying and holding the stocks of companies that were well-positioned for long-term growth in sales and profits. And he felt this positioning could best be determined by examining factors that are difficult to measure through ratios and other mathematical formulations—the quality of management, the potential for future long-term sales growth, and the firm's competitive edge.

Growth Stocks: The Overall Philosophy

Fisher first and foremost was a growth stock investor. He felt the greatest investment returns did not come from the purchase of stocks that were undervalued, since even a stock that is undervalued by as much as 50% would only double in price once it reached fair market value. Instead, he sought much higher returns from those companies that could achieve growth in sales and profits greater than the overall market over a long period of time. On the other hand, once those companies were found, he favored buying their stock opportunistically, either when the market temporarily undervalues the company due to unexpected bad news, or when the markets are depressed.

Fisher did not seek companies that showed promise of short-term growth due to cyclical events or one-time factors, feeling that the timing was too risky and the promised returns too small. Instead, he focused on long-term growth, which he felt could only come from companies that were strong in three dimensions:

- The company is producing goods or services with the potential for future long-term sales growth,

- The company has special characteristics that will allow it to retain a favorable competitive edge over existing competitors and newcomers, and
- The company has excellent management with both a determination to grow the company and the ability to implement its plans.

True long-term growth companies, he felt, were not necessarily small and relatively young firms, although he did not exclude these companies (as long as they had some operating history upon which he could judge—he did not favor new firms). On the other hand, he noted that the qualities that constitute excellent management vary considerably based on firm size.

Finding Companies Worthy of Consideration

Although Fisher wrote for the average individual investor, his approach is not one that is easy to implement.

To begin with, Fisher did not begin his search through any methodical screening system. Instead, he maintained that most of his original ideas came from "key investment men" (other investment advisers) whom he had come to respect in terms of their knowledge of the kinds of stocks he preferred. Other sources included trade and financial periodicals.

The primary type of company he saw as a potential for further investigation was one that was either already in or entering into an area with opportunities for unusual sales growth, but in which other newcomers or competitors would have a more difficult time entering. Once a prospective firm was found, Fisher said his next step was to determine whether the company measured up to his 15-point criteria. To determine this, he first examined the financial statements for a thorough understanding of the nature of the business, including: its capitalization and financial position, profit margins, a breakdown of total sales by product lines, the extent of research activity, income statement figures that throw light on depreciation and abnormal or non-recurring costs in prior years' operations, and the major owners of the stock including the degree of ownership by management. Then, he used what he terms the "scuttlebutt" approach to help answer his 15 points, talking to competitors, analysts, and anyone who may have knowledge of the company. Lastly, he sought information to analyze his 15 points through a discussion with management.

The 15 Points

What are the 15 points?

Fisher used a 15-point system to rate a prospective company, and he limited his investments to firms that fulfilled most of them:

Functional factors:

1) **Is the company providing a product or service that has sufficient market poten-**

tial for a sizable increase in sales for several years? In this instance, Fisher is discussing sales over the long term, and warns against firms that may show spurts due to one-time factors. On the other hand, he notes that the problems of marketing new products often causes sales increases to come in a series of uneven spurts rather than a smooth progression and suggests judging sales growth over a series of years rather than single years.

2) **Does the company have superiority in production**—is it the lowest-cost producer (for manufacturing firms) or does it have the lowest-cost operations (for service firms or retailers)? Low production costs will allow a company to survive during hard times when higher-cost competitors are weeded out, he notes. In addition, low-cost producers are better able to build funds internally for future growth.

3) **Does the company have a strong marketing organization?** Fisher's definition of a strong marketing organization is broad and includes the ability to recognize changes in public tastes, an effective advertising effort, and an efficient product distribution system.

4) **Does the company have outstanding research and development efforts?** Fisher was a strong believer in research efforts to produce new and better products in a better way or at lower cost. Sometimes, he noted, these efforts would even lead to new lines of business. He suggested examining the amount expended on research relative to its size, but warned against simple comparisons among companies because of differences in what is included in reported research and development figures. Fisher was also concerned about the effectiveness of a firm's research effort indicated by its ability to bring research ideas to production and eventually to market—that is, its teamwork with the other parts of the firm. The most important question, he said, is how much in net profits over the past 10 years has been a result of research efforts? Firms that have done well in this regard in the past, he said, will most likely do so in the future.

5) **How effective is the company's cost analysis and accounting controls?** Good management and the efficient use of resources can only come from good information, according to Fisher. In addition, the finance function should provide an early-warning system for problems that could affect profitability.

6) **Does the company have financial strength?** Fisher was concerned here with a firm's ability to finance growth without the need to use equity financing, since increasing the number of shares outstanding would dilute an existing shareholder's benefits of investing in the firm.

Excellence in management and labor relations:

7) **Does management have the determination, leadership and skills necessary to continue to develop products or services that will further increase sales?** Fisher strongly believed that good management was key to long-term growth—by spotting

new opportunities, adapting to changing market environments, developing plans, and coordinating the efforts of the organization to carry out those plans.

8) **Is there a good working relationship among the management team?** Fisher felt that good teamwork was crucial among the major divisions, and that this was best fostered by a strong effort to develop and promote its managers from within the organization.

9) **Does the company have enough depth to its management?** Even smaller firms, Fisher noted, need enough depth in management to prevent a "corporate disaster" should something happen to the key person.

10) **Does the company have good labor relations?** Fisher felt that the entrepreneurial atmosphere and teamwork within a firm should permeate through all aspects of a company, including rank and file workers. Mediocre relations, he stated, tends to produce high labor turnover and greater costs in training new workers.

11) **Does management have a sufficiently long-range outlook?** Fisher noted that long-term growth sometimes comes at the expense of short-term profits, and managements that are unwilling to forego current profits can hurt the future growth of a firm.

12) **Does the firm practice good investor relations?** To Fisher, good investor relations means a management that is willing to be honest and forthcoming when troubles and disappointments arise. Evasions, he stated, tend to be a sign of weak management—either they do not have a plan to deal with an unexpected difficulty, or they do not have a sense of responsibility toward shareholders.

13) **Does the management have unquestionable integrity?** "The management of a company is always far closer to its assets than is the stockholder," Fisher states. And managers can benefit themselves at the expense of shareholders in an "infinite" number of ways, including salaries and perks high above the norm. The only protection shareholders have against management abuses of position is to invest in companies whose managers have unquestioned integrity.

Business characteristics

14) **Does the firm have above-average profitability?** In a rare instance, Fisher actually suggests a mathematical comparison—profit margins per dollar of sales, compared against similar firms in the same industry. Older and larger firms should have among the best figures in their industry, he states. On the other hand, younger firms may elect to speed up growth by spending all or a large part of profits on research or sales; for these firms, Fisher suggested that investors make sure that narrow profit margins are due to spending in these areas alone. Firms operating in areas with high profits will attract competition, but operating at extremely high efficiency levels will reduce the incentive for competitors to enter the market.

15) **Is there some aspect to the business that will allow the company to keep its relative competitive edge?** Innovations, special skills or services, patent protections

and similar advantages give companies a strong ability to fend off competitors or newcomers to the area.

Secondary Factors: When to Buy

Fisher did not necessarily favor the purchase of an "outstanding company" at any price. Instead, he suggested that investors exploit buying opportunities, which can take several forms:

- **Short-term troubles:** Even companies that are under the guidance of exceptionally able managers are bound to have troubles, plans that fail to unfold or new products with "kinks" that need to be worked out, and once that trouble produces a price decline, investors can purchase the stock.
- **Market blindness:** Earnings increases that have not yet been reflected in price changes.
- **Market declines:** When the overall market drops and pulls the stock down with it, investors are faced with a buying opportunity.

Fisher noted that investors can still make money if these kinds of opportunities don't arise, but they must have more patience with the chosen stock and recognize that their profits will be smaller.

Although Fisher recognized opportunities in market declines, he suggested that investors in general ignore business and economic trends, investing funds as soon as an "appropriate buying opportunity" arises. For particularly conservative investors, he recommended dollar cost averaging.

Stock Monitoring and When to Sell

Fisher provided a number of helpful rules both for purchasing and selling.

For stock purchases, Fisher warned against agonizing over eighths and quarters when placing a trade. Attempting to shave points off the price, he noted, often results in a trade not going through, and the investor loses out on investing long term in an outstanding firm. And any savings, he pointed out, will be insignificant compared to long-term returns.

Fisher was a strong advocate of long-term investing, advising investors to hold onto their stocks until there is a fundamental change in the firm's nature, or it has grown to a point where it will no longer be growing faster than the overall economy. He warned, however, that when companies grow, managements need to change and adapt, and investors may need to sell if management doesn't keep pace. Fisher recommended against selling for short-term reasons—for example, to take profits if a temporary downturn is expected.

Fisher suggested that investors use a three-year rule for judging results if a stock is underperforming the market but nothing else has happened to change the investor's original view. If after three years it is still underperforming, he recommended that investors sell the stock.

On the other hand, Fisher advised selling "mistakes" quickly, once they are recognized.

Fisher felt that the size and quality of the companies used in constructing an investor's stock portfolio should determine the optimal balance. Smaller and riskier firms require more diversification, and while a 10% to 20% portfolio position may be optimal for a larger, more stable firm, a 5% position may be more appropriate for smaller, riskier, firms. However, Fisher warned against overdiversification, which he felt caused investors to lower their standards and to put money in companies that they do not thoroughly understand or haven't thoroughly researched. Sufficient diversification, he said, would be an investment in 10 or 12 larger companies in a variety of industries with different characteristics, and portfolio holdings of over 20 companies is probably too much.

Fisher in Summary

While Fisher does not provide an easy-to-follow methodical approach for individual investors to implement, his discussion of the qualitative factors within "outstanding companies" serves as a useful outline that adds some color to strict mathematical approaches. Becoming acquainted with all of a company's financial statements—the 10-K and annual reports—as well as gaining an understanding of the industry in which a company is operating and knowledge of the firm's competitors are all necessary components of Fisher's approach.

Fisher wrote of the complaints he received concerning the amount of time and effort necessary to implement his approach. However, he was unsympathetic:

"Is it either logical or reasonable that anyone could [achieve the kind of reward gained from selecting growth stocks successfully] with an effort no harder than reading a few simply worded brokers' free circulars in the comfort of an armchair one evening a week? . . . So far as I know, no other fields of endeavor offer these huge rewards this easily."

Philip Fisher's Approach in Brief

Philosophy and style
Investment in "outstanding" companies that over the years can grow in sales and profits more than the market as a whole. The key features of "outstanding" companies are: strong management that has a disciplined approach designed to achieve dramatic long-term growth in profits, with products or services that have the potential for sizable sales long term, and with other inherent qualities that would make it difficult for competitors and newcomers.

Universe of stocks
No restrictions on universe of stocks from which to select. Over-the-counter stocks should not be overlooked, but "outstanding" companies are not necessarily young and small.

Criteria for initial consideration
Prospective companies should pass most of the following 15 points:
Functional factors:
- Products or services with sufficient market potential for sizable increase in sales for several years. Major sales growth, judged over a series of years.
- Superiority in production—lowest-cost production (for manufacturing firms) or lowest-cost operation (for service firms or retailers).
- Strong marketing organization—efficiency of sales, advertising, and distributive organizations.
- Outstanding research and development efforts—amount expended relative to its size, effectiveness of effort as indicated by ability to bring research ideas to production and to market and by how much research contributed to net profits.
- Effectiveness of company's cost analysis and accounting controls, and choice of capital investments that will bring the highest return.
- Financial strength or cash position—sufficient capital to take care of needs to exploit prospects for next several years without the need to raise equity capital.

Excellence in Management
- Attitude of management to continue to develop products or services that will further increase sales.
- Development of good in-house management and teamwork.

- Management depth.
- Good labor and personnel relations.
- Long-range outlook by management even at the expense of short-term profits.
- Good investor relations, and willingness to talk freely about problems.
- Management of unquestionable integrity—salaries and perks in line with those of other managers.

Business characteristics
- Above-average profitability: Compare profit margins per dollar of sales—compare within industry and examine for several years, not just single years. Older and larger firms are usually the best in their industry. Younger firms may elect to speed up growth by spending all or a large part of profits on research or sales; for these, make sure a narrow profit margin is due to spending in these areas alone.
- Ability to maintain good profit margins: Good position relative to competition—for instance, skill in a particular line of business, or patent protection for a small business.

Secondary factors
Once an "outstanding" company is found, purchase stock when it is out-of-favor either because the market has temporarily misjudged the true value of the company, or because of general market conditions. "Outstanding" companies can also be purchased at fair value, but investors should expect a lower (but respectable) return.

Stock monitoring and when to sell
- Use a three-year rule for judging results if a stock is underperforming but no fundamental changes have occurred.
- Hold stock until there is a fundamental change in its nature or it has grown to a point where it will no longer be growing faster than the overall economy.
- Don't sell for short-term reasons.
- Sell mistakes quickly, once they are recognized.
- Don't overdiversify—10 or 12 larger companies is sufficient, investing in a variety of industries with different characteristics.

STOCK SCREENS: APPLYING THE PHILIP FISHER APPROACH

The qualitative factors Fisher focused on requires detailed analysis to determine whether a company is positioned for long-term growth. The challenge for an investor is to come up with a list of stocks that merit that type of in-depth analysis. Our goal was to perform a basic series of screens that identified companies worthy of study using Fisher's 15 qualitative factors.

Although Fisher feels that his growth stock techniques can be applied to any industry, he confines his research to manufacturing companies because he understands their character-istics. In our own screens using the Fisher approach, we do not limit the search to any specific industry. However, an investor considering the incorporation of the Fisher approach into their own style would be wise to make a realistic appraisal of the industries in which they should consider investing directly.

Competitive Advantage

Fisher sought companies with inherent characteristics that should lead to above-average profitability over the long term. He preferred to use profit margin, which compares net income to sales, to identify companies with strong competitive positions because he believed it to be more reliable than measures such as return on assets. Return on assets can be easily distorted by factors such as uneven age and historical cost of assets. However, care must also be taken when comparing companies by profit margin. Industries with commodity items and high turnover typically have a lower profit margin; firms with more specialized niche products usually have a higher margin, but lower turnover. Profit margin screens should be tailored to compare companies in very similar lines of work if you wish to identify truly outstanding companies.

Our first screen specifies that profit margins should be above industry norms for each of the last five fiscal years, as well as the most recent 12 months. Beyond looking at any one year, it is important to examine the profit margin over time. A long string of strong profit margins may indicate a company that has a competitive advantage it is somehow protecting. Fisher likened a high profit margin to an open jar of honey that attracts a swarm of angry insects bent on devouring it.

Fisher believed that there are two primary ways for a company to protect an above-average margin—either establish a monopoly or become a dominant low-cost producer. The only real growth monopoly opportunities in the U.S. are found in companies that have some patent protection preventing competitors from exactly copying some product or technology. These opportunities are rare and usually short-lived. Fisher preferred to concentrate on firms that have established themselves as the clear market leaders, are low-cost producers, and are in an industry segment where success depends on the interplay of many unique disciplines. Low-cost producers are better positioned to weather economic slowdowns and generate more funds internally for expansion and research. When looking at companies from this perspective, Fisher always asked what the company was doing that could not be duplicated well by others.

Consistent Sales Growth

Fisher preferred to invest in companies that showed consistent strong and steady growth over firms that showed great variability. Our screen looks for positive year-to-year sales growth for each of the last three fiscal periods and requires that sales have not slowed down over the last 12 months compared to the last fiscal year. We also screen for firms growing faster than their industry, indicating a potential competitive advantage.

Dividend Payments

Fisher felt that investors looking for companies with maximum potential for capital gains should confine their investments to those paying a low dividend or no dividend, and also those having strong earnings power and attractive places to reinvest their earnings. Fisher looked for companies with sufficient capital to take care of needs to exploit prospects for the next several years without raising new capital.

Our screen specified that firms should not pay any dividends. We decided to be fairly restrictive in our screen; alternative, less-restrictive screens might look for low dividend yields or low dividend payout ratios.

A Great Firm at a Great Price

Fisher explained the desirability of pursuing a long-term growth strategy, but also emphasized the advantages of buying these growth firms when they are out of favor. However, he believed that the only value in looking at historical price-earnings ratios was to help gain a perspective on the base valuation over time. The key was looking forward and anticipating future earnings growth. Comparing the price-earnings ratio to the earnings growth rate is a common valuation technique. Companies with higher expected earnings growth should trade with higher price-earnings ratios. Stocks with a price-earnings ratio half the level of the earnings growth rate are considered attractive.

For the Fisher screen, we construct our price-earnings to earnings growth (PEG) ratio using expected earnings for the next fiscal year for the price-earnings ratio, which is often termed the forward price-earnings ratio, and the expected long-term growth rate in earnings based

Screening Criteria for the Philip Fisher Screen

Definitions for screens and terms can be found in the glossary starting on page 191.

Screening Criteria:

- Net profit margin for the last 12 months and each of the last 5 fiscal years greater than industry median*
- Sales for the last 12 months and each of the last 3 fiscal years greater than prior year*
- 3-year sales growth greater than industry median
- No dividends*
- PEG ratio (based on estimated EPS for next fiscal year for P/E and 5-year estimated EPS growth rate) less than or equal to 0.5 and greater than 0.1

Data not shown in table. Also note that the table shows additional data columns that may be of interest to those using this approach.

on analysts' consensus earnings estimates collected by I/B/E/S, a brokerage estimate research firm. Our final screen looks for companies with a PEG ratio less than or equal to 0.5.

Studies show that extremely low PEG are not very good predictors of strong stock performance. Very low PEG ratios occur with unusually low price-earnings ratios and high growth rates that are not sustainable. We therefore require that the PEG ratio be above 0.1.

Table 1 shows the results of our interpretation of how screens can be applied to a Philip Fisher approach. It is based on data as of February 25, 2000, using AAII's *Stock Investor Professional*. Screening tips for the Fisher approach are on pages 88 and 89.

Table 1.
Stocks Passing the Philip Fisher Screening*

Company (Exchange: Ticker)	Price ($)	52-wk Price High ($)	52-wk Price Low ($)	Mkt Cap. ($ mil)	Net Profit Margin (12 mo) (%)	Total Liab. to Assets (%)	PEG Ratio EPS Est. 5-yr (x)	Curr P/E (x)	3-yr EPS Cont Grth (%)	EPS Grth Est (%)	3-yr Sales Grth (%)
Zindart Limited (M: ZNDT)	5.00	14.50	4.75	44.1	9.2	53.4	0.2	4.2	–0.7	17.5	10.9
Drew Industries, Inc. (A: DW)	8.31	13.25	8.25	94.4	5.0	49.3	0.2	5.5	18.4	35.0	48.9
Pediatrix Medical Group (N: PDX)	7.19	37.13	6.00	112.0	12.8	34.3	0.2	4.5	49.6	20.2	61.6
Consolidated Graphics (N: CGX)	14.31	64.25	12.94	225.6	7.3	53.2	0.2	5.4	86.9	23.0	72.4
Century Business Services (M: CBIZ)	3.00	16.13	2.94	273.8	10.5	31.0	0.2	4.8	18.6	28.0	62.9
Travis Boats&Motors, Inc. (M: TRVS)	9.75	21.50	8.25	42.2	3.6	70.1	0.3	7.4	25.2	23.3	41.3
Analytical Surveys, Inc. (M: ANLT)	8.00	29.50	6.50	55.6	8.2	40.4	0.3	6.2	49.1	22.0	71.0
Dave & Buster's, Inc. (N: DAB)	6.56	29.38	5.06	85.0	2.8	41.8	0.3	7.7	45.2	25.6	51.4
Tarrant Apparel Group (M: TAGS)	8.00	48.63	6.00	126.4	5.7	49.8	0.3	5.6	51.1	20.0	22.6
Action Performance Co's (M: ACTN)	9.63	42.38	7.75	163.0	8.3	48.5	0.3	5.9	49.1	22.6	97.9
Fairfield Communities (N: FFD)	8.94	17.13	7.00	397.7	11.2	44.4	0.3	7.2	38.4	22.5	26.9
ShopKo Stores Inc. (N: SKO)	16.50	40.75	16.13	501.5	2.6	69.3	0.3	4.6	21.3	14.8	14.7
Avant! Corporation (M: AVNT)	14.44	25.25	10.50	556.2	13.5	26.2	0.3	10.0	33.9	35.5	48.8
Tommy Hilfiger, Inc. (N: TOM)	11.31	41.06	11.06	1,072.8	11.4	46.1	0.3	4.9	29.8	18.8	50.7
Display Technologies, Inc (M: DTEK)	4.13	5.57	2.38	32.2	3.0	54.6	0.4	15.9	8.2	45.0	70.7
Argosy Education Group (M: ARGY)	5.19	14.38	3.53	33.6	9.9	27.7	0.4	8.1	34.6	21.5	27.5
A.C. Moore Arts & Crafts (M: ACMR)	5.56	6.88	4.00	41.2	1.9	35.7	0.4	7.3	–15.9	20.0	23.2
Healthcare Recoveries (M: HCRI)	4.44	8.69	2.56	49.7	11.1	46.5	0.4	9.6	31.9	22.5	29.4
Schlotzsky's, Inc. (M: BUNZ)	7.19	12.69	6.00	53.3	12.6	36.2	0.4	8.6	23.1	23.5	48.0
AVTEAM, Inc. (M: AVTM)	6.00	10.00	4.25	68.6	6.7	56.4	0.4	8.2	45.2	20.0	60.3
Matrix Bancorp, Inc. (M: MTXC)	10.50	18.00	7.63	70.7	13.3	94.6	0.4	6.6	14.8	17.5	77.8
P.A.M. Transportation (M: PTSI)	9.00	12.88	6.88	76.0	5.6	69.8	0.4	6.8	–1.3	17.0	16.1
Suburban Lodges of Amer. (M: SLAM)	5.69	7.75	4.75	80.8	15.4	33.7	0.4	10.5	28.6	28.6	107.6
Prime Medical Services (M: PMSI)	8.88	10.63	6.63	147.0	14.5	61.3	0.4	9.4	4.4	21.2	65.2
Tractor Supply Company (M: TSCO)	16.88	30.50	12.75	148.0	2.5	59.9	0.4	8.4	6.5	19.0	16.1
Lason, Inc. (M: LSON)	8.06	59.88	7.94	152.4	2.6	47.7	0.4	10.5	60.2	28.7	81.8
Covenant Transport, Inc. (M: CVTI)	11.44	20.00	10.25	170.6	4.9	46.6	0.4	7.6	22.0	18.6	27.1
Crossmann Communities (M: CROS)	15.38	33.63	14.19	177.3	6.8	49.6	0.4	4.5	29.2	12.5	33.4
Pomeroy Computer Res. (M: PMRY)	16.50	23.13	9.56	194.8	3.2	55.9	0.4	7.9	31.7	20.3	39.6
Friede Goldman Halter (N: FGH)	5.56	20.13	4.88	221.9	4.6	65.6	0.4	6.3	104.8	15.0	168.0
Wackenhut Correction Corp (N: WHC)	10.25	21.94	8.00	229.5	5.1	32.9	0.4	10.3	43.0	24.3	46.5
Stoneridge, Inc. (N: SRI)	10.38	19.50	9.31	232.4	6.0	67.9	0.4	5.6	26.8	15.5	21.9

(cont'd on next page)

Table 1.
Stocks Passing the Philip Fisher Screening *(cont'd)*

Company (Exchange: Ticker)	Price ($)	52-wk Price High ($)	52-wk Price Low ($)	Mkt Cap. ($ mil)	Net Profit Margin (12 mo) (%)	Total Liab. to Assets (%)	PEG Ratio EPS Est. 5-yr (x)	Curr P/E (x)	3-yr EPS Cont Grth (%)	EPS Grth Est (%)	3-yr Sales Grth (%)
NCI Building Systems, Inc (N: NCS)	15.31	27.00	14.50	284.3	4.9	67.6	0.4	6.2	16.8	15.0	41.2
US Oncology, Inc. (M: USON)	4.06	12.81	3.81	348.9	4.2	42.6	0.4	8.8	24.1	20.5	66.3
Toll Brothers, Inc. (N: TOL)	16.63	23.44	15.56	606.9	6.9	63.0	0.4	5.7	20.9	14.6	24.4
AmeriCredit Corp. (N: ACF)	12.94	18.94	11.00	968.3	20.7	61.7	0.4	10.6	46.3	24.4	60.6
Abercrombie & Fitch Co. (N: ANF)	14.00	50.75	12.88	1,428.0	13.3	42.8	0.4	10.1	79.9	28.6	51.3
Smithway Motor Xpress (M: SMXC)	3.50	10.69	3.50	17.6	2.7	68.6	0.5	4.5	6.4	9.4	27.8
ASI Solutions, Inc. (M: ASIS)	4.13	10.06	2.63	27.2	5.0	50.0	0.5	9.6	54.5	20.0	77.9
Technisource, Inc. (M: TSRC)	5.25	9.25	3.50	54.4	3.2	12.5	0.5	16.4	34.4	30.0	53.7
SOS Staffing Services (M: SOSS)	4.38	9.63	3.75	55.5	1.5	41.7	0.5	10.2	13.0	19.3	55.7
Del Global Technologies (M: DGTC)	7.69	11.00	7.19	60.1	9.9	21.4	0.5	9.2	13.8	18.0	15.9
PJ America, Inc. (M: PJAM)	10.75	25.63	10.00	61.1	6.2	13.0	0.5	10.9	19.2	23.5	60.2
Exactech, Inc. (M: EXAC)	14.25	16.25	9.13	71.1	8.8	23.3	0.5	13.6	15.4	25.0	38.2
Natrol, Inc. (M: NTOL)	6.50	9.50	5.69	87.5	11.3	15.1	0.5	10.2	30.8	22.5	42.4
Hibbett Sporting Goods (M: HIBB)	15.63	31.00	12.50	100.5	4.7	42.0	0.5	12.9	36.2	26.3	28.8
Innotrac Corporation (M: INOC)	9.81	26.75	6.13	110.0	5.0	33.3	0.5	9.5	31.9	20.0	46.0
Hot Topic, Inc. (M: HOTT)	15.88	27.13	6.34	149.1	6.9	26.1	0.5	15.6	106.9	30.0	63.6
FPIC Insurance Group, Inc (M: FPIC)	17.38	50.88	13.81	168.5	14.2	71.7	0.5	8.2	14.7	15.0	20.1
AmeriPath, Inc. (M: PATH)	8.56	10.69	7.00	184.8	10.1	55.3	0.5	8.2	109.5	17.5	122.9
Chattem Inc. (M: CHTT)	19.00	41.69	16.25	186.6	5.9	91.2	0.5	8.4	82.0	16.2	29.8
Discount Auto Parts (N: DAP)	11.50	26.44	10.00	192.0	5.0	55.8	0.5	7.0	4.2	15.0	18.5
Helen of Troy Limited (M: HELE)	7.06	20.00	7.02	203.5	8.2	31.6	0.5	8.5	25.2	16.8	20.8
DVI, Incorporated (N: DVI)	15.00	18.06	11.25	213.3	14.0	83.9	0.5	10.5	19.2	20.0	32.8
Deltek Systems, Inc. (M: DLTK)	13.19	17.88	8.06	223.9	17.6	30.6	0.5	13.5	19.2	26.0	34.3
Quiksilver, Inc. (N: ZQK)	10.81	30.83	9.25	242.1	6.0	41.5	0.5	9.4	28.2	20.0	31.9
Triad Guaranty Inc. (M: TGIC)	20.25	23.69	11.50	269.4	38.9	40.3	0.5	9.1	45.8	17.3	45.4
Buckle, Inc. (N: BKE)	13.25	32.56	12.56	281.1	10.0	20.1	0.5	8.3	47.8	15.7	25.2
StaffMark, Inc. (M: STAF)	9.94	14.13	5.75	292.1	1.1	58.2	0.5	9.6	–8.2	18.3	184.9
Ocular Sciences, Inc. (M: OCLR)	15.63	35.25	13.50	358.1	20.5	17.9	0.5	10.0	35.6	19.8	30.7
Palm Harbor Homes, Inc. (M: PHHM)	16.06	26.00	13.75	367.6	5.4	53.6	0.5	9.0	31.1	20.0	22.2
Boyds Collection, Ltd (N: FOB)	6.31	18.69	5.94	378.2	25.8	90.9	0.5	6.0	58.7	12.5	41.3
IMRglobal Corp. (M: IMRS)	11.88	23.25	7.00	457.9	14.6	20.7	0.5	15.2	104.1	28.8	91.1

(cont'd on next page)

Table 1.
Stocks Passing the Philip Fisher Screening *(cont'd)*

Company (Exchange: Ticker)	Price ($)	52-wk Price High ($)	52-wk Price Low ($)	Mkt Cap. ($ mil)	Net Profit Margin (12 mo) (%)	Total Liab. to Assets (%)	PEG Ratio EPS Est. 5-yr (x)	Curr P/E (x)	3-yr EPS Cont Grth (%)	EPS Grth Est (%)	3-yr Sales Grth (%)
Pre-Paid Legal Services (N: PPD)	27.13	39.94	19.88	611.6	21.9	40.0	0.5	16.2	75.2	35.0	39.3
Republic Services, Inc. (N: RSG)	11.31	25.50	8.88	1,984.8	11.5	55.6	0.5	9.8	46.5	19.4	19.4
RSA Security Inc. (M: RSAS)	63.06	80.00	14.25	2,431.4	76.4	27.4	0.5	16.8	44.2	32.3	50.0

Screening criteria used to produce table results can be found on page 84.

Exchange Key: N = New York Stock Exchange
A = American Stock Exchange
M = Nasdaq

Statistics are based on figures as of February 25, 2000.
Data Source: AAII's Stock Investor/Market Guide, Inc, and I/B/E/S.

Screening Tips: The Philip Fisher Approach

Functional and Management Factors

The functional and management factors described by Fisher require largely qualitative judgment. However some can be quantified into screens.

Products or services with sufficient market potential for sizable increases in sales for seven years: While it is difficult to screen for expected sales growth, Fisher also liked consistent historical sales growth. You can screen for recent year-to-year sales increases to capture recent sales patterns. A screen for sales growth above industry growth levels can help to locate firms with a competitive advantage.

Superiority in production and effectiveness of cost control: Can be measured through operating efficiency ratios such as asset and inventory ratios and profitability ratios such as gross, operating, and net profit margins. Optimally, the ratios should be steady and improving over time, and they should be favorable compared to industry norms.

Outstanding research and development efforts: Measures such as research and development as a percent of sales will help to indicate the relative importance placed on future company investment, but this element does not measure the effectiveness of R&D. Looking at the percent of sales from products introduced in the last few years is sometimes used as an indication of successful R&D implementation, especially with technology firms. No screening program will capture this type of ratio, so contacting investor relations will be necessary.

Financial strength or cash position: Many measures and screens are available for financial strength and cash levels. Cash levels are normally compared to market cap to calculate cash as a percent of price. Higher percentages indicate high relative cash levels. Some investors calculate a net cash figure that adjusts cash downward for liabilities. Financial strength is normally measured through ratios such as current, quick, debt-to-liability, and debt-to-equity ratios. Most screening programs will have a few of these basic ratios and you should try to screen for favorable ratios relative to industry norms.

Business Characteristics

Above-average profitability: Most screening programs will have a mix of top (gross) to bottom (net) profitability ratios. Optimally, you should screen for ratios that are increasing and better than the industry norm. Not all screening program support comparison against industry norms, so you may have to screen on basic levels, then manually compare the ratio to the appropriate industry level.

Good profit margins and good position relative to competition: Company performance should be measured relative to competition. Profit margins above industry norms for the last few years should help to identify firms that have had a competitive advantage in the past. Growth in sales and earnings can complement the profit margin screens to identify companies gaining at the expense of the competition. Increasing market share would also highlight strong performance, but few screening programs will have market share figures. However, market share and the competitive environment is usually discussed in a company's 10-K filings.

(cont'd on next page)

Screening Tips: The Philip Fisher Approach *(cont'd)*

Secondary factors

A great firm at a great price: Fisher liked to invest in good companies that were out-of-favor. Beyond traditional screens for low price multiples to factors such as earnings, sales, or book value, you may wish to consider a screening variable such as the price-earnings relative to growth rate (PEG) ratio. This ratio equates the earnings growth level to the valuation level of the firm, allowing firms with higher growth rates to trade at higher price-earnings levels yet still carrying an attractive price level. Normally, you should screen for PEG ratios of 1.0 or less; for the Fisher screen we used 0.5 or less.

THE PETER LYNCH APPROACH TO INVESTING IN "UNDERSTANDABLE" STOCKS

No modern-day investment "winner" is better known than Peter Lynch, who gained his considerable fame managing the Fidelity Magellan Fund. The fund was among the highest-ranking stock funds throughout Lynch's tenure, which began in 1977 at the fund's launching, and ended in 1990, when Lynch retired. Although Lynch achieved success as an institutional investor, he strongly believes that individual investors have a distinct advantage over Wall Street and large money managers when using his approach. Individual investors, he feels, have more flexibility in following this basic approach because they are unencumbered by bureaucratic rules and short-term performance concerns.

Peter Lynch's approach is strictly bottom-up, with selection from among companies with which the investor is familiar, and then through fundamental analysis that emphasizes a thorough understanding of the company, its prospects, its competitive environment, and whether the stock can be purchased at a reasonable price.

The Philosophy: Invest in What You Know

Lynch is a "story" investor. That is, each stock selection decision is based on a well-grounded expectation concerning the firm's growth prospects that can easily be explained. The expectations are derived from the company's "story"—what it is that the company is going to do, or what it is that is going to happen, to bring about the desired results.

The more familiar you are with a company, and the better you understand its business and competitive environment, the better your chances of finding a good "story" that will actually come true. For this reason, Lynch is a strong advocate of investing in companies with which one is familiar, or whose products or services are relatively easy to understand. Thus, Lynch says he would invest in "pantyhose rather than communications satellites," and "motel chains rather than fiber optics."

Lynch does not believe in restricting investments to any one type of stock. His "story" approach, in fact, suggests the opposite, with investments in firms with various reasons for favorable expectations. In general, however, he tends to favor small, moderately fast-growing companies that can be bought at a reasonable price.

Selection Process

Lynch's bottom-up approach means that prospective stocks must be picked one-by-one and then thoroughly investigated—there is no formula or screen that will produce a list of prospective "good stories." Instead, Lynch suggests that investors keep alert for possibilities based on their own experiences—for instance, within their own business or trade, or as consumers of products.

The next step is to familiarize yourself thoroughly with the company so that you can form reasonable expectations concerning the future. However, Lynch does not believe that investors can predict actual growth rates, and he is skeptical of analysts' earnings estimates.

Instead, he suggests that you examine the company's plans—how does it intend to increase its earnings, and how are those intentions actually being fulfilled? Lynch points out five ways in which a company can increase earnings: It can reduce costs; raise prices; expand into new markets; sell more in old markets; or revitalize, close, or sell a losing operation. The company's plan to increase earnings and its ability to fulfill that plan are its "story," and the more familiar you are with the firm or industry, the better edge you have in evaluating the company's plan, abilities, and any potential pitfalls.

Categorizing a company, according to Lynch, can help you develop the "story" line, and thus come up with reasonable expectations. He suggests first categorizing a company by size. Large companies cannot be expected to grow as quickly as smaller companies.

Next, he suggests categorizing a company by generalized "story" lines, and he identifies six:

- **Slow Growers:** Large and aging companies expected to grow only slightly faster than the U.S. economy as a whole, but often paying large regular dividends. These are not among his favorites.

- **Stalwarts:** Large companies that are still able to grow, with annual earnings growth rates of around 10% to 12%; past examples include Coca-Cola, Procter & Gamble, and Bristol-Myers. If purchased at a good price, Lynch says he expects good but not enormous returns—certainly no more than 50% in two years and possibly less. Lynch suggests rotating among the companies, selling when moderate gains are reached, and repeating the process with others that haven't yet appreciated. These firms also offer downside protection during recessions.

- **Fast-Growers:** Small, aggressive new firms with annual earnings growth of 20% to 25% a year. These do not have to be in fast-growing industries, and in fact Lynch prefers those that are not. Fast-growers are among Lynch's favorites, and he says that an investor's biggest gains will come from this type of stock. However, they also carry considerable risk.

- **Cyclicals:** Companies in which sales and profits tend to rise and fall in somewhat predictable patterns based on the economic cycle; examples include companies in the auto industry, airlines and steel. Lynch warns that these firms can be mistaken for stalwarts by inexperienced investors, but share prices of cyclicals can drop dramatically during hard times. Thus, timing is crucial when investing in these firms, and Lynch says that investors must learn to detect the early signs that business is starting to turn down.

- **Turnarounds:** Companies that have been battered down or depressed—Lynch calls these "no-growers"; past examples include Chrysler, Penn Central and General Public Utilities (owner of Three Mile Island). The stocks of successful turnarounds can move back up quickly, and Lynch points out that of all the categories, these upturns are least related to the general market.
- **Asset opportunities:** Companies that have assets that Wall Street analysts and others have overlooked. Lynch points to several general areas where asset plays can often be found—metals and oil, newspapers and TV stations, and patented drugs. However, finding these hidden assets requires a real working knowledge of the company that owns the assets, and Lynch points out that within this category, the "local" edge—your own knowledge and experience—can be used to greatest advantage.

Selection Criteria

Analysis is central to Lynch's approach. In examining a company, he is seeking to understand the firm's business and prospects, including any competitive advantages, and evaluate any potential pitfalls that may prevent the favorable "story" from occurring. In addition, an investor cannot make a profit if the story has a happy ending but the stock was purchased at a price that is too high. For that reason, he also seeks to determine reasonable value.

Here are some of the key numbers Lynch suggests investors examine:

Year-by-year earnings: The historical record of earnings should be examined for stability and consistency. Stock prices cannot deviate for very long from the level of earnings, so the pattern of earnings growth will help reveal the stability and strength of the company. Ideally, earnings should move up consistently.

Earnings growth: The growth rate of earnings should fit with the firm's "story"—fast-growers should have higher growth rates than slow-growers. Extremely high levels of earnings growth rates are not sustainable, but continued high growth may be factored into the price. A high level of growth for a company and industry will attract a great deal of attention from both investors, who bid up the stock, and from competitors, who provide a more difficult business environment.

The price-earnings ratio: The earnings potential of a company is a primary determinant of company value, but at times the market may get ahead of itself and overprice a stock. The price-earnings ratio helps you keep your perspective, by comparing the current price to most recently reported earnings. Stocks with good prospects should sell with higher price-earnings ratios than stocks with poor prospects.

The price-earnings ratio relative to its historical average: Studying the pattern of price-earnings ratios over a period of several years should reveal a level that is "normal" for the company. This should help you avoid buying into a stock if the price gets ahead of the earnings, or sends an early warning that it may be time to take some profits in a stock you own.

The price-earnings ratio relative to the industry average: Comparing a company's price-earnings ratio to the industry's may help reveal if the company is a bargain. At a minimum, it leads to questions as to why the company is priced differently—is it a poor performer in the industry, or is it just neglected?

The price-earnings ratio relative to its earnings growth rate: Companies with better earnings growth prospects should sell with higher price-earnings ratios, but the ratio between the two can reveal bargains or overvaluations. A price-earnings ratio of half the level of historical earnings growth is considered attractive, while relative ratios above 2.0 are unattractive. For dividend-paying stocks, Lynch refines this measure by adding the dividend yield to the earnings growth [in other words, the price-earnings ratio divided by the sum of the earnings growth rate and dividend yield]. With this modified technique, ratios above 1.0 are considered poor, while ratios below 0.5 are considered attractive.

Ratio of debt to equity: How much debt is on the balance sheet? A strong balance sheet provides maneuvering room as the company expands or experiences trouble. Lynch is especially wary of bank debt, which can usually be called in by the bank on demand.

Net cash per share: Net cash per share is calculated by adding the level of cash and cash equivalents, subtracting long-term debt, and dividing the result by the number of shares outstanding. High levels provide a support for the stock price and indicate financial strength.

Dividends & payout ratio: Dividends are usually paid by the larger companies, and Lynch tends to prefer smaller growth firms. However, Lynch suggests that investors who prefer dividend-paying firms should seek firms with the ability to pay during recessions (indicated by a low percentage of earnings paid out as dividends), and companies that have a 20-year or 30-year record of regularly raising dividends.

Inventories: Are inventories piling up? This is a particularly important figure for cyclicals. Lynch notes that, for manufacturers or retailers, an inventory buildup is a bad sign, and a red flag is waving when inventories grow faster than sales. On the other hand, if a company is depressed, the first evidence of a turnaround is when inventories start to be depleted.

When evaluating companies, there are certain characteristics that Lynch finds particularly favorable. These include:

- *The name is boring, the product or service is in a boring area, the company does something disagreeable or depressing, or there are rumors of something bad about the company*—Lynch likes these kinds of firms because their ugly duckling nature tends to be reflected in the share price, so good bargains often turn up. Past examples include: Service Corporation International (a funeral home operator—depressing); and Waste Management (a toxic waste clean-up firm—disagreeable).
- *The company is a spin-off*—Lynch says these often receive little attention from Wall Street, and he suggests that investors check them out several months later to see if insiders are buying.

- **The fast-growing company is in a no-growth industry**—Growth industries attract too much interest from investors (leading to high prices) and competitors.
- **The company is a niche firm controlling a market segment or an area that would be difficult for a competitor to enter.**
- **The company produces a product that people tend to keep buying during good times and bad**—*such as drugs, soft drinks, and razor blades*—These firms are more stable than companies whose product sales are less certain.
- **The company is a user of technology**—These companies can take advantage of technological advances, but don't tend to have the high valuations of firms directly producing technology.
- **There is a low percentage of shares held by institutions, and there is low analyst coverage**—Bargains can be found among firms neglected by Wall Street.
- **Insiders are buying shares**—A positive sign that insiders feel particularly confident about the firm's prospects.
- **The company is buying back shares**—Buybacks become an issue once companies start to mature and have cash flow that exceeds their capital needs. Lynch prefers companies that buy their shares back over firms that choose to expand into unrelated businesses. The buyback will help to support the stock price and is usually performed when management feels share prices are favorable.

Characteristics Lynch finds unfavorable are:

- Hot stocks in hot industries.
- Companies (particularly small firms) with big plans that have not yet been proven.
- Profitable companies engaged in diversifying acquisitions. Lynch terms these "diworseifications."
- Companies in which one customer accounts for 25% to 50% of their sales.

Portfolio Building and Monitoring

As portfolio manager of the Magellan Fund, Lynch held as many as 1,400 stocks at one time. Although he was successful in juggling this many stocks, he does point to significant problems in managing such a large number of stocks. Individual investors, of course, will hold nowhere near that number, but he is wary of over-diversification just the same. There is no point in diversifying simply for the sake of diversifying, he argues, particularly if it means less familiarity with the firms. Lynch says investors should own however many "exciting prospects" that they are able to uncover that pass all the tests of research. Lynch also suggests investing in several categories of stocks as a way of spreading the downside risk, and he warns against investment in a single stock.

Lynch is an advocate of maintaining a long-term commitment to the stock market. He does not favor market timing, and indeed feels that it is impossible to do so. But that doesn't necessarily mean investors should hold onto a single stock forever. Instead, Lynch says investors should review their holdings every few months, rechecking the company "story" to see if anything has changed either with the unfolding of the story or with the share price. They key to knowing when to sell, he says, is knowing "why you bought it in the first place." Lynch says investors should sell if:

- The story has played out as expected and this is reflected in the price; for instance, the price of a stalwart has gone up as much as could be expected.
- Something in the story fails to unfold as expected, the story changes, or fundamentals deteriorate; for instance, a cyclical's inventories start to build, or a smaller firm enters a new slower-growth stage.

For Lynch, a price drop can be an opportunity to buy more of a good prospect at cheaper prices. It is much harder, he says, to stick with a winning stock once the price goes up, particularly with fast-growers where the tendency is to sell too soon rather than too late. With these firms, he suggests holding on until it is clear the firm is entering a different growth stage.

Rather than simply selling a stock, Lynch suggests "rotation"—selling the company and replacing it with another company with a similar story, but better prospects. The rotation approach maintains the investor's long-term commitment to the stock market, and keeps the focus on fundamental value.

Summing It Up

Lynch offers a practical approach that can be adapted by many different types of investors, from those emphasizing fast growth to those who prefer more stable, dividend-producing investments.

Lynch sums up stock investing and his outlook best:

"Frequent follies notwithstanding, I continue to be optimistic about America, Americans, and investing in general. When you invest in stocks, you have to have a basic faith in human nature, in capitalism, in the country at large, and in future prosperity in general. So far, nothing's been strong enough to shake me out of it."

The Peter Lynch Approach in Brief

Philosophy

Investment in companies in which there is a well-grounded expectation concerning the firm's growth prospects and in which the stock can be bought at a reasonable price. A thorough understanding of the company and its competitive environment is the only "edge" investors have over other investors in finding reasonably valued stocks.

Universe of stocks

All listed and over-the-counter stocks—no restrictions.

Criteria for initial consideration

Select from industries and companies with which you are familiar and have an understanding of the factors that will move the stock price. Make sure you can articulate a prospective stock's "story line"—the company's plans for increasing growth and any other series of events that will help the firm—and make sure you understand and balance them against any potential pitfalls. Categorizing the stocks among six major "story" lines is helpful when evaluating prospective stocks.

Specific factors depend on the firm's "story," but at a minimum these factors should be examined:

- Year-by-year earnings: Look for stability and consistency, and an upward trend.
- P/E relative to historical average: The price-earnings ratio should be in the lower range of its historical average.
- P/E relative to industry average: The price-earnings ratio should be below the industry average.
- P/E relative to earnings growth rate: A price-earnings ratio of half the level of historical earnings growth is attractive; relative ratios above 2.0 are unattractive. For dividend-paying stocks, use the price-earnings ratio divided by the sum of the earnings growth rate and dividend yield—ratios below 0.5 are attractive, ratios above 1.0 are poor.
- Debt-equity ratio: The company's balance sheet should

be strong, with low levels of debt relative to equity financing; be particularly wary of high levels of bank debt.
- Net cash per share: The net cash per share (cash less long-term debt) relative to share price should be high.
- Dividends and payout ratio: For investors seeking dividend-paying firms, look for a low payout ratio (earnings per share divided by dividends per share) and long records (20 to 30 years) of regularly raising dividends.
- Inventories: Particularly important for cyclicals, inventories that are piling up are a warning flag, especially if growing faster than sales.

Other favorable characteristics

- The name is boring, the product or service is in a boring area, the company does something disagreeable or depressing, or there are rumors of something bad about the company.
- The company is a spin-off.
- The fast-growing company is in a no-growth industry.
- The company is a niche firm controlling a market segment.
- The company produces a product that people tend to keep buying during good times and bad.
- The company can take advantage of technological advances, but is not a direct producer of technology.
- There is a low percentage of shares held by institutions and there is low analyst coverage.
- Insiders are buying shares.
- The company is buying back shares.

Unfavorable characteristics

- Hot stocks in hot industries.
- Companies (particularly small firms) with big plans that have not yet been proven.
- Profitable companies engaged in diversifying acquisitions.
- Companies in which one customer accounts for 25% to 50% of sales.

(cont'd on next page)

The Peter Lynch Approach in Brief *(cont'd)*

Stock monitoring and when to sell

- Do not diversify simply to diversify, particularly if it means less familiarity with the firms. Invest in whatever number of firms is large enough to still allow you to fully research and understand each firm. Invest in several categories of stock for diversification.
- Review holdings every few months, rechecking the company "story" to see if anything has changed. Sell if the "story" has played out as expected or something in the story fails to unfold as expected or fundamentals deteriorate.
- Price drops usually should be viewed as an opportunity to buy more of a good prospect at cheaper prices.
- Consider "rotation"—selling played-out stocks with stocks with a similar story, but better prospects. Maintain a long-term commitment to the stock market and focus on relative fundamental values.

STOCK SCREENS: APPLYING THE PETER LYNCH APPROACH

Peter Lynch is a bottom-up, kick-the-tires type of stockpicker. As a result, much of his criteria is qualitative in nature, where analysis must be done on each stock individually, and screening a large universe does not work, However, some of his principles are useful screening criteria and that is what we focus on here.

Examine the Price-Earnings Ratio

Our first screen excludes financial firms. Although Peter Lynch is a big fan of financial stocks, we had to exclude them from the general screen because their financial statements cannot be directly compared to other firms.

Finding a good company is only half of the battle in making a successful investment. Lynch is a strong proponent of buying good companies at a reasonable price. The earnings potential of a company is a primary determinant of company value. At times, the market may get ahead of itself and even overprice a stock with great prospects. The price-earnings ratio helps to keep your perspective in check. Lynch examines price-earnings ratios in several ways:

- *How does the price-earnings ratio compare to its historical average?* By studying the pattern of price-earnings ratios over a period of several years, you can develop a sense of the normal level for the company. Requiring that a company's current price-earnings ratio be lower than its own five-year average price-earnings ratio can be a very effective screen in narrowing down a large list of prospective stocks. Beyond examining the company's current valuation level, it requires a company to have five years of positive earnings and five years of price data. Most software programs can easily perform this screen.
- *How does the price-earnings ratio compare to the industry norm?* Comparing a company's price-earnings ratio to the industry may help reveal whether the company is a bargain. This is relatively simple to screen: Our screen requires that the company have a price-earnings ratio lower than normal for its industry.
- *How does the price-earnings ratio compare to its earnings growth rate?* Companies with better prospects should sell with higher price-earnings ratios. So how can you compare the price-earnings ratios of companies with different growth prospects? A useful valuation technique is to measure the price-earnings ratio relative to the earnings growth rate (PEG ratio). Lynch considers a price-earnings ratio of half the level of historical earnings growth attractive, while ratios above 2.0 are unattrac-

tive. Lynch refines this measure by adding the dividend yield to the earnings growth. This adjustment acknowledges the contribution that dividends make to an investor's return. The ratio is calculated by dividing the price-earnings ratio by the sum of the earnings growth rate and the dividend yield. With this modified technique, ratios above 1.0 are considered poor, while ratios below 0.5 are considered attractive. Our screen uses this ratio of price-earnings to the earnings growth rate plus the dividend yield; a ratio less than or equal to 0.50 is specified as a cut-off.

How Stable and Consistent Are the Earnings?

It is important to examine the historical record of earnings. Stock prices cannot deviate very long from the level of earnings, so the pattern of earnings growth will help to reveal the stability and strength of the company. Ideally, earnings should move up consistently. We did not use any earnings stability screens, but this can be done manually by examining year-by-year earnings per share data over a long-term time period of at least five years.

Avoid Hot Companies in Hot Industries

Lynch prefers to invest in companies with earnings expanding at moderately fast rates (20% to 25%) in non-growth industries. Extremely high levels of earnings growth rates are not sustainable. In addition, a high level of growth for a company and industry will attract a great

Table 1.
Peter Lynch Screening Results*

Company (Exchange: Ticker)	Price ($)	P/E (x)	5-Yr Avg. P/E (x)	PEG Ratio (Div-Adj 5-Yr) (x)	Mkt Cap ($ mil)	Total Liab to Assets (%)	EPS Grth (5-Yr) (%)	Div Yield (%)	5-Yr Avg. Div Yield (%)	% of Shares Held by Inst. (%)	% of Shares Held by Insiders (%)	Cash Per Share ($)
AMREP Corporation (N: AXR)	5.38	6.3	8.7	0.3	38.9	50.1	24.6	0.0	na	14.6	62.7	2.4
Analytical Surveys, Inc. (M: ANLT)	8.00	6.2	27.8	0.1	55.6	40.4	46.7	0.0	na	16.9	26.7	1.0
Ballantyne of Omaha, Inc. (N: BTN)	6.25	10.4	19.6	0.3	77.7	35.9	33.3	0.0	na	17.7	29.2	0.1
Cagle's, Inc. (A: CGL.A)	10.81	3.8	16.8	0.2	51.3	48.7	21.6	1.1	0.7	14.6	66.3	0.0
Chase Corporation (A: CCF)	10.88	8.2	10.6	0.2	42.5	44.5	30.1	2.9	1.7	12.6	51.4	0.1
Chicago Rivet & Machine (A: CVR)	21.50	7.3	10.7	0.3	24.7	28.3	19.5	3.3	4.2	13.2	30.5	1.5
Continental Materials (A: CUO)	22.38	8.6	13.4	0.3	44.1	43.4	33.3	0.0	na	17.5	49.2	0.1
DeWolfe Companies (A: DWL)	6.88	4.9	52.1	0.3	23.2	74.5	16.8	0.0	na	5.7	64.4	2.2
Disc Graphics, Inc. (M: DSGR)	3.81	8.3	12.7	0.2	21.0	60.9	34.1	0.0	na	10.0	74.6	0.0
ELXSI Corporation (M: ELXS)	13.00	3.3	7.7	0.5	55.7	28.7	7.8	0.0	na	11.5	62.6	0.3
Emons Transportation Grp. (M: EMON)	2.00	7.7	34.1	0.2	15.7	58.2	42.5	0.0	na	15.2	54.1	0.3
Farrel Corporation (M: FARL)	2.06	4.0	25.7	0.2	10.8	50.1	13.7	7.8	5.4	14.1	69.5	0.7
Flamemaster Corporation (M: FAME)	6.75	12.1	16.5	0.3	11.0	8.3	46.5	1.9	2.8	0.8	38.5	1.2
Flanigan's Enterprises (A: BDL)	5.00	4.3	6.2	0.1	9.8	35.2	41.9	2.2	na	9.6	48.7	0.8
Friedman Industries (A: FRD)	3.63	10.1	10.2	0.5	26.1	37.0	16.3	5.5	4.4	16.1	48.5	0.1
General Employment Ent. (A: JOB)	4.38	7.3	15.5	0.2	22.3	25.0	33.8	1.1	na	4.1	35.1	2.2
Great Northern Iron Ore (N: GNI)	52.00	8.5	9.8	0.3	78.0	14.7	13.1	12.3	10.0	2.9	6.7	0.3
Hi-Tech Pharmacal Co. (M: HITK)	5.00	11.1	18.8	0.4	22.0	28.2	30.3	0.0	na	10.8	40.8	1.0
Humphrey Hospitality Tr. (M: HUMP)	6.81	8.6	13.5	0.4	76.1	56.0	7.9	13.2	na	0.4	55.3	0.5
IPI Inc. (A: IDH)	2.38	6.1	11.9	0.4	11.2	9.8	14.3	0.0	na	12.5	81.0	0.4
Liberty Homes, Inc. (M: LIBHA)	6.75	6.4	10.6	0.5	26.4	33.8	10.1	4.1	2.6	13.9	59.0	2.5
Lifschultz Industries Inc (M: LIFF)	10.38	7.2	12.9	0.3	11.6	16.4	23.3	0.0	na	0.1	64.3	0.9
Mesa Laboratories, Inc. (M: MLAB)	4.44	8.7	13.8	0.5	16.6	5.0	17.3	0.0	na	12.3	22.5	1.6
Napco Security Systems (M: NSSC)	3.19	6.1	14.7	0.3	11.1	42.8	19.6	0.0	na	11.8	39.9	0.5
National Beverage Corp. (A: FIZ)	7.50	10.9	12.2	0.3	137.1	50.7	36.5	0.0	na	5.5	79.2	1.8
P & F Industries (M: PFINA)	6.63	6.3	9.6	0.2	23.2	55.8	45.3	0.0	na	17.9	71.5	0.2
Sel-Leb Marketing Inc. (M: SELB)	3.00	8.3	162.3	0.3	6.8	52.4	24.6	0.0	na	5.2	55.7	0.0
Smithfield Companies (M: HAMS)	7.00	14.0	18.1	0.3	15.4	23.6	44.0	2.0	2.0	9.3	81.9	2.6
Systemax Inc. (N: SYX)	9.00	8.8	26.9	0.3	320.0	42.1	27.5	0.0	na	13.6	84.0	1.2
Taylor Devices, Inc. (M: TAYD)	2.53	9.7	19.8	0.4	7.0	41.8	26.6	0.0	na	0.0	46.1	0.3
Tech/Ops Sevcon, Inc. (A: TO)	11.50	12.6	16.1	0.5	35.8	38.1	18.1	6.3	4.2	17.3	32.6	1.0
Village Super Market, Inc (M: VLGEA)	12.75	7.0	17.0	0.2	38.1	58.4	42.1	0.0	na	14.7	69.9	7.2
Westerbeke Corporation (M: WTBK)	2.50	6.6	9.5	0.5	4.8	26.0	16.0	0.0	na	0.6	68.7	0.9

na = not available

Exchange Key: N = New York Stock Exchange
A = American Stock Exchange
M = Nasdaq

*Screening criteria used to produce table results can be found on opposite page.

Data Source: AAII's Stock Investor/Market Guide, Inc. and I/B/E/S. Statistics are based on figures as of February 25, 2000.

deal of attention from both investors, who bid up the stock price, and from competitors, who provide a more difficult business environment. Our screen specifies a maximum annual earnings per share growth rate of 50% over the last five years.

What Is the Level of Institutional Holdings?

Lynch feels that the bargains are located among stocks neglected by Wall Street. The lower the percentage of shares held by institutions and the lower the number of analysts following the stock, the better. Our screen requires a lower percentage of shares held by institutions than the median. This criterion will tend to filter out larger firms.

How Large Is the Firm?

Small firms have more upside potential than large firms. Small firms can easily expand in size while large firms are limited. The table of passing companies lists the market capitalization of the firms. Big companies have small moves, small companies have big moves.

How Strong Is the Balance Sheet?

A strong balance sheet provides maneuvering room as the company expands or experiences trouble. Our screen requires that the company's ratio of total liabilities to assets is below its industry norm. We looked at total liabilities because it considers all forms of debt. Comparing the company's ratio against industry levels is important because acceptable levels vary by industry. Lynch is also especially wary of bank debt, which can usually be called in by the bank on demand. Small-cap stocks have a more difficult time raising capital through the bond market than larger stocks and often turn to banks for capital. A close examination of the financial statements, especially in the notes to the financial statement, should help to reveal the use of bank debt.

Table 1 is a list of stocks passing the screens we used to illustrate how Peter Lynch's approach could be implemented. It is based on data as of February 25, 2000, using AAII's *Stock Investor Professional*. Screening tips for the Peter Lynch approach are on pages 103 and 104.

Screening Tips: The Peter Lynch Approach

Year-by-year earnings: Lynch likes to see stability and consistency in earnings. Basic screens could look for positive year-to-year changes in earnings or positive annual earnings. Some services such as Value Line and Standard & Poor's provide earnings stability rankings that can be used in screens.

Earnings growth: When screening for earnings growth you should require reasonable, but not excessive rates of growth. In most cases, if you have already entered criteria looking year-to-year earnings increases, there is no need to establish minimum earnings growth screens. However, you may wish to establish a maximum earnings growth for passing firms. For our screen we require that the earnings growth be less than 50% annually over the last five years. Lynch stays away from extremely high levels of earnings growth because even though it is sustainable, continued high growth may be factored into the price, pushing it too high. A high level of growth for a company and industry will attract a great deal of attention from both investors, who bid up the stock, and competitors, who provide a more difficult business environment.

The price-earnings ratio relative to its historical average: Studying the pattern of price-earnings ratios over a period of several years should reveal a level that is "normal" for the company. Screen for a current price-earnings ratio below its five- or 10-year average. Make sure that the average has not been skewed by a very high price-earnings ratio for a given year. You may also wish to eliminate firms with a price-earnings ratio more than twice the average for any of the past five or 10 years.

The price-earnings ratio relative to the industry average: Comparing a company's price-earnings ratio to the industry's average may help reveal if the company is a bargain. More programs are allowing for such a comparison. A simple screen would look for company price-earnings ratios below the industry average or median price-earnings ratio.

The price-earnings ratio relative to its earnings growth rate: Companies with better prospects should sell with higher price-earnings ratios, but the ratio between the two can reveal bargains or overvaluations. Many screening systems provide a price-earnings to growth (PEG) ratio, but the exact construction of the ratio differs from program to program. Generally, as a minimum, you should screen for a PEG ratio below 1.0. Lynch indicates that he looks for PEG ratios below 0.5. If your program allows for custom fields, you can create your own PEG ratio following Lynch's example of adding the dividend yield to the growth rate [in other words, the price-earnings ratio divided by the sum of the earnings growth rate and dividend yield]. The interpretation of this modified PEG ratio is the same: Lynch considers ratios below 0.5 to be attractive.

Ratio of debt to equity: Lynch looks for strong balance sheets and is especially wary of bank debt, which can usually be called in by the bank on demand. Few screening program will indicate if debt is bank debt, so it is best to use traditional financial strength screens such as low debt-to-equity, debt as a percentage of capital, or total liabilities to assets. Acceptable debt levels vary from industry to industry, so you may wish to require ratios better than the industry norm.

Net cash per share: Lynch calculates net cash per share by adding cash and cash equivalents, subtracting long-term debt, and dividing the result by the number of shares outstanding. High levels provide a support for the stock price

(cont'd on next page)

Screening Tips: The Peter Lynch Approach *(cont'd)*

and indicate financial strength. Few programs will have this calculation available, but if your program supports custom fields, you should be able to calculate the variable. Normally, you would look for high levels of net cash per share relative to stock price.

Dividends & payout ratio: Dividends are usually paid by the larger companies, and Lynch tends to prefer smaller growth firms. However, Lynch suggests that investors who prefer dividend-paying firms should seek firms with the ability to pay during recessions (indicated by a low percentage of earnings paid out as dividends), and companies that have a 20-year or 30-year record of regularly raising dividends. Few software programs will provide such a long history of dividend payments, but if dividends are important to you, screen for dividend payments for each of the years tracked by your program. Also look for low payout ratios (85% or less for utilities, 50% or less for other firms) over time.

Inventories: Are inventories piling up? Look out for increases in the ratio of inventory as a percent of assets, or decreases in the inventory turnover rate.

Diversifying Among Investing Styles: The James O'Shaughnessy Approach

One of the longest-running debates among stockpickers concerns whether selection criteria should focus on growth characteristics or value characteristics. In other words, should you buy stocks for their superior growth potential, or because they are undervalued?

James O'Shaughnessy, president of the investment advisory firm O'Shaughnessy Capital Management, set out several years ago to try to settle the argument once-and-for-all by testing a series of growth and value screens on a sufficiently large database of stocks (S&P's Compustat data for stocks of $150 million or greater market capitalization) that covers a long time period—40 years. His goal also was to determine which screens within each strategy produced the best returns.

The results of his analyses were published in the highly popular "What Works on Wall Street: A Guide to the Best-Performing Investment Strategies of All Time" (see References on page 201 for more information).

What Works? O'Shaughnessy's Philosophy

Based on his analyses, O'Shaughnessy developed an approach that diplomatically marries the two strategies. He found that both strategies can work, but they work best on different kinds of stocks. A value strategy tends to work best on large-capitalization stocks, while a more growth-focused approach is useful for a stock universe that emphasizes smaller stocks. He also found the two strategies to be complementary, with the value strategy offering less volatility, and the growth strategy offering greater potential for capital appreciation.

Within each strategy, O'Shaughnessy found the most effective approach was to use "multifactor" screens, and he therefore advises that investors seek stocks that pass several criteria, including at least one value screen that prevents an investor from paying too much for a stock.

O'Shaughnessy states, however, that the most important aspect is discipline—sticking with a proven strategy over long periods of time, even when going through rough times. And simpler strategies, he notes, are easier to stick with than complex strategies. Simple, disciplined strategies work because they take the emotions out of stock investing and force an investor to buy stocks at those times when they offer the best buys.

Universe of Stocks

O'Shaughnessy suggests that investors select stocks from two different universes, depending on their investment style.

For value-based strategies, O'Shaughnessy suggests buying stocks in firms with a large market capitalization, similar to those in the S&P 500; within his own database, this group consisted of roughly the top 16% of all companies by market cap.

For growth-based strategies, he suggests investors broaden their focus to encompass smaller stocks as well as larger-capitalization stocks, rather than focusing exclusively on small firms. However, he puts a floor of $150 million (which should be adjusted for inflation) on smaller stocks.

Why? O'Shaughnessy found that the largest gains came from the smallest stocks—those that are below $25 million in market capitalization (these figures are adjusted for inflation, since the study covers 40 years of data). However, he argues that the extremely large number of stocks within this category—over 2,000 in the Compustat database—makes it very difficult for an investor to choose among them. In addition, O'Shaughnessy is concerned with higher trading costs associated with very small-capitalization stocks, although his focus is more on institution-sized investors. He notes that professional money managers would have difficulty investing in stocks below $150 million in market capitalization, and he therefore suggests investors concentrate on stocks with market capitalizations above $150 million.

What Works: Value Strategies

Value strategies seek to identify out-of-favor investments that are attractively priced in relation to some measure of value for the firm. O'Shaughnessy tested a number of basic value strategies on stocks of all market capitalizations, and he found that most of these screens were effective in identifying both winners and losers—the best-valued portfolios tended to produce the highest returns, and the worst-valued portfolios tended to produce the lowest returns. There were differences among the screens, however:

- **Price-earnings ratios:** Low price-earnings ratios were most effective as a screen for large-capitalization stocks, which O'Shaughnessy believes is due to the fact that many smaller firms are more likely to have strong earnings growth several years running, and are therefore likely to have higher price-earnings ratios. On the other hand, buying stocks with the highest price-earnings ratios is a losing proposition regardless of firm size.
- **Price-to-book-value ratios:** Low price-to-book-value ratios were most effective as a screen for large-capitalization stocks, although it worked with smaller firms as well. On the other hand, high price-to-book-value is closely associated with growth stocks, and O'Shaughnessy suggests that high ratios alone should not keep you

from buying a stock.

- **Price-to-cash-flow (income before extraordinary items plus depreciation and amortization) ratios:** Low ratios were effective as a screen for both small- and larger-capitalization stocks. High ratios should be avoided unless there are other compelling reasons for purchase, such as strong growth that can mitigate some of the cash-flow risk.
- **Price-to-sales ratios:** O'Shaughnessy found this to be a very effective screen for stocks of all sizes. Low ratios consistently produced higher returns, and high ratios are "toxic" and should be avoided.
- **Dividend yield:** High yields were very effective as a screen for large-capitalization stocks and not at all effective for smaller stocks. O'Shaughnessy suggests that investors who use this screen stick to larger, better-known companies with strong balance sheets and longer operating histories. For small stocks, O'Shaughnessy warns that high dividend yields may be a sign of more trouble to come.

O'Shaughnessy states that value screens tend to reward investors who stick with them through all kinds of market environments, and thus they are particularly useful for more risk-averse investors. Conversely, he warns that highly valued stocks tend to go through certain periods of spectacular returns, which often prove enticing to investors who do not focus on the longer term.

The best approach, O'Shaughnessy argues, is to require that a stock pass several screens. In addition, he suggests that value strategies work best with large-capitalization stocks. Based on his analysis of various combinations, he recommends a value approach that focuses on stocks with:

- **Large (higher than average) market capitalizations**—These firms are less volatile, tend to have long operating histories, and are more likely to survive adverse environments.
- **More common shares outstanding than average**—This offers excellent liquidity for investors.
- **Higher-than-average cash flows**—This helps screen out potentially weak companies that may cut dividends, a conditioning screen for a high dividend yield criteria.
- **Sales that are 1.5 times the average**—This helps identify market-leading companies.
- **High dividend yields**—This is the best value screen for large-capitalization stocks, although other value criteria could be substituted. This screen should be performed after the list of market-leading firms is identified using the first four screens. In his analysis, O'Shaughnessy selected the 50 highest-yielding stocks, but excluded utilities.

This kind of portfolio, he argues, tends to provide considerable downside protection during bear markets, yet can provide competitive returns during bull markets. For that reason, it is particularly well-suited for risk-averse investors.

What Works: Growth Strategies

Growth strategies seek to invest in companies that will continue to produce above-average earnings growth. O'Shaughnessy tested a number of basic growth strategies on stocks of all market capitalizations, including high rates of one- and five-year earnings growth, high profit margins, high returns on equity and high relative strength. Most of these simple growth strategies proved to be very risky. For instance, O'Shaughnessy found that purchasing firms with the largest increases in earnings growth, whether over one year or five, is a losing proposition because investors tend to pay too much for these stocks. And although growth stocks go through spurts of very high returns, especially during bull markets, they also go through very bearish periods. Over the long term, the returns do not adequately compensate for the high risk. The one exception, however, was:

- **Relative strength (one-year price changes):** Stocks with the highest relative strength (the highest price changes over the prior year) produced the highest returns the following year. O'Shaughnessy found this screen to be one of the most effective for stocks of all sizes, although he warns that it is a very volatile approach that can severely test investor discipline. Why does a momentum indicator work? O'Shaughnessy speculates that the market is simply "putting its money where its mouth is." Conversely, O'Shaughnessy suggests that investors avoid the biggest one-year losers, since most likely they will continue to lose.

Growth strategies, O'Shaughnessy notes, are more consistent with smaller stocks, although he prefers not to exclude large firms from consideration. And although the magnitude of growth appears to be of little use in identifying high-returning stocks, high relative strength provides a useful growth screen. O'Shaughnessy combines this factor with a low price-to-sales screen for his growth approach focusing on stocks with:

- **Market capitalizations of $150 million or greater**
- **Earnings gains in the current year compared to the previous year**
- **Price-to-sales ratios of 1.5 or below**—O'Shaughnessy relaxes the value criteria (below 1.0) slightly to allow more of the growth stocks to make the final cut, yet ensure that valuations are not extreme
- **Ranking among the highest in one-year price increase for all stocks**

The low price-to-sales ratio requirement combined with the high relative strength screen assures that growth stocks are bought when they are cheap, but at a time when the market is starting to realize that they have been overlooked.

O'Shaughnessy warns that this growth approach tends to be volatile, but its higher returns compensate for the greater risk. Thus, the approach is more useful for investors who can tolerate higher risk.

Portfolio Strategies

O'Shaughnessy argues that investors should not choose between growth versus value, but rather they should invest in both—they are complementary. Thus, an investor is best-served by diversifying among these two styles—dividing a stock portfolio into two parts, one focusing on finding value among market-leading companies, and the other seeking growth among consistently growing firms with low price-sales ratios and high price momentum. The value portion of an investor's portfolio offsets the volatility produced by the growth portion, which introduces the potential for greater gains. O'Shaughnessy recommends a 50/50 split for risk-tolerant investors, while risk-averse investors should weight their portfolios more heavily with stocks selected using the value approach.

O'Shaughnessy does not suggest specific rules for portfolio size and when to sell a stock. But he strongly argues against strategies that encourage frequent trading due to the costs, which are a drag on returns, and he emphasizes the importance of consistently following a relatively simple approach. Presumably, an investor could do well adopting the simple rules he used for the portfolios in his analyses:

- Each portfolio was rebalanced once a year, dropping stocks that no longer met the criteria, and adding those that did.
- Each portfolio consisted of 50 stocks held in equal amounts. He does mention that investors need not hold as many as 50 stocks per portfolio, but he points out that academic studies indicate a minimum of 16 stocks in various industries are required to achieve adequate diversification. Thus, at a minimum, an investor purchasing individual stocks who combines a growth portfolio with a value portfolio would need to hold at least 32 stocks.

In Summary

O'Shaughnessy's examination of investment screens is a useful guide for any investor who picks his own stocks. And he stands firmly in the stock-picking camp, arguing that it is possible to beat the market as long as a disciplined and emotion-free approach is followed.

O'Shaughnessy suggests that investors be guided by the Taoist concept of Wu Wei—let things occur as they are meant to occur. Translated into investment terms, this means:

"Pick good strategies, understand their nature and let them work. Don't try to second-guess or outsmart them. Don't abandon them because they're experiencing a rough patch. Take ego out of decisions. Don't make the simple complex. And most of all, be consistent."

The James O'Shaughnessy Approach

Philosophy and style

There is no single strategy that works best at all times and for all stocks. Both value and growth strategies can be useful, as long as the approach is consistently applied, is disciplined, and uses rules that have been proven to be successful over long time periods. Value strategies tend to work best on large-capitalization stocks, while a more growth-focused approach is useful for a stock universe that emphasizes smaller stocks. Successful value and growth strategies are complementary, with the value strategy offering less volatility and the growth strategy offering greater potential for capital appreciation.

Universe of stocks

- For value-based strategies: Stocks in firms with a large market capitalization (greater than overall average), similar to those in the S&P 500; within O'Shaughnessy's database, this group consisted of roughly the top 16% of all companies by market cap.
- For growth-based strategies: All stocks greater than $150 million in market capitalization (adjusted for inflation).

Criteria for initial consideration

Value Approach:
- Large market capitalizations (greater than overall average)
- More common shares outstanding than average
- Sales that are 1.5 times the average
- Higher-than-average cash flows (to screen out potentially weak companies that may cut dividends)

- High dividend yields (should be performed after the list of market-leading firms is identified using the first four screens); exclude utilities. This proved to be the best value screen, but other value criteria could be substituted.

Growth Approach:
- Market capitalization of $150 million or greater
- Earnings gains in current year compared to previous year
- Price-to-sales ratios of 1.5 or below
- Ranked among the highest in one-year price increase for all stocks (this should be performed after the first three growth screens).

Stock monitoring and when to sell

Investors should diversify among growth-based and value-based approaches. For risk-tolerant investors, a 50/50 split among the two strategies is a starting point; risk-averse investors should weight their portfolios more heavily with stocks selected using the value approach. Do not use strategies that encourage frequent trading, which will increase costs. Use simple rules that can be consistently applied. The rules for portfolios used in O'Shaughnessy's analyses included:
- Each portfolio consisted of 50 stocks held in equal amounts
- Portfolios were rebalanced annually—stocks that no longer met the criteria were dropped and those that did were added
- Although investors may not want to hold as many as 50 stocks, academic studies indicate a minimum of 16 stocks in various industries are required to achieve adequate diversification

Stock Screens: Applying the O'Shaughnessy Approach

In his book, O'Shaughnessy argues that the majority of investors fail to beat market averages because they do not follow a disciplined approach to investing. Instead, investors let the emotions surrounding the market overpower their judgment and push them off their planned investment course. O'Shaughnessy suggests disciplined approaches that follow growth and value strategies, depending on the universe of stocks selected. Both approaches lend themselves well to stock screening programs.

The Value Approach for Large-Cap Stocks

Testing revealed that the value approach was better suited for the large-cap universe. Large caps were also less volatile than the all-stocks universe, which fits nicely into the more conservative goal of the value screen. O'Shaughnessy established a screen for large-cap market leaders and tested a number of value factors to determine which additional factor produced consistent and strong performance over the long haul.

- **Universe:** The large-cap universe is defined as stocks whose market capitalization exceeded the average for the complete universe. The software package we used, *Stock Investor Professional*, has a database that covers over 9,000 stocks with an average market capitalization of $2 billion.
- **Common shares outstanding:** The next value filter specifies that a company should have more common shares outstanding than the average stock in the database, a screen for adequate liquidity.
- **Cash flow:** The next filter requires that cash flow per share exceed the database average.
- **Sales:** O'Shaughnessy also targets firms with total sales that are 1.5 times the database average.
- **Dividend Yield:** O'Shaughnessy recommends the use of dividend yield to build a value portfolio. The final screen selects the 50 highest-yielding stocks, but excludes utilities to keep them from dominating the dividend yield screen.

Table 1 is a list of stocks passing the screens we used to illustrate how O'Shaughnessy's value approach could be implemented. It is based on data as of February 25, 2000, using AAII's *Stock Investor Professional.*

The Growth Approach

With the exception of relative price strength, the growth strategies tested by O'Shaughnessy were not very promising. O'Shaughnessy's single factor tests screened for companies with extreme values—factors such as highest earnings growth, highest margins, and highest returns on equity. By reducing these extreme growth requirements and establishing moderate value requirements, O'Shaughnessy was able to construct a portfolio that had the desired combination of strong price growth and reasonable risk.

- **Universe:** The growth stock screen has a more encompassing universe than the value screen because smaller stocks have greater growth potential than their large-cap counterparts. Our screen looks for stocks with a market capitalization above $150 million. However, this figure should be adjusted annually for inflation.
- **Earnings growth:** O'Shaughnesssy's growth screen requires that current annual earnings be higher than the previous year. Our screen looks for a positive change in earnings per share for the latest four quarters compared to the previous four quarters. About half of the stocks pass this criterion.
- **Price-to-sales:** O'Shaughnessy balances the growth requirement by establishing a maximum price-to-sales ratio ceiling of 1.5. The price-to-sales ratio is the current price divided by the sales per share for the most recent 12 months, and is a measure of stock valuation relative to sales. A high ratio might imply an overvalued situation; a low ratio might indicate an undervalued stock. When used independently as a value screen, more restrictive ceilings of 0.75 or 1.0 are common. The price-to-sales

Table 1.
Stocks Passing the O'Shaughnessy Value Screening*

Company (Exchange: Ticker)	P/E (x)	Shares Out- Stand'g (Mil)	Cash Flow per Share ($)	Price-to- Book- Value (x)	Price-to- Sales (x)	Curr. Div Yield (%)	Earnings Grth Rate (5-Yr) (%)	Sales Grth Rate (5-Yr) (%)	Mkt Cap ($ mil)	Rel. Strgth Rank (52-wk) (%)
Albertson's Inc. (N: ABS)	21.3	423.60	14.60	1.88	0.33	2.9	11.5	7.2	10,378.9	8
Allstate Corporation (N: ALL)	6.0	790.90	5.50	1.02	0.61	3.3	21.4	4.7	16,410.0	12
American General Corp. (N: AGC)	11.6	248.05	15.30	1.78	1.19	3.4	26.3	16.2	12,649.6	23
Aon Corporation (N: AOC)	16.1	260.00	10.90	1.76	0.81	3.9	11.0	18.6	5,485.6	12
Atlantic Richfield Co. (N: ARC)	16.6	322.50	11.70	2.71	1.82	4.2	11.2	−10.2	21,945.6	62
Bank of America Corp. (N: BAC)	9.8	1,722.31	8.60	1.66	2.04	4.5	5.2	11.4	75,329.5	22
Bank of Montreal (N: BMO)	9.4	266.76	7.10	1.26	0.89	4.6	na	na	8,111.0	26
Bank One Corporation (N: ONE)	8.4	1,167.00	7.40	1.46	1.70	6.8	1.8	23.7	28,457.5	9
BB&T Corporation (N: BBT)	12.4	316.68	10.20	2.32	2.53	3.5	33.7	15.6	7,227.0	17
Bell Atlantic Corp. (N: BEL)	17.9	1,553.00	7.10	4.76	2.26	3.2	3.3	19.1	73,855.2	36
Campbell Soup Company (N: CPB)	15.9	429.00	12.80	52.36	1.86	3.2	5.4	−0.7	11,833.3	22
Canadian Imperial Bank (N: BCM)	17.6	442.70	17.00	1.71	1.08	3.1	na	na	10,252.3	54
Caterpillar, Inc. (N: CAT)	13.7	355.00	6.70	2.37	0.64	3.6	21.0	12.5	12,764.5	31
Chevron Corporation (N: CHV)	22.6	657.19	12.80	2.70	1.42	3.7	1.1	−3.8	46,636.2	43
ConAgra, Inc. (N: CAG)	24.4	476.20	9.30	2.52	0.31	5.0	−3.5	0.9	7,940.7	12
Conoco Inc. (N: COC.B)	16.5	627.00	8.90	2.74	0.49	3.9	−9.7	3.3	12,094.8	na
Conseco, Inc. (N: CNC)	5.0	327.00	2.70	0.89	0.61	4.1	−9.0	24.0	4,784.1	9
Eastman Kodak Company (N: EK)	13.3	316.20	9.00	4.70	1.32	3.0	24.0	0.8	18,265.4	40
Emerson Electric Co. (N: EMR)	15.6	430.40	10.50	3.31	1.42	3.0	11.5	10.6	20,529.7	34
Equity Office Properties (N: EOP)	18.0	253.63	8.80	0.98	3.16	7.0	83.5	60.2	6,020.6	45
First Union Corporation (N: FTU)	8.5	946.80	6.00	1.69	1.82	6.8	6.7	17.8	28,089.4	12
Firstar Corporation (N: FSR)	20.9	985.78	17.60	2.76	3.48	3.6	12.3	38.5	17,643.4	19
Fleet Boston Corporation (N: FBF)	12.1	569.52	5.90	1.57	2.07	4.7	11.4	6.1	23,518.9	16
Ford Motor Company (N: F)	7.3	1,206.00	3.40	1.92	0.33	4.7	51.6	5.9	51,864.2	24
General Mills, Inc. (N: GIS)	17.3	303.50	13.00	38.82	1.54	3.3	3.3	3.2	9,937.2	34
GTE Corporation (N: GTE)	13.6	978.00	7.20	5.05	2.17	3.3	19.4	5.7	54,784.7	40
H.J. Heinz Company (N: HNZ)	18.3	357.87	18.30	5.88	1.26	4.5	−3.6	5.7	11,593.3	15
J.C. Penney Company, Inc. (N: JCP)	13.6	260.00	3.60	0.60	0.13	7.2	−10.2	9.4	4,150.9	7
Kellogg Company (N: K)	25.3	405.20	14.90	10.45	1.22	4.7	−3.5	1.4	8,513.5	14
KeyCorp (N: KEY)	6.9	448.74	5.20	1.19	1.36	6.6	9.5	5.6	7,604.2	12
May Department Stores (N: MAY)	9.8	331.00	6.90	2.21	0.60	3.6	5.6	7.0	8,478.3	18
Nabisco Group Holdings (N: NGH)	11.5	325.19	3.80	0.94	0.28	5.5	−19.3	2.4	2,894.6	4
National City Corporation (N: NCC)	8.3	613.50	6.80	1.99	1.92	6.2	13.0	5.1	11,230.6	11
Norfolk Southern Corp. (N: NSC)	22.2	381.00	6.20	0.88	1.10	5.8	1.0	−1.1	5,233.6	10
Occidental Petroleum Corp (N: OXY)	10.3	357.60	6.60	1.75	0.83	6.3	4.4	−4.1	5,789.4	54
Philip Morris Companies (N: MO)	6.1	2,386.00	6.10	2.95	0.60	9.8	13.6	4.1	46,435.5	10
Phillips Petroleum Co. (N: P)	15.4	253.31	6.90	2.13	0.76	3.7	−0.2	−1.1	9,339.7	47
PNC Bank Corporation (N: PNC)	9.1	294.50	6.80	1.89	2.19	4.8	6.8	5.7	11,072.7	26

(cont'd on next page)

Table 1. *(cont'd)*
Stocks Passing the O'Shaughnessy Value Screening*

Company (Exchange: Ticker)	P/E (x)	Shares Out- Stand'g (Mil)	Cash Flow per Share ($)	Price-to- Book- Value (x)	Price-to- Sales (x)	Curr. Div Yield (%)	Earnings Grth Rate (5-Yr) (%)	Sales Grth Rate (5-Yr) (%)	Mkt Cap ($ mil)	Rel. Strgth Rank (52-wk) (%)
Raytheon Company (N: RTN.B)	15.1	338.02	4.60	0.59	0.32	4.1	0.0	16.2	6,536.0	5
Royal Bank of Canada (N: RY)	12.2	313.77	10.00	1.80	1.30	5.1	63.6	8.4	13,152.3	39
Sara Lee Corp. (N: SLE)	11.9	886.00	8.00	8.86	0.66	3.6	48.7	5.2	13,382.4	14
Sears, Roebuck & Co. (N: S)	6.8	379.80	4.50	1.57	0.24	3.5	−15.1	6.3	9,874.0	17
SunTrust Banks, Inc. (N: STI)	12.1	318.24	12.00	2.02	2.71	3.0	10.3	19.2	15,938.4	26
Texaco, Inc. (N: TX)	21.7	543.67	11.30	2.16	0.77	3.9	−11.9	−1.4	25,648.2	48
Toronto-Dominion Bank (N: TD)	19.8	596.04	19.80	2.78	2.08	3.3	na	na	14,930.3	62
U.S. Bancorp (NEW) (N: USB)	8.9	726.51	9.00	1.98	2.40	4.7	16.9	20.4	13,325.5	14
Unocal Corporation (N: UCL)	53.6	242.40	6.90	2.93	1.07	3.1	−5.9	−8.1	6,242.3	44
USX-Marathon Group (N: MRO)	10.1	309.39	5.00	1.41	0.30	4.0	61.0	13.0	6,602.8	54
Washington Mutual Inc. (N: WM)	7.0	565.36	7.40	1.42	1.08	4.8	11.3	38.5	12,881.4	14
Xerox Corporation (N: XRX)	10.2	664.49	5.60	2.84	0.68	4.0	30.0	6.4	13,368.2	5

na = not available

Exchange Key: N = New York Stock Exchange
A = American Stock Exchange
M = Nasdaq

*Screening criteria used to produce table results can be found on page 112.

Statistics are based on figures as of February 25, 2000.
Data Source: AAII's Stock Investor/Market Guide, Inc. and I/B/E/S.

ratio is loosened here to 1.5 to allow more growth-oriented companies to pass, yet filter those companies with extreme valuations.

• **Relative strength**: O'Shaughnessy's final filter is for relative price strength. Relative price strength is a price momentum indicator; it confirms investor expectations and interest by comparing the performance of a stock relative to the market. Our final screen seeks the 50 companies with the highest relative price strength over the past year.

Table 2 is a list of stocks passing the screens we used to illustrate how O'Shaughnessy's growth approach could be implemented. It is based on data as of February 25, 2000. Screening tips for the O'Shaughnessy approaches appear on page 117.

Table 2.
Stocks Passing the O'Shaughnessy Growth Screening*

Company (Exchange: Ticker)	P/E (x)	Shares Out-Stand'g (Mil)	Cash Flow per Share ($)	Price-to-Book-Value (x)	Price-to-Sales (x)	Curr. Div Yield (%)	Earnings Grth Rate (5-Yr) (%)	Sales Grth Rate (5-Yr) (%)	Mkt Cap ($ mil)	Rel. Strgth Rank (52-wk) (%)
4Front Technologies, Inc. (M: FFTI)	39.1	11.08	24.90	4.45	1.27	0.0	20.7	121.4	315.9	83
ACT Manufacturing, Inc. (M: ACTM)	119.4	12.99	63.00	4.92	0.80	0.0	-15.2	45.1	547.6	82
Advanced Marketing Serv. (M: ADMS)	13.7	12.84	12.10	2.33	0.35	0.3	150.7	13.6	217.8	78
Air Canada, Inc. (M: ACNAF)	16.6	188.20	6.00	1.75	0.46	0.0	na	na	1,990.2	88
Allen Telecom, Inc. (N: ALN)	na	27.48	15.00	1.51	1.14	0.0	-19.1	15.8	376.7	85
Amphenol Corporation (N: APH)	30.6	17.86	16.50	na	1.35	0.0	29.0	8.8	1,524.3	80
Arch Comunications Group (M: APGR)	na	48.06	20.00	na	1.03	0.0	-69.3	43.8	595.2	84
Argosy Gaming Company (N: AGY)	6.2	28.06	4.70	9.08	0.52	0.0	-9.6	49.7	299.2	85
Asia Pacific Res. Int'l. (N: ARH)	na	318.70	21.90	0.38	1.12	0.0	-21.2	33.4	418.6	89
Audiovox Corporation (M: VOXX)	40.8	19.33	36.90	5.12	0.95	0.0	39.3	19.0	1,220.1	97
AutoTote Corporation (A: TTE)	52.8	36.27	8.10	na	0.82	0.0	15.0	7.2	173.3	85
Aztar Corporation (N: AZR)	22.8	44.35	5.60	0.87	0.49	0.0	-5.6	9.2	387.9	75
C&D Technologies, Inc. (N: CHP)	22.1	12.86	12.80	3.81	1.39	0.2	28.8	14.2	579.3	77
C.H. Robinson Worldwide (M: CHRW)	37.9	41.18	32.30	9.50	0.86	0.7	20.5	13.2	1,890.2	76
Channell Commercial Corp. (M: CHNL)	16.8	9.10	10.40	2.55	1.33	0.0	18.3	31.4	154.1	78
Chesapeake Energy Corp. (N: CHK)	21.9	97.13	na	na	0.89	2.6	-163.3	67.3	297.9	92
Damark International Inc. (M: DMRK)	164.6	5.55	25.80	7.45	0.51	0.0	-19.5	-2.0	217.6	93
Domtar Inc. (N: DTC)	19.7	184.40	8.20	1.76	0.99	0.0	23.4	14.1	2,103.4	77
Dynegy, Inc. (N: DYN)	48.6	154.94	30.60	5.73	0.49	0.4	18.8	38.6	6,823.7	90
Enron Corp. (N: ENE)	51.7	714.00	27.30	5.70	1.27	0.8	10.1	31.4	46,962.1	78

(cont'd on next page)

Table 2. *(cont'd)*
Stocks Passing the O'Shaughnessy Growth Screening*

Company (Exchange: Ticker)	P/E (x)	Shares Out- Stand'g (Mil)	Cash Flow per Share ($)	Price-to- Book- Value (x)	Price-to- Sales (x)	Curr. Div Yield (%)	Earnings Grth Rate (5-Yr) (%)	Sales Grth Rate (5-Yr) (%)	Mkt Cap ($ mil)	Rel. Strgth Rank (52-wk) (%)
ePlus, Inc. (M: PLUS)	33.5	7.89	19.80	4.89	1.12	0.0	45.9	30.0	265.8	92
Factory 2-U Stores, Inc. (M: FTUS)	38.6	12.23	17.90	7.95	0.70	na	−23.5	28.5	281.6	78
Fisher Scientific Int'l. (N: FSH)	76.7	40.10	28.40	na	0.69	0.0	−38.5	18.1	1,659.6	83
Four Media Company (M: FOUR)	30.7	19.69	6.30	2.21	1.36	0.0	14.3	36.0	284.3	83
Hall, Kinion & Associates (M: HAKI)	29.2	10.39	21.30	4.58	1.16	0.0	na	66.2	189.3	83
Imation Corp. (N: IMN)	25.9	36.50	6.80	1.50	0.70	0.0	−4.1	−2.4	1,077.7	78
Indus International, Inc. (M: IINT)	7.3	32.20	6.20	2.19	1.33	0.0	na	na	270.1	81
Kent Electronics Corp. (N: KNT)	83.0	28.06	32.50	2.79	1.06	0.0	−53.7	27.0	934.3	86
Laboratory Corp. of Amer. (N: LH)	31.3	127.07	3.80	2.76	0.28	0.0	−30.8	16.2	482.9	79
MasTec, Inc. (N: MTZ)	34.9	28.33	15.20	6.04	1.46	0.0	39.0	56.9	1,549.8	81
Material Sciences Corp. (N: MSC)	12.7	15.05	4.60	1.34	0.42	0.0	−7.8	20.1	215.0	78
Matria Healthcare, Inc. (M: MATR)	7.8	36.67	13.00	3.00	1.00	0.0	na	na	220.6	77
Mitchell Energy & Develp. (N: MND.A)	65.9	49.12	5.70	2.73	1.21	2.3	−32.6	−5.9	1,003.9	76
MYR Group, Inc. (N: MYR)	17.0	5.98	12.40	3.66	0.38	0.5	37.2	33.5	179.6	86
Nera AS (M: NERAY)	74.2	90.17	31.30	5.08	1.46	na	−50.3	9.9	570.6	87
Nu Horizons Electronics (M: NUHC)	23.9	8.90	25.00	2.34	0.45	0.0	−4.2	22.4	154.0	92
Nuevo Energy Company (N: NEV)	na	19.61	12.10	1.38	1.02	0.0	−54.5	18.6	295.5	82
Olsten Corporation (N: OLS)	56.5	81.31	9.10	1.23	0.19	1.3	18.7	13.9	965.5	77
Pioneer-Standard Electr. (M: PIOS)	14.3	26.40	10.40	1.52	0.19	0.7	6.1	31.2	555.4	81
QAD Inc. (M: QADI)	na	30.27	na	4.68	1.23	0.0	−64.8	23.8	288.1	82
Rica Foods, Inc. (A: RCF)	38.7	7.17	10.80	10.69	0.98	0.0	24.0	212.2	208.8	79
Salton, Inc. (N: SFP)	9.3	11.18	7.80	3.63	0.68	0.0	59.2	59.6	511.0	82
SCI Systems, Inc. (N: SCI)	32.1	144.03	18.20	4.26	0.74	0.0	42.3	29.4	5,391.7	83
Sensormatic Electronics (N: SRM)	30.8	76.10	12.90	1.82	1.28	0.0	−21.0	9.2	1,371.5	76
SITEL Corporation (N: SWW)	na	67.54	14.80	3.81	0.87	0.0	−17.6	53.5	600.4	87
Technitrol, Inc. (N: TNL)	17.1	16.06	13.30	3.69	1.47	0.6	47.3	34.9	757.0	79
Vans, Inc. (M: VANS)	20.5	13.54	12.60	1.90	0.85	0.0	36.4	20.6	201.3	83
WFS Financial Inc. (M: WFSI)	7.2	25.74	2.30	1.77	1.30	na	−22.5	16.5	384.9	78
Wilsons The Leather Exp. (M: WLSN)	12.6	11.00	9.40	3.18	0.54	0.0	30.2	−0.8	269.9	82
Workflow Mgmt., Inc. (M: WORK)	18.5	12.62	11.80	3.69	0.60	0.0	−3.3	20.5	277.2	88

na = not available

Exchange Key: N = *New York Stock Exchange*
A = *American Stock Exchange*
M = *Nasdaq*

Screening criteria used to produce table results can be found on page 115.

Statistics are based on figures as of February 25, 2000.
Data Source: AAII's Stock Investor/Market Guide, Inc. and I/B/E/S.

Stock Market Winners: What Works and Why

Screening Tips: The James O'Shaughnessy Approach

Value Strategy

Large-Cap Universe: O'Shaughnessy defines the large-cap universe as stocks whose market capitalization exceeded the average for the complete universe. At the beginning of 2000, the average market capitalization of O'Shaughnessy's universe was $2.5 billion. If your program supplies the market average you can specify market cap above the current level. The O'Shaughnessy Web site (www.oshaughnessyfunds.com) can serve as a source for market average if your screening program does not provide it.

Shares Outstanding: A company should have more common shares outstanding than the average stock in the market. At the beginning of 2000, we were screening for companies with at least 237.6 million shares outstanding.

Cash Flow: Cash flow per share should exceed the market average. At the beginning of 2000, we were screening for companies with cash flow per share of at least $0.95.

Sales: O'Shaughnessy specifies that a firm must have total sales 1.5 times the market average. This average sales figure does not fluctuate as widely as some of the other averages. At the beginning of 2000, we were screening for companies with at least 1.5 times the average sales figure of $1,092.0 million.

Exclude Utilities: O'Shaughnessy excludes utilities to keep them from dominating the dividend yield screen. Most screening programs easily allow you to exclude or include specific industry segments.

Dividend Yield: Once you have narrowed down your universe from the previous screens, you should select the top-yielding stocks. You can start off with a low dividend yield and keep specifying higher and higher dividend yields until only 50 companies pass.

Growth Strategy

Large-Cap Universe: The growth stock screen is based upon a larger universe because smaller stocks have greater growth potential than their large-cap counterparts. The growth stock universe looks for stocks with a market capitalization above $150 million. This figure should be adjusted annually for inflation. The O'Shaughnessy Web site (www.oshaughnessyfunds.com) provides the minimum market-cap figure annually.

Earnings Growth: The growth screen looks for a positive change in earnings per share for the latest four quarters compared to the previous four quarters. Most screening programs will provide a range of growth rate periods available for screening. If a one-year growth rate is not provided, try to construct a screen comparing the earnings per share for the latest 12 months (four quarters) to the comparable period one year ago.

Reasonably Priced: O'Shaughnessy balances the growth requirement by establishing a maximum price-to-sales ratio ceiling of 1.5. Price-to-sales has become a fairly common screening variable, so you should be able to screen easily for it.

One Year Relative Price Strength: Once you have narrowed down your growth stock universe from the previous screens, you should screen for the 50 companies with the highest relative price strength over the last year. Any of the one-year price change or relative strength measures should work for this screening element. The key is finding out which stocks have had the strongest price increases over the last year.

THE T. ROWE PRICE APPROACH TO INVESTING IN GROWTH STOCKS

It's hard to argue with long-term success, and one of the earliest investors who met with long-term success was T. Rowe Price.

T. Rowe Price, who died in 1983, was the founder of T. Rowe Price Associates, the Baltimore investment advisory firm that manages the T. Rowe Price family of no-load mutual funds. In the process of managing private accounts, Price started several mutual funds using his approach (the family's Growth Stock, New Horizons and New Era funds). He sold the firm when he retired in the early '70s.

Price developed his investment philosophy in the 1930s, when the prevailing approach was to jump in and out of stocks based on the cyclical nature of the stock market. Price, however, felt that investors should mimic the owners of successful business enterprises, who "do not attempt to sell out and buy back again their ownerships of the businesses through the ups and downs of the business and stock market cycles."

T. Rowe Price's approach focused on growth stocks. Of course, "growth industries" change over time; the growth industries at the time he formulated his philosophy would be considered mature today. Some of Price's secondary rules would therefore need to be adapted to today's—and tomorrow's—circumstances.

Price himself would have been the first to do so. "Change is the investor's only certainty," he stated in 1937, a statement that he repeated over the years, unchanged.

Why Growth Stocks: The Philosophy

T. Rowe Price essentially sought stocks among all stocks listed—he did not restrict his growth stock search among any subset of stocks. His growth stock approach was based on the theory that, over time, both dividend payments and market values will increase as earnings grow, which he felt to be particularly attractive as protection against inflation. At the time he developed his approach, many investors preferred high-dividend-yielding stocks for steady returns in the form of dividends. However, Price felt that these stocks showed less promise for gains and dividend increases and, thus, in the long-term, real growth could be threatened by inflation. Interestingly, Price recognized the threat of inflation in the '30s, despite the prior devastating experience faced by investors—the Depression, a time of deflation.

The search for growth stocks was based on Price's "life cycle" theory of corporations, which held that companies go through a cycle of growth, maturity, and decline. The greatest possibility for gain and least risk, he felt, is when the long-term earnings trend in a company is positive. And the best time to invest in a company, he stated, is when it is small, before its shares "gain in stature" and sell at high price-earnings ratios.

During the earlier years, many of the stocks that Price considered to be growth candidates paid at least some dividends, which explains in part Price's mention of dividends in his growth approach. Over the years, however, many growth companies, particularly those with smaller market capitalizations, chose to forgo dividends. These firms, of course, were certainly considered within Price's approach. In 1960 he extended his growth stock criteria to smaller, emerging growth companies (through the T. Rowe Price New Horizons Fund). This particular fund picks from a universe of smaller capitalization companies.

Growth Stock Criteria

Price defined a growth stock as: "A share in a business enterprise that has demonstrated long-term growth of earnings, reaching a new high level per share at the peak of each succeeding major business cycle, and that gives indications of reaching new high earnings at the peaks of future business cycles."

In addition, he stated that earnings per share should be increasing faster than the rate of inflation to offset any erosion in the purchasing power of the dollar.

Price did not focus on year-to-year earnings growth because of possible distortions in the reported earnings pattern caused by business cycles and developments within the industry or firm. He noted, for instance, that a cyclical decline in earnings due to a general economic slowdown could be misinterpreted as an end of growth for the firm, or similarly a cyclical recovery in earnings could be mistaken for a resumption in earnings growth. Most importantly, a non-growth company enjoying a cyclical recovery in earnings as the overall economy improves could be mistaken for a growth stock. Price spent a considerable amount of time examining a firm's industry and the firm itself to identify the ongoing cycles, so that real changes in earnings could be detected from within those cycles. The true test for Price, therefore, was growth in earnings during successive business peaks.

Buying Growth, But at a Reasonable Price

Price's approach concentrated on growth, but he would not pay any price for growth. In fact, part of his reasoning in selecting growth stocks was to find firms before they became "glamorized," particularly by institutions. Thus, although institutional ownership or scrutiny was never a factor in his selection process, he was clearly concerned about it, and favored stocks that were not in the market's spotlight.

Price used price-earnings multiples in his valuation analysis. He evaluated the price-earnings ratios of firms relative to their historical norms—preferring, for instance, not to buy stocks selling at high levels relative to their historical average. Interestingly, Price became alarmed at the valuation levels of most growth stocks in the early 1970s, and in particular, he disagreed with the managers of the funds he himself had started, which he no longer managed. He didn't convince the managers—but he correctly anticipated one of the worst downturns in 50 years.

Top-Down Factors

Price was a careful observer of overall trends concerning social, political, and economic influences that could affect the market and particular industries, and he invested accordingly—a top-down approach.

His view of trends, however, was broad and very long-term. For instance, in the mid-1960s he predicted that inflation would accelerate, and he therefore developed an investment strategy that concentrated on natural resource companies, the T. Rowe Price New Era Fund.

However, he also viewed trends in a somewhat shorter-term context, although he was not a market timer, nor a cyclical investor who jumped from sector to sector depending on the economic cycle. In particular, he felt that it was important to select companies in growing industries. He defined his ideal "growing industry" as one that was growing both in volume and earnings. For example, in one article written in the '30s, he contrasted the railroad industry, which had increasing earnings but was not increasing passenger miles, with the power and light industry, which was expanding its customer base and increasing its earnings at the same time. (Interestingly, he had other reasons—fear of government regulation—that made him cautious of the latter industry).

In Price's view, industries that offered the most "fertile fields" for growth were:
- New industries;
- Divisions of old industries that are experiencing vigorous growth as a result of new products, or new uses for old products, and
- Specialty industries with expanding products and markets.

Management and Other Factors

In any approach many other factors are important, and Price listed a number of secondary characteristics he sought. Of these, Price felt that the first—good management—was the most important, since good management can cope with many of the other factors that may be unfavorable and possibly turn those factors around.

To evaluate good management, Price posed these questions:
- **Are directors and officers actively on the job?**
- **Do they have a substantial stock interest in the firm, or is their sole compensation from big salaries and pensions?**
- **Are they planning for the future growth of the company through intelligent research?**

- **Do they understand social trends and have the good will of their employees?**

Other secondary factors include:

- **Intelligent research:** Companies that are looking to ensure their future growth through efforts to develop new products, new markets for existing products, or both.
- **Strong finances** that would allow a company to survive short-term downturns in earnings. Two items he examined in this area include increases in capital from retained earnings, as well as the availability of additional financing.
- **Relatively high return on invested capital** and returns on invested capital that are not declining over the long term. In particular, he felt that companies should be able to lower production costs and develop expanding markets without reducing return on invested capital. [Return on invested capital is earnings before interest, taxes and dividends divided by total capital, which is stockholder's equity plus preferred stock and long-term debt.]
- **Favorable profit margins** relative to the firm's industry, and a favorable trend in profit margins. [Profit margin is net income divided by revenue.] Favorable profit margins relative to the industry provide an indication of the competitive advantage a firm has against its peers, while a favorable trend in profit margins provides an indication of the strength of management and its abilities over time.
- **Absence of cut-throat competition** in the industry, which would cut down on growth prospects.
- **Companies that are not subject to government regulation,** which tends to restrict earnings.
- **Companies with good employee relations**, but in which total payroll is not large in relation to gross revenue. This would allow a company to more easily adjust to any fluctuations that may occur in its business.

Monitoring Stocks

Price believed in a long-term buy-and-hold strategy, in which growth stocks would be held until they were no longer growth stocks. That, of course, means monitoring the holdings to determine if the long-term growth in earnings will continue. To do that, he focused on many of the factors used in the original selection process and, in particular, a study of the trends in sales, profit margin, and return on invested capital.

He noted it was important when trying to detect the end of earnings growth to measure both growth in volume of sales and the trend in return on invested capital. High profit margin companies, he said, do not always prove to be better growth stocks; companies with low profit margins are sometimes able to increase sales volume without increasing capital investment. On the other hand, if increasing capital investment does not increase the profits, a decline in the return on invested capital results. This declining trend, he said, is a warning signal.

Price said that the causes of these changes in trend could often be seen before the results could actually be measured, and therefore he scrutinized companies to see if certain changing circumstances could lead to a change in trends. The changing circumstances he kept an eye on included:

- Saturation of markets
- New inventions
- Expiration of patents
- Increased competition
- Adverse legislation
- Unfavorable court decisions
- Sharp rise in cost of materials
- Sharp rise in labor costs
- Increase in taxes

When to Sell

The time to sell a stock holding, according to Price, was when the company no longer appeared to have favorable future growth prospects. Significant price declines did not trigger any sales as far as Price was concerned, but rather offered an opportunity to add to a holding, assuming the stock still filled the growth criteria.

T. Rowe Price also felt that if prices reached "excessively high levels," investors should sell enough shares to permit the withdrawal of the original capital invested in the stock, plus the amount needed to cover capital gains taxes; the original capital could then be invested elsewhere.

Summarizing Price

As a final note, Price also discussed the need for diversification in a growth stock portfolio. In fact, he felt that as many as 60 stocks would be necessary, which would allow an investor to participate in a wide range of basic industries and natural resources. He also felt that such a large number would act as a hedge against almost any conceivable crisis that could stem from changes in social, political, and even international developments.

The best summarization of the Price approach is his own:

"Invest money in a business that must cope with the minimum of consumer, labor, and government interference, that is managed by men with vision who understand the significance of the social and economic trends, and who are preparing for the future through intelligent research and development."

The T. Rowe Price Approach in Brief

Philosophy and style
Investment in stocks of companies with long-term earnings growth prospects, under the theory that growth in earnings will ultimately be reflected in growth of market values and dividends; also investment in stocks in the early, growth stages of their life cycle before they become "glamorized."

Universe of stocks
No restrictions, but smaller capitalization stocks viewed as particularly fertile ground.

Criteria for initial consideration
- Earnings per share increasing at the peak of each succeeding major business cycle, as well as increased projected earnings per share at peak of future business cycles. Earnings are examined relative to industry and overall market to find distortions caused by business cycles to determine the real trend in earnings and to rule out non-growth "cyclicals." To ensure long-term growth of earnings, companies should be in growing industries. Areas of possibility include: new industries, divisions of old industries experiencing vigorous growth as a result of new products or new uses for old products, and specialty industries with expanding products and markets.
- Long-term earnings per share growth greater than inflation.
- Price-earnings ratio not high relative to historical average.

Secondary factors
- Management is key. Look for management with substantial interest in the firm, and that appears to be planning intelligently for the future
- Strong finances: increase in capital from retained earnings; availability of additional financing
- Relatively high return on invested capital
- Favorable profit margins relative to industry; favorable trend in profit margins
- Absence of cut-throat competition in the industry
- Little government interference
- Good labor relations, but total payroll not large relative to gross revenue

Stock monitoring and when to sell
- Monitor for changes in trends of sales, profit margin and return on invested capital
- Monitor for changes in management, competitive stance, regulatory changes, and changes in industry
- Sell when company no longer fits definition of "growth" company, when the outlook does not continue to be favorable, when there is a break in trend of sales, profit margin, and return on invested capital
- Trim when prices reach excessively high levels, as measured by price-earnings ratios relative to historical levels

Stock Screens: Applying the T. Rowe Price Approach

Primary Factors

T. Rowe Price's approach is to identify growth companies by looking for increasing earnings per share at the peak of each succeeding major business cycle, as well as increased projected earnings per share at the peak of future business cycles. Screening programs geared to individual investors do not provide data going back far enough in time to screen for this. Currently the U.S. is in an economic expansion that began in March of 1991. The peak of the previous expansion occurred in July of 1990, and you would have to go back nearly 19 years for the peak of a prior expansion, which occurred in July of 1981. (The Survey of Current Business published by the U.S. Department of Commerce is a good source of data on measures of economic activity.)

The filter makes sense—it is trying to exclude cyclical companies that currently may look like growth stocks. However, it cannot be applied automatically. After a prolonged economic expansion, the growth rates of cyclical companies may look extremely high because you are comparing earnings against a very low base level. Current seven-year and three-year growth rates are well into the double digits for many cyclical firms. Industries that make heavy use of fixed assets and financial leverage can show tremendous earnings growth once they get past their breakeven point.

Growth firms represent companies growing well beyond the level of the overall economy. A mature firm such as General Motors, in a cyclical industry such as autos, will roughly grow and contract at the rate of the overall economy. While it may be possible to expand market share and grow at a slightly higher rate than the industry, there are still severe restraints on the firm's long-term growth potential.

In screening for growth stocks, it may be possible to focus on industries in the early stages of their life cycle, which can be fairly easy to accomplish with screening programs. Alternatively, you can explicitly exclude industries known to be in their mature stage; however, Price also expressed interest in looking at divisions of old industries experiencing vigorous growth as a result of new products or new uses for old products. In the end, when applying this screen it may be better to screen for reasonable levels of growth and manually exclude firms that do not have strong long-term growth potential.

Growth Greater Than Inflation

Price was an early proponent of buying a good company at reasonable price and holding it for a long time. He recognized the potential for inflation to erode the value of his holdings and specified that earnings per share should be increasing faster than the rate of inflation.

In the last five years, inflation as measured by the consumer price index has grown at about 3.0% per year—roughly in line with the long-term inflation rate. Specifying a minimum historical growth rate of 3.0% or 4.0% would not be a very restrictive screen. Since we are trying to identify companies with above-average growth rates and are not specifying any other minimum growth levels, the screen here seeks seven-year and five-year growth rates better than half the companies covered by the stock database, and a three-year growth better than 75% of all firms.

Growth at a Reasonable Price

While Price concentrated on growth, he would not pay any price for it. When looking at price-earnings ratios, he would prefer not to buy stocks selling at levels high relative to their historical average. A current price-earnings ratio lower than its historical average would be a potential sign that a stock is undervalued, while a current price-earnings ratio that is high compared to its historical average might indicate an overvalued firm. This assumes that the growth prospects of the firm have not changed fundamentally over the period of study and that based upon the historical relationship of price to earnings, the market is not correctly discounting the future earnings potential of the firm.

For that reason, the screen here requires that the current price-earnings ratio be below its five-year average price-earnings ratio.

Many firms do not have a five-year average price-earnings ratio. To calculate this figure a company needs five years of price data and five years of positive earnings. Negative earnings lead to non-meaningful price-earnings ratios, so positive earnings for each of the last five years are required.

Beyond negative earnings, unusually low earnings may also throw off standard price-earnings ratio screens. Short-term drops in earnings due to events such as special charges, extraordinary events, or even general slowdowns can lead to unusually high price-earnings ratios. As long as the market perceives the earnings decline as temporary, the high price-earnings ratio will be supported. Because the average price-earnings screen relies on a normal situation, these outlier ratios must be excluded. When performing a hands-on evaluation you can manually exclude years with negative or unusually low earnings. However, when screening a large universe of stocks, it is best to establish conditioning criteria that eliminate companies with extreme price-earnings ratios.

For our screens, five filters are included that exclude companies whose price-earnings ratio exceeded 40 for any of the last five years.

Management

Price felt that good management was an important consideration when selecting firms, believing that managers should have substantial interest in the firm and not receive compensation primarily from big salaries and pensions. We include a filter requiring that insiders own at least 20% of outstanding shares. The primary weakness with this filter is that the SEC defines an insider as a "beneficial owner" who maintains at least a 5% position in the firm. Under this definition, an investment adviser who owns at least 5% of a firm's shares will be included as an insider. To make the best use of this screen, it would be a good idea to look at the proxy statements of the companies that pass the complete screen and see how many shares the officers and directors actually own.

Strong Finances

Price thought that a company should have strong finances to be considered for purchase. The failing of many growth firms is the inability to obtain more capital for future expansion. Price focused on the ability to increase capital from retained earnings and on the ability to obtain further financing. These two criteria deal with the primary sources of company funds—internal cash flow from operations and additional outside sources of capital. At its most basic level, an increase in capital from retained earnings simply means the company is profitable and is not paying out all of its earnings in the form of dividends. Since we have already screened for positive earnings, we simply need to screen for a payout ratio (dividends per share divided by earnings per share) below 100%. Since earnings can be reduced by non-cash charges such as depreciation, a screen for positive cash flow is also included.

Availability of additional external financing is more of a qualitative examination than a quantitative screen. It would consider the ability of the company to raise capital from the equity markets by floating additional stock. Here the market environment for initial public offerings would play a role. Beyond equity financing, companies can try to float debt or look toward bank lending. If you were interested in considering the type of factors a lender would require, you could add screens that look at the current levels of debt (financial leverage), cash positions, cash flow, and coverage ratios.

Return on Invested Capital

Price looked for high and expanding return on invested capital (earnings before interest, taxes and dividends divided by common equity, preferred stock and long-term debt) when selecting stocks. He was trying to capture firms that made effective use of their capital by keeping a lid on production costs and expanding into new markets. The software program used here, *Stock Investor Professional*, does not include this calculation, so return on assets is substituted. Return on assets is calculated by dividing net income by total assets, and using it represents the type of adjustments often required when applying a computer screen. Return on assets is used instead of return on equity because it includes preferred

T. Rowe Price Growth Approach Screening Criteria

Definitions for screens and terms can be found in the glossary starting on page 191.

Screening Criteria:

- 3-year EPS growth among the top 25% in stock database
- 5-year EPS growth among the top 50% in stock database*
- 7-year EPS growth among the top 50% in stock database
- P/E ratio less than 5-year average P/E ratio
- Average annual P/E ratio less than 40 for each of the last 5 years*
- Insider ownership greater than or equal to 20% of shares outstanding
- Payout ratio (last 12 months) less than 100%*
- Postive cash flow*
- Return on assets (last 12 months) greater than industry median
- Net profit margin (last 12 months) greater than industry median
- Net profit margin (last 12 months) greater than or equal to net profit margin (last fiscal year)*
- Net profit margin (last 12 months) greater than net profit margin 5 fiscal years prior*
- Operating profit margin (last 12 months) greater than industry median
- Operating profit margin (last 12 months) greater than or equal to operating profit margin (last fiscal year)*
- Operating profit margin (last 12 months) greater than operating profit margin 5 fiscal years prior*

Data not shown in table. Also note that the table shows additional data columns that may be of interest to those using this approach.

stock, long-term debt, common equity, and short-term liabilities, which more closely match the return on invested capital calculation. Our screen looks for a return on assets that is higher than industry medians.

Favorable Profit Margins

Favorable profit margins may provide an indication that a company has a competitive advantage over its peers. However, because profit margins are very industry specific, they must be compared against industry norms. Two screens, one that looks for operating margins above industry medians and another that compares net profit margins against industry medians, are included.

Beyond margins that are currently high, it is important that the company be able to maintain its profit margins. A declining profit margin can point to increased competition and lower prices or weak cost control. Therefore, screens are provided that look for current net

Table 1.
Stocks Passing the T. Rowe Price Growth Screening*

Company (Exchange: Ticker)	Price ($)	52-Wk Price High ($)	52-Wk Price Low ($)	EPS Grth 3-yr (%)	EPS Grth 7-yr (%)	Curr P/E (x)	5-yr Avg. P/E (x)	Insider Owner-ship (%)	Inst'l Owner-ship (%)	Trailing 12 Months Ret. on Assets (%)	Trailing 12 Months Net Profit Mrgin (%)	Trailing 12 Months Oper'g Profit Mrgin (%)
AAON, Incorporated (M: AAON)	17.50	19.19	8.13	35.2	45.8	11.7	16.7	42.5	27.0	15.0	6.8	11.4
Centex Construction Prod. (N: CXP)	25.81	41.81	24.88	36.1	99.2	4.9	12.3	62.0	36.2	24.0	25.4	39.9
CNF Transportation, Inc. (N: CNF)	30.88	45.88	28.38	35.3	21.1	9.2	16.6	20.0	85.2	5.6	3.0	6.2
Control Chief Holdings (M: DIGM)	4.25	5.50	3.97	65.1	25.5	7.7	12.1	50.0	0.0	11.9	6.8	12.3
Fairfield Communities (N: FFD)	8.94	17.13	7.00	38.4	16.5	7.2	19.3	30.1	52.5	11.0	11.2	17.7
Family Dollar Stores, Inc (N: FDO)	16.38	26.75	14.00	31.0	13.7	19.3	21.5	22.0	73.5	13.1	5.2	8.2
Fossil, Inc. (M: FOSL)	22.25	36.58	15.81	36.4	21.2	14.3	19.3	61.0	45.7	18.8	12.1	20.8
J&J Snack Foods Corp. (M: JJSF)	17.25	24.44	15.50	34.5	16.3	11.4	16.1	57.8	70.9	6.7	5.0	8.6
M.D.C. Holdings, Inc. (N: MDC)	14.44	22.00	13.38	54.5	55.9	3.7	7.7	68.0	66.2	10.2	5.7	9.5
M/I Schottenstein Homes (N: MHO)	14.38	22.00	12.75	43.4	21.2	3.1	8.2	45.1	51.4	7.3	4.6	7.7
Miller Building Systems (M: MBSI)	5.13	8.75	4.63	65.1	45.8	5.1	22.0	34.3	19.1	11.0	5.4	8.5
National RV Holdings, Inc (N: NVH)	13.38	29.50	12.75	92.4	33.3	4.5	16.7	26.7	61.0	19.9	7.7	12.4
Pomeroy Computer Res. (M: PMRY)	16.50	23.13	9.56	31.7	35.5	7.9	17.1	22.9	50.4	7.6	3.2	5.8
Rent-A-Wreck of America (M: RAWA)	1.94	9.00	1.13	39.5	26.4	11.4	20.6	69.6	0.1	23.3	16.7	21.7
Ross Stores, Inc. (M: ROST)	13.69	26.13	12.00	47.8	26.1	8.2	16.3	21.1	95.0	16.0	6.4	10.4
STV Group, Incorporated (M: STVI)	7.00	8.88	6.00	104.1	38.1	5.3	17.1	92.2	69.1	8.6	3.7	6.9
Sybron International Corp (N: SYB)	28.13	30.81	20.69	32.7	25.6	22.5	23.5	26.0	78.2	7.7	12.9	24.3
Target Corporation (N: TGT)	55.88	77.00	53.75	45.2	18.3	23.6	24.3	20.0	1.0	6.0	3.2	5.4
Thor Industries, Inc. (N: THO)	24.13	32.00	22.25	31.2	18.5	8.5	13.0	63.8	47.0	13.4	4.0	6.7
Winnebago Industries (N: WGO)	21.38	28.75	12.88	59.5	31.3	10.2	15.3	39.9	31.7	16.7	6.8	9.8

na = not available

Exchange Key: N = New York Stock Exchange
A = American Stock Exchange
M = Nasdaq

*Screening criteria used to produce table results can be found on opposite page.

Source: AAII's Stock Investor and Market Guide. Data as of February 25, 2000.

and operating margins above levels five years ago.

Little Government Interference

The level of government interference is a difficult screen to implement. The best mechanical approach would be to exclude industries with known regulatory issues, such as the utility group. Alternatively, companies that pass the screen can be examined one by one and the impact of government interference could be assessed individually. This is the type of discussion that would be covered in a company's annual 10-K filings with the SEC. These can be obtained directly from the company or they can be downloaded from the Internet for public companies at the SEC Web site (www.sec.gov).

Good Labor Relations

Much of Price's work was written when industrial companies were the strength and growth of our economy. With the shift toward the service sector in the U.S., the analysis of the typical union-based work force is less relavant. This screen is also more of a qualitative evaluation than a quantitative analysis. While it is an important concern, it would be best addressed when analyzing the passing companies individually.

The Results

Table 1 presents the results of our interpretation of how a screening process can be applied to the T. Rowe Price approach. It is based on data as of February 25, 2000, using AAII's *Stock Investor Professional*. Screening tips for the T. Rowe Price approach on are page 131.

Screening Tips: The T. Rowe Price Approach

Primary Factors:

Earnings per share increasing at the peak of each succeeding major business cycle:
Few screening programs maintain enough data to establish such a perspective. This type of filter would be best applied manually after the computerized screening process.

To ensure long-term growth of earnings, companies should be in growing industries:
In screening, you can include only perceived growth industries or exclude industries with few growth prospects. However, there are often segments of growth within a mature industry. Alternatively, companies with few growth opportunities can be excluded manually after the screen is performed.

Long-term earnings per share growth greater than inflation:
The current low inflationary environment (3%–4%) makes this a rather loose filter in screening for growth stocks. We looked for companies with 3-year earnings growth greater than 75% of all firms and five-year and seven-year earnings growth greater than 50% of all firms.

Price-earnings ratio not high relative to historical average:
Use a filter in which the price-earnings ratio based upon trailing 12 months' earnings is below the average price-earnings ratio over the last five years. The calculation of the five-year price-earnings average required positive earnings over each of the last five years (price-earnings ratios are not meaningful for negative numbers) as well as price data for each of those years. The historical average can be skewed upward by one year of weak earnings, so a screen excluding companies whose price-earnings ratio was above 40 for any of the last five years was added.

Secondary Factors:

Substantial management interest in the firm:
Screen for companies with insiders holding at least 20% of outstanding shares.

Strong finances—increase in capital from retained earnings:
Given the other filters, this is not a very restrictive screen. However, you could add a requirement for payout ratio to be below 100%. Modern interpretations may call for positive cash flow or free cash flow, which would be more restrictive.

Strong finances—availability of additional financing:
More of a qualitative examination than a quantitative screen. If you are interested in considering the type of factors a lender would require, a focus on financial leverage, cash positions, cash flow, and coverage ratios would be appropriate.

Relatively high return on invested capital:
T. Rowe Price examined return on invested capital (earnings before interest, taxes and dividends divided by equity and long-term debt). A screen for company return on assets higher than industry norms can be substituted.

Favorable profit margins relative to industry:
Screen for operating and net profit margins that exceed industry norms.

Favorable trend in profit margins:
Screen for operating and net profit margins below levels last year and five years ago.

(cont'd on next page)

Screening Tips: The T. Rowe Price Approach *(cont'd)*

Absence of cut-throat competition in the industry:
   Screen for above-industry average profit margins and improving profit margins.
Little government interference:
   Difficult screen to implement except by excluding industries with known regulatory issues such as the utility group.
Good labor relations, but total payroll not large relative to gross revenues:
   More of a qualitative evaluation than a quantitative analysis. Reference to payroll relative to revenues is better suited toward industrial firms rather than those in the service sector.

GROWTH AT A REASONABLE PRICE:
THE RALPH WANGER APPROACH

How do you find the green grass of opportunity among stocks that have been picked over by heavy competition from other smart, full-time investors? Ralph Wanger's answer is to stand apart from the herd to find the choice pickings by focusing on smaller-capitalization stocks, a stance many investors won't take because of the greater risks.

As the portfolio manager of the highly successful Acorn Fund, Ralph Wanger has been a consistent promoter of small-stock investing, and has held to his investment philosophy through the best and worst market environments. Although there are numerous small-cap funds today, the Acorn Fund is one of the oldest, having been launched by Wanger in 1970.

His investment approach primarily focuses on finding the opportunities and limiting the risks of investing in smaller-capitalization stocks.

Why Small-Cap Stocks: The Philosophy

Aside from offering less-exploited opportunities, Wanger points to several other advantages offered by investing in smaller-capitalization stocks, which he defines as companies below $1 billion in market capitalization (share price times number of shares outstanding).

First, smaller companies have more room to grow. No company can sustain a high growth rate forever, and eventually a firm's size starts to weigh it down. Large companies simply cannot sustain the high growth rates achievable by a small but fast-growing company.

In addition, Wanger likes to focus on long-term trends and change. He notes that change creates opportunities for investors who can perceive them and points out that smaller companies can adapt more readily to change.

There are also more actions that can cause the prices of small-cap companies to rise. Stock prices will rise due to: earnings growth; acquisition by a larger company at an above-market price; stock repurchases by the company; and an increase in the price the market is willing to pay for one dollar of earnings due to increased institutional interest. Typically, though, large-company stock prices rise only for the first reason.

And, Wanger finds smaller companies that are in only one or two lines of business to be more easily understandable than large companies in many lines of business.

Lastly, Wanger points to numerous academic studies indicating that smaller-cap stocks have provided higher rates of return over long time periods, even after adjusting for the risk.

Nonetheless, Wanger does acknowledge that investing in small-cap stocks is a riskier strategy, particularly since misjudgments are bound to occur.

Risk reduction, in Mr. Wanger's view, is in the careful selection of specific stocks. To lower the risk of small-cap investing, he suggests investing in companies that are established, with managements that have proven their capabilities over time, that have a sound balance sheet and a strong position in their industry. For that reason, he suggests avoiding stocks that are start-ups, initial public offerings, and turnarounds. He also warns against overpaying for a stock. Lastly, for individual investors, a small-cap portfolio should have at least 12 stocks.

Growth Stocks: Trend-Spotting

Wanger seeks companies with growth potential, and he does so first by determining broad areas for potential future growth. Thus, his approach starts with a top-down outlook: He first identifies general "themes"—strong social, economic, or technological trends that will last longer than one business cycle (at least five years or more). The advantage of focusing on long-term trends, he says, is that most other investors are focused more on shorter-term predictions of two years or less, and it is difficult to outguess the competition, particularly since most investors are basing their decisions on the same information. The other advantage of focusing on long-term trends is that it forces you to be a long-term investor, which is particularly important in the smaller-cap area because of high trading costs.

What does Wanger mean by a trend or long-term theme? One past example he points to is underdeveloped countries and their development. These countries have been investing in telephone systems, a trend he says was obvious for many years and which has already benefited many investors in companies such as Mexico's Telefonos de Mexico. He also notes that individuals in developing countries will have more discretionary spending—and will therefore be buying more discretionary items.

Other possible theme areas Wanger points to:
- Rebuilding of infrastructure in countries worldwide
- Expansion of communications and transportation networks worldwide
- Energy exploration of older marginal oil fields by smaller energy companies
- Outsourcing of services and jobs that require technological and skilled personnel
- Money management, particularly as public pension systems are privatized

Wanger says that to identify trends, you must "develop an observing mind-set," that can draw generalizations from many different particulars. He suggests that trends can best be spotted from reading and one's everyday general experience, including the work environment. He notes, though, that it is easy—and likely—that mistakes will be made, which is why diversification is important.

Once a trend has been spotted, Wanger selects companies that will benefit from these themes. That doesn't mean that the investment is directly in the theme itself, particularly if it is a strong technological trend. In fact, he points out that most companies that are directly involved in "trend-setting" are the ones that will least benefit from the trend. His best example is firms that are directly involved in technology, which is certainly the most obvious and strongest long-term trend today. Competition among technology firms is strong, and even though there are many "geniuses" running these companies, they are competing with other geniuses.

Instead, Wanger prefers to invest in companies that will benefit from the technological advance—the downstream users of technology, rather than the technology companies themselves. Past examples include the banking industry, which has been transformed through the use of ATM machines, the credit card industry, and the database and data processing industries.

Of course, a trend-spotting approach dictates that you must learn to recognize when the trend has "played out"—it no longer offers growth potential. The signs that a trend is ending include: the stocks of firms in the area become too pricey, there are many new issues coming out, and marginal players are starting to enter the field.

While trend-spotting is Wanger's primary source for ideas, he also considers a company to be promising if it is not part of a theme but has a near-monopoly in a special market niche that is likely to last more than one business cycle. That, he says, is a theme in itself.

Criteria for Purchase

The hardest work, in Wanger's view, is the actual selection process. Selecting a company consists of understanding the company, its products, its industry position, its financials, and its management. Then, you must make a decision as to whether the market price for the stock fairly reflects the company's real value and its prospects.

Finding value is an important part of Wanger's approach—he believes in growth investing, but only at a reasonable price. However, to find value, you must have a different perspective than others in the marketplace, and you must bring that fresh perspective with you when analyzing a company.

Wanger's selection approach emphasizes three areas: growth potential, financial strength, and fundamental value.

The growth potential comes from a company's ability to exploit its long-term theme. Thus, Wanger looks for companies that have good products, an expanding market, and the ability to efficiently manufacture and market their products. In addition, companies should have a special niche in an area of the market that is not easily entered by competitors. "Boring" stocks are more likely to fit this description than glamour stocks.

Wanger focuses considerable attention on management, seeking a team that is capable of fully exploiting the company's niche. However, Wanger notes that this is a qualitative judgment that cannot be made by looking at statistics. Instead, he prefers talking to competitors, suppliers, and management itself (which he acknowledges is difficult for individual investors to do on their own). Signs of good management include:

- The management team is small and has considerable knowledge of the industry.

- Its plans for the company's future are reasonable, but not inflexible, and the management is adaptable to changing market conditions.
- A large share of company stock is owned by the managers.

To reduce the risks of investing in smaller-capitalization stocks, Wanger seeks companies with financial strength. Usually, companies that have survived various economic environments have some form of financial strength, and for that reason he avoids start-ups, IPOs, and turnarounds.

He avoids companies with high levels of debt and where debt is rising, but notes that debt levels must be judged relative to other companies in the industry. For manufacturing or retail businesses, debt should be less than half of the company's total capitalization. He also seeks companies with adequate working capital and firms that use conservative accounting practices.

Wanger suggests examining other balance sheet items to make note of other liabilities (for instance, pension liabilities), other "hidden" assets (goodwill and other intangibles and under-valued real estate) and to determine if the company is actually generating cash or if reported earnings are primarily due to an accounting function. Inventories and receivables should be examined relative to revenues to note any changes over time; rising ratios are a warning sign that inventories are building up.

The third leg of Wanger's approach is to seek fundamental value—the share price should be cheap relative to indications of growth prospects such as earnings, sales or cash flow, or relative to the asset value of the firm. He notes that companies that are recognized for their growth potential by the market will have high multiples no matter which measure—price-earnings, price-to-sales, or price-to-cash-flow—is used. He finds advantages and disadvantages with each measure, and notes that investors who use the different measures should be wary of potential problems with each—for instance, price-earnings ratios can be misleading due to accounting manipulations of earnings. He suggests that operating profitability is best judged by using cash flow (which he defines as earnings before interest, taxes, depreciation, and amortization). And he says that the share price should be cheap relative to a company's asset value, which takes everything into consideration including long-term and short-term liabilities, as well as intangibles such as brands and patents.

Wanger's approach examines many different valuation measures, but he also uses a valuation model that helps judge a stock's value relative to its growth potential. The model is based on his own predicted earnings growth rate (not more than two years out) and a predicted price-earnings multiple that is adjusted for the expected level of interest rates (since at high interest rate levels, multiples tend to be lower than when interest rates are at low levels). The valuation model provides a price for stock two years hence, and thus an expected rate of return over two years. This is compared to what most analysts are expecting, and the stock is considered cheap if expectations are higher than consensus analyst expectations.

Monitoring and Selling Stocks

Wanger is a long-term investor, which is particularly important in the smaller-cap area because illiquidity in that area tends to drive up trading costs. Therefore, stocks should be purchased with the intent to hold for a long time period that is measured in years; if the stock performs as expected, liquidity will be less of a concern when it comes time to sell.

Wanger suggests that when a stock is purchased, the motivating reason for the purchase should be written down. Stocks should then be carefully monitored to make sure that the reason for purchasing the stock is still valid. That means continuously revising the expected earnings outlook for the firm. If the unexpected occurs—for instance, if earnings come in lower than expected or other analysts' expectations turn out to be markedly different from your own—a re-evaluation of the stock is in order to find out if you have made an error in judgment, or if you have missed important information. If the original premise remains valid and yet the price has dropped, Wanger views it as a buying opportunity.

Stocks should be sold when the reason for purchasing the stock is no longer valid—either it has achieved its expected potential, or it has failed. In general, however, Wanger prefers to let profits run to avoid the mistake of selling too soon.

Wanger in Summary

While Wanger makes a strong case for investing in smaller-capitalization stocks, he does not feel that these should be an investor's only holdings. Instead, he emphasizes the need to diversify holdings among larger-capitalization stocks. Aside from simply ensuring you get adequate performance at all times, he notes you are more likely to stick with a small-cap approach during lean times if other parts of your portfolio are doing well.

Wanger is also a strong proponent of international investing and, in fact, many of the growth opportunities Wanger seeks are international in nature. However, he points out that investing in foreign markets directly is very difficult for individual investors to accomplish and he suggests the mutual fund route for most investors who want to invest overseas.

Lastly, Wanger states that his own approach is not necessarily the only approach to successful investing. The most important aspect of investing, he says, is to stick with stocks that you really understand, and to stick with a disciplined approach that suits your needs and personality.

Wanger summarizes his own philosophy:

"Maintain independence of thought and a healthy degree of skepticism, so you won't be drawn into the herd. Don't overpay, no matter how much you like a company. Invest in themes that will give a company a long-term franchise. Invest downstream from technology. Think and invest globally. Find stocks to own, not trade."

The Ralph Wanger Approach in Brief

Philosophy and style

Investment in companies in which there is a well-grounded expectation concerning the firm's growth prospects, and in which the stock can be bought at a reasonable price. The best area for finding stocks that meet these criteria is in the small-capitalization market, in companies with financial strength and market dominance.

Universe of stocks

Smaller-capitalization companies (less than $1 billion in market capitalization) that are seasoned; no start-ups or initial public offerings.

Criteria for initial consideration

Identify general "themes"—strong social, economic, or technological trends—that will last five years or longer, and select companies that will benefit from these themes. In addition, a company is promising if it has a near-monopoly in a special market niche.

Criteria for purchase

Companies must show evidence of: growth potential, financial strength, and fundamental value:

- Growth potential: Company should have a special niche and should be in an area of the market that is not easily entered by competitors. Company also should have a good management team capable of fully exploiting that niche. Management is judged by talking to competitors, suppliers and management itself. Signs of good management include: The management team is small, with considerable knowledge of the industry; it has reasonable plans for the future but is adaptable to changing markets; and it owns a large share of company stock.
- Financial strength: Low debt relative to its industry, adequate working capital and conservative accounting practices. For manufacturing or retail businesses, debt should be less than half of company's total capitalization. Balance sheet should be scrutinized for liabilities other than debt (for instance, pension liabilities) and additional "hidden" assets (for instance, goodwill or intangibles). Inventories and receivables relative to revenues should be examined for stability; rising ratios may indicate problems with sales and warrant further investigation. Companies that have weathered various economic environments tend to have financial strength; turnarounds, start-ups and initial public offerings are more shaky and should be avoided.
- Fundamental value: Share price should be cheap relative to indications of earnings-growth prospects such as earnings, sales or cash flow; companies with recognized growth potential will have high multiples no matter which measure is used. Be wary of potential problems with each measure—for instance, price-earnings ratios can be misleading due to accounting manipulations of earnings. Operating profitability is best judged by cash flow (earnings before interest, taxes, depreciation, and amortization). Also, price should be cheap relative to company's asset value, which takes everything into consideration including long-term and short-term liabilities, as well as intangibles such as brands and patents; book value (assets less depreciation) is not a useful measure.

Valuation

To help judge value relative to growth potential, a valuation model is used, based on the predicted earnings growth rate (not more than two years out), and a predicted price-earnings multiple (adjusted for the expected level of interest rates, since at high interest rate levels, multiples tend to be lower than when interest rates are at low levels). The model provides a price for the stock two years hence, and thus an expected rate of return over two years; this is compared to what most analysts are expecting, and the stock is considered cheap if expectations are higher than consensus analyst expectations.

(cont'd on next page)

The Ralph Wanger Approach in Brief *(cont'd)*

Stock monitoring and when to sell

Stocks should be held for the long-term, particularly given high trading costs associated with small caps. For adequate diversification, a small-cap portfolio should hold at least 12 stocks. However, an investor's total savings portfolio should not be invested only in small-cap stocks, but should consist of large-capitalization stocks and international stocks.

When purchasing a stock, the reason for the purchase should be written down. Stock should be sold when the reason for purchasing the stock is no longer valid—either it has acheived its expected potential, or it has failed. However, stocks should be continually re-evaluated. If the unexpected occurs, for instance, earnings come in lower than expected or other analysts' expectations are markedly different, re-evaluate management and its abilities; if original premise remains and the price has dropped, buy more, but if original premise turns out to be incorrect, sell. In general, let profits run.

STOCK SCREENS: APPLYING THE RALPH WANGER APPROACH

Ralph Wanger concentrates his investments in the stocks of smaller companies. Our first screen excludes companies with market capitalization (shares outstanding times market price) of greater than $1 billion. Wanger's definition of small-cap stocks is not as restrictive as the academic studies concerning the small-stock effect, but roughly follows the standards used by other small-cap mutual funds.

Wanger chooses to avoid extremely small companies, termed micro caps, because he feels that they can be too risky—"one misstep and they are out." He does not state a limit, but our screen specifies $100 million as a lower market capitalization limit.

He also prefers established companies with proven management over start-ups, near venture capital stocks, and initial public offerings (IPOs). We therefore established a screen that filters out companies that do not have a stock price four years ago—a figure that can be easily adjusted to suit your personal preferences. Note that we constructed a screen based upon stock price because a screen for historical sales or earnings going back a number of years is no guarantee of excluding IPOs (which will typically have financial statements going back a number of years when they go public). Many data services will enter this historical data when the company is added to the database, enhancing the analysis of these companies.

Niche Players

Ralph Wanger seeks companies with a dominant market position, and suggests that it is best to stick with only the leaders in the industry. It is better to own the best company in a marginal industry than the third runner-up in a major industry.

To screen for firms that might hold dominant market positions, we first search for companies with profit margins above the median for their industry. Profit margins can be very industry-specific, so you cannot simply seek high absolute levels. To help guard against companies with just a strong one-time showing, we also screen for companies whose current profit margins are greater than or equal to their profit margins two years ago.

As with all preliminary screening criteria, you should closely examine the stocks passing the profit margin screen. Does the company actually have a strong position in the industry that will continue to hold over the long run? Perhaps it passed the screen because it was misclassified and grouped with other firms that are not that similar.

Financial Strength

Wanger avoids marginal, underfunded companies of any size. He feels that financial strength makes corporate growth sustainable, and he looks for companies with low debt, adequate working capital, and conservative accounting.

Prudent use of debt allows companies to expand and increase return on shareholder equity. However, the balance sheet should be examined to see if the company has too much debt or to see if debt is rising to dangerous levels. Appropriate debt levels vary from industry to industry, so it's best to screen based on industry norms. For example, utilities typically carry higher levels of debt than highly cyclical firms.

We screen out firms that have higher levels of total liabilities to total assets than their industry median. The ratio of total liabilities to total assets is more encompassing than just looking at long-term debt-to-equity ratios.

Secondary screens should include an examination of the balance sheet to compare the levels of liabilities over time, study the relationship of inventories and receivables to sales, etc. If inventories, for example, are increasing faster then sales, it may point to a shift in the buying habits of customers to products of competitors. You should also read the financial statement notes to study the size of pension liabilities.

Traditional screens for working capital look at ratios such as the quick and current ratios, which compare short-term assets to short-term liabilities. However, these measures are very static and not as useful as measures that test the company's ability to meet current and future obligations.

As a test of both working capital and confirmation of the quality of earnings, we screen for positive cash flow over the last 12 months and each of the last three fiscal years. Earnings can be influenced by many management assumptions trickling through the accounting books. Cash flow is less influenced by these types of varying assumptions, making it more comparable across a wide range of companies. A study of cash flows has the added benefit of being more comparable across industries.

Growth at a Reasonable Price

When determining if an investment represents an attractive purchase, it is important to separate the company from the stock. While Ralph Wanger seeks sound companies, he will only consider them for purchase if they are available at an attractive price. The share price should be cheap relative to indications of growth prospects for items such as earnings, sales or cash flow, or relative to the asset value of the firm.

For our screen, we decided to focus on the price-earnings ratios. The price-earnings ratio (stock price divided by earnings per share for the most recent 12 months) embodies the market's expectation of future earnings potential for a company. Typically, companies with higher growth potential trade with higher ratios because investors are willing to pay a higher multiple of current earnings for the prospect of higher future earnings. Stocks with lower prospects or greater risk of achieving future earnings typically trade with lower price-earnings ratios.

The ratio of price-earnings to earnings growth (known as the PEG ratio) is a common valuation tool that equates the assumptions built into the price-earnings ratio to the actual earnings growth rate of the firm. Firms with price-earnings ratios equal to their growth rate (for instance, a price-earnings ratio of 15 and an earnings growth rate of 15%, a ratio of 1.0) are considered fairly valued. When the price-earnings ratio is above the growth rate (a ratio above 1.0) the stock is considered overvalued, while a price-earnings ratio below the company's growth rate (a ratio less than 1.0) may point to an undervalued stock.

We screen for companies with a PEG ratio below 1.0.

The price-earnings to growth screen does not free you from a careful study of the earnings prospects for the companies passing the filter. Its strength lies in equating growth to valuation levels.

Valuation Alternatives

Other useful screens for value include comparing a company's current price-earnings ratio to its historical average or the average for its industry. You can screen for low ratios to these averages and try to discover why the company is trading at a discount.

Table 1.
Stocks Passing the Ralph Wanger Screening*

Company (Exchange: Ticker)	Price ($)	Market Cap ($ mil)	Net Profit Margin (12 mo.) (%)	Total Liab. to Total Assets (%)	PEG Ratio (EPS Grth 5-yr) (x)	P/E (x)	7-yr Avg. P/E (x)	5-yr EPS Grth (%)	EPS Grth Est (%)	% of Shares Held by Insiders (%)	% of Shares Held by Inst'l (%)
Bel Fuse, Inc. (M: BELFA)	21.25	223.6	17.2	12.0	0.4	10.7	na	30.4	na	27.8	7.7
Centennial Bancorp (M: CEBC)	9.50	186.6	21.9	89.5	0.6	15.8	19.5	28.3	16.0	27.2	10.9
Dataram Corporation (M: DRAM)	17.38	137.6	7.0	39.0	0.4	24.8	na	64.0	na	25.5	10.5
HEICO Corporation (N: HEI)	15.69	247.3	11.6	49.0	0.2	16.5	32.6	78.9	26.3	74.0	12.0
Irwin Financial Corp. (M: IRWN)	14.38	307.7	26.9	87.6	0.6	9.9	14.7	15.9	16.0	56.1	10.4
National Beverage Corp. (A: FIZ)	7.50	137.1	3.2	50.7	0.3	10.9	12.9	36.5	na	79.2	5.5
Palm Harbor Homes, Inc. (M: PHHM)	16.06	367.6	5.4	53.6	0.2	9.0	na	40.4	20.0	62.0	16.4
Pilgrim's Pride Corp. (N: CHX)	8.00	331.1	4.7	52.8	0.3	5.2	na	16.1	11.3	75.4	16.9
Schawk, Inc. (N: SGK)	7.75	164.3	8.8	62.7	0.8	13.8	24.7	16.9	15.0	55.2	15.3
Seaway Food Town, Inc. (M: SEWY)	21.88	146.0	1.2	65.4	0.7	18.7	13.9	26.2	10.0	58.0	11.4
State Auto Financial (M: STFC)	7.88	312.1	9.8	57.4	0.4	7.8	15.0	18.2	11.3	71.0	14.9

na = not available

Exchange Key: N = New York Stock Exchange
A = American Stock Exchange
M = Nasdaq

*Screening criteria used to produce table results can be found on opposite page.

Source: AAII's Stock Investor/ Market Guide Inc. and I/B/E/S. Statistics are based on figures as of February 25, 2000.

Beyond studying multiples of earnings, you can also look at price-to-sales ratios, price-to-cash-flow ratios, price-to-book-value ratios, and dividend yields. Wanger finds advantages and disadvantages with each measure, and investors should be aware of potential problems with each.

Earnings can be influenced by management assumptions. Temporary developments such as new product rollout costs and cyclical slowdowns can influence earnings more than sales. However, some industries traditionally sell with low price-to-sales ratios. Typically these industries have low profit margins.

Asset-based ratios, such as the price-to-book-value ratio, can be influenced by company factors such as specific depreciation schedules, age of assets, and even inventory accounting methods. Furthermore, unequal treatment of intangible assets across companies may lead to uneven results.

The price-to-cash-flow ratio can be helpful as a confirmation of the quality of earnings. It is suitable for analysis of companies with high levels of depreciable assets such as cable TV firms. Cash flow analysis is useful for companies with no earnings, yet that are generating high levels of cash. However, price-to-cash-flow measures are industry-sensitive. Cyclical firms and companies with long development construction cycles may have periods of slow sales, inventory build-up, and high capital expenditures. It is also less suited to analysis of growth stocks not generating cash from operations.

Management

Good management is critical. In his company visits, Wanger tries to get a sense of the ability and the honesty of the people running the firm. Management must be shareholder-oriented, and management owning a large chunk of the firm is desirable.

For our next screen, we look for companies in which the insiders own at least 20% of the outstanding shares. Most stock database programs rely on SEC filings made by beneficial owners to calculate the number of insiders holding shares. Since any shareholder who owns 5% of the outstanding shares is classified as an insider under the system, care must be taken in interpreting the results. A useful follow-up would be a careful reading of the proxy statement and 10-K filings to confirm that the managers are the owners with significant interest.

Neglected Stocks

As a final check, we screen out stocks with excessive institutional ownership, since Ralph Wanger's goal is to purchase neglected quality stocks at reasonable prices. The smaller the analyst interest when the stock is researched and purchased, the greater the chance that you are buying a mispriced stock. If the stock is eventually discovered by Wall Street, the premium investors are willing to pay for the company's earnings may increase, leading to a handsome profit.

Many measures of institutional interest exist. Percentage of outstanding shares held by institutions indicates the control possible by institutions along with the possible stock price correction if the herd heads for the exit door all at once. This figure may be skewed by a few large institutions such as an endowment fund, so many investors also look at the number of institutions holding the stock or the number of analysts providing estimates for recommendations as proxies for institutional interest.

We screen out companies where the percentage of shares held by institutions was greater than the database median—currently about 25%.

Table 1 is a list of stocks passing the screens we used to illustrate how Ralph Wanger's small-cap approach could be implemented. It is based on data as of February 25, 2000, using AAII's *Stock Investor Professional.* Screening tips for the Wanger small-cap approach are on pages 145 and 146.

Screening Tips: The Ralph Wanger Small-Cap Approach

Themes
Wanger first identifies long-term social, economic, or technological trends and selects companies poised to benefit from these trends. Computer software programs can easily screen for specific sectors or industries that look particularly interesting. Wanger prefers to invest in companies that have a "downstream" benefit from "hot" themes such as technology.

Size
Wanger has a preference for smaller-capitalization companies, but wishes to avoid extremely small firms, termed micro caps, because he feels that they are too risky—one misstep and they are out. While Wanger does not state the lower end of the scale, a minimum market capitalization of $100 million would exclude micro-cap firms. Wanger establishes $1 billion in market capitalization as the upper end of his universe, which also includes some medium-sized firms. These ranges can be easily screened in most software programs.

Established Firms
Wanger prefers seasoned companies with established management; no start-ups, initial public offerings, or troubled firms. Start-ups and initial public offerings can be screened out by requiring five years of stock price history.

Strong Niche Position
Wanger prefers companies with strong positions in their industries. These companies may be operating in a special niche (geographical, technological, marketing, etc.) that makes it difficult for other firms to compete. Profit margins can reveal possible market niches—companies with net profit margins above their industry norms over the last 12 months would be a good preliminary screen. Another indicator would be to screen for an increase in profit margins from two years back to the most recent 12 months. Follow-up examinations should include a detailed study of the firm's position in the industry and how it might change over time.

Financially Strong
Companies with strong financials are preferred. Wanger looks for firms with low debt relative to their industry average, adequate working capital, and conservative accounting practices. Most software programs can easily screen for companies with total liabilities to total assets below industry norms. Alternative screens might look for low debt-to-total-capitalization or low debt-to-equity. To help check for adequate working capital, screen for positive cash flow for the most recent 12 months and over each of the last three fiscal years. Companies passing the initial financial screens should be examined for factors such as hidden liabilities (for instance, pension obligations), stable relationship of inventories and receivables to sales levels, and conservative accounting practices.

Reasonably Priced
Companies with better growth prospects deserve to trade at higher price-earnings ratios, but investors should avoid paying too much for the stock. To compare ratios among companies with different growth rates, examine the price-earnings ratio relative to the earnings growth rate (the PEG ratio); ratios below 1.0 generally represent good value. Most screening programs can easily calculate these ratios. We screened for companies with a PEG

(cont'd on next page)

Screening Tips: The Ralph Wanger Small-Cap Approach *(cont'd)*

ratio below 1.0. Alternative value screens would include low price multiples for earnings, book value, sales, or cash flow. Ratios should be examined at an absolute level or compared to market values, industry medians, or historical levels.

Ownership Interest

Wanger prefers companies with entrepreneurial owners. Smaller growth firms are often run by managers with significant stock ownership. Most screening programs allow you to screen for the percentage of shares held by insiders. As a primary screen, we looked for companies in which insiders own at least 20% of the outstanding shares. As a follow-up, examine the proxy statement to confirm that the managers have significant ownership positions.

Neglected Stocks

Smaller firms have less analyst coverage than larger firms. The smaller the analyst coverage when you first buy into a stock, the more likely the stock is mispriced. We screened for companies with percentage of shares held by institutions below the overall universe median—currently about 25%. Alternative screens would include the number of institutions owning stocks and the number of analysts providing earnings estimates.

Investing in Technology: The Michael Murphy Approach

Growth stock investing typically starts with a broad analysis of the economy in a search for sectors that are growing more quickly than average. But one well-known growth investor, Michael Murphy, finds this analysis unnecessary. Why? He firmly believes that today's true growth opportunity is quite obvious—the world of high-technology.

Murphy is editor of the California Technology Stock Letter (800/998-2875; www.ctsl.com), a well-followed investment advisory newsletter that tracks and makes recommendations on technology stocks.

Murphy regards technology not so much as a sector, but rather as *the* growth driver of the U.S. economy, covering a relatively diversified group of companies. His approach seeks to identify technology stocks that are most likely to be the future leaders, and then buy those stocks when they become undervalued relative to their growth potential.

Why Technology Stocks?

Murphy believes that the U.S. economy is currently in the midst of a paradigm shift—a "once-in-a-century revolution" that is creating massive changes in almost all areas of the U.S. economy, creating new infrastructures, jobs and sources of wealth, while destroying old ones. The changes are similar to those brought about by other major innovations—for instance, the industrial revolution and later the introduction of mass production and a consumer-based economy. In today's economy, the change is being brought about by technology—electronics and computer technology, as well as medical and biotechnology.

The result of this shift, says Murphy, is that the technology sector is the fastest-growing and will quickly dominate all other sectors in terms of size. It is also a sector that is becoming very diversified, with seven major industry groups.

He also explicitly rejects investment guru Peter Lynch's dictum that individuals should not invest in things that can't be easily understood. He believes individuals don't need to understand the underlying technology, only the company and its competitive environment—the same way an individual may invest in a car manufacturer without understanding the technology behind how a car actually runs.

Identifying the Stocks

The real basis of a technology company's success, according to Murphy, stems from its commitment to research and development.

R&D is aimed at identifying advances, incorporating the advances into specific products and then bringing them to market. The result is either new products or new variations of old products. These new or significantly improved products drive rapid sales growth, often by creating their own demand—the World Wide Web being a perfect example. New products also carry higher profit margins, he notes, because there is usually little competition when they are first introduced. Thus, R&D spending is the company's investment in its future growth.

For that reason, heavy spending on R&D is the key to identifying profitable high-tech companies under Murphy's approach.

How can you identify "heavy spending?" If R&D spending is significant, it will be listed as a separate line item on the company's income statement (found in the firm's annual report and usually in its quarterly reports). Dividing the company's R&D spending by its annual sales tells you in percentage terms how much a company is spending on R&D.

Murphy requires a company to spend a minimum of 7% of revenues on R&D spending.

Of course, companies need to be spending their R&D funds and managing their business *wisely.* Other factors Murphy seeks include:

- *Sales growth of at least 15% per year.* Murphy regards this as a crucial test and suggests that companies failing this are not worth pursuing. This level of sales growth indicates that the company has a growing market for its products, and that its investments in new products are paying off.
- *Pretax profit margins (operating income less interest expense divided by revenues) of 15% or better.* This indicates that the company's products are delivering a substantial profit, and that sales growth is not being driven by "giveaways."
- *Return on equity (net income divided by shareholder's equity) of 15% or more.* Murphy regards this as more important in capital-intensive technology sectors such as semiconductor manufacturing. The figure indicates that a company is capable of financing its own growth without resorting to outside financings that dilute earnings.

On a more qualitative level, Murphy suggests asking: Does the company turn out a steady stream of new, successful products? Annual reports will provide some answers to this question. If research discussed one year turns into a product launch the following year and is a success the third year, it is a good indication the company is able to turn out a steady stream of new products.

Murphy also suggests calling the investor relations department of the prospective company and asking what percentage of revenues today come from products introduced in the last three years. If the company's research is productive, the answer should be over 50%.

The Growth-Flow Model

Identifying a potentially profitable technology stock is the first step, but Murphy does not believe in paying any price for growth. Instead, he prefers to follow potential companies and then purchase them once valuations reach attractive levels.

The problem, however, is that traditional valuation approaches can be misleading for technology firms. R&D spending directly cuts into a company's current earnings, so that the more a company spends on R&D, the worse its current reported earnings will be. The result will be a relatively higher price-earnings ratio for companies that spend more heavily on R&D.

However, from a shareholder's viewpoint, earnings invested for tomorrow in the form of R&D are as important as reported earnings today. Murphy therefore adds per share R&D spending [R&D spending divided by the number of shares outstanding] to aftertax earnings per share to determine what he terms a company's "growth flow." Dividing the current price of a stock by the growth flow per share provides the price-to-growth-flow ratio. It is this ratio that Murphy uses to measure the underlying investment value of a technology stock.

Murphy says the price-to-growth-flow ratio identifies cheap stocks both earlier and more accurately: R&D spending is usually stable, and does not drop when earnings suffer. Thus, when share prices drop due to disappointing earnings, the price-earnings ratio will tend to change little, whereas the stock will immediately look cheaper on a price-to-growth-flow basis.

As a guideline, Murphy views technology stocks as fairly priced when price-to-growth-flow ratios are around 10 to 14; anything under 8 is cheap and below 5 is a real bargain; 16 and over is too expensive.

Murphy provides a number of other useful rules of thumb for using the price-to-growth-flow model:

- **Compare the price-earnings ratio with the price-to-growth-flow ratio.** If the price-to-growth-flow figure is a small fraction of the price-earnings ratio, it is a strong indication that the market is mispricing the stock by placing too much emphasis on current earnings.
- **Compare the price-earnings ratio to the percent of sales spent on R&D**—for example, a price-earnings ratio of 13.3 and 19.6% of sales spent on R&D. In general, if a company's price-earnings ratio is below its percentage of sales spent on R&D, the stock is worth a look.
- **When examining R&D spending, pay attention to the actual number of dollars being spent.** Many firms can spend $3 million; a lot fewer can spend $30 million. As the sheer dollar amounts get larger, there are few companies that can afford to spend at those levels, and with less competition, the payback should be even greater.

Taming Risk

The volatility of technology stocks is obvious, and Murphy does not try to play it down.

One approach Murphy suggests to quantify risk is to examine the downside—the price to which a technology stock may plummet if everything turns sour. To estimate this, Murphy uses three worst-case valuation estimates:

- The price-to-sales ratio drops to 1.0.
- The price-to-book-value ratio drops to 1.5.
- The price-earnings ratio drops to one-third of the growth rate for the last three years—for instance, if the growth rate were 30% over the last three years, the worst-case price-earnings ratio would drop to 10.

Murphy determines the price level for each of these scenarios and then takes an average of the three. For instance, if sales per share were $7.84, the first downside price would be $7.84; if book value per share was $7.23, the second downside price would be $10.85 (7.23 × 1.5); and if the growth rate was 36.3% and earnings per share were $1.92, the price-earnings ratio would drop to 12.1 [36.3 ÷ 3] and the third downside price would be $23.23 (12.1 × 1.92). The average downside price would be $13.97 [(7.84 + 10.85 + 23.23) ÷ 3].

The difference between the current price and the downside price, divided by the current price, produces the percentage risk of the stock—in other words, the percentage amount the current price would fall if the worst were to happen. Obviously, the lower the percentage risk, the better. A downside risk of 50% is common, and a good buying opportunity is when the downside risk is only 25%.

Portfolio Building

Another important aspect to controlling risk in technology stocks, according to Murphy, is to diversify among the seven major groups:

- Semiconductor equipment producers (companies that make the equipment that makes semiconductors);
- Semiconductor producers;
- Large computers;
- Personal computers;
- Software;
- Communications, including data communications (computer-to-computer data) and telecommunications; and
- Medical technology, including both biotechnology and medical devices.

Murphy suggests that investors build a portfolio of at least 10 stocks, with companies from each of the seven industry groups. Keeping an eye on diversification among the various industries is particularly important, he notes, because at any point in time, the cheaper technology stocks are likely to be within one group; paying attention only to valuations, and not to your portfolio mix, can lead to a dangerously concentrated group of holdings.

For portfolios up to $300,000, he suggests holding up to 12 stocks, and for portfolios over $300,000, he would increase the number of holdings to 20. However, he says 20 is a good upper limit, since it is difficult for individuals to track more than that number. If new money is added to the portfolio, he suggests adding proportionately to the existing holdings, or putting more in those that are more undervalued rather than buying a new stock. If you simply must buy a new stock, he suggests selling your least attractive stock. This approach, he says, not only keeps the portfolio to a manageable level, but also is a good way of pruning shares.

When to Sell

Murphy provides one sell signal on the upside: sell if the stock's price-to-growth-flow ratio gets as high as the growth rate. However, in general, he suggests that investors use relativity to guide their stock sales—sell when there is a better stock to buy, rather than simply because the stock has gone up in price. On the other hand, if the stock grows so much that it represents more than a third of your portfolio, it should be trimmed back, with the proceeds reinvested in the most attractive other holdings.

What if prices fall? If the stock is still attractive on a price-to-growth-flow basis, Murphy says these are great buying opportunities. However, if the fundamentals have changed, or if management appears to be failing—for instance, new products do not get out, or management seriously misleads shareholders—sell.

Murphy in Summary

Murphy summarizes his approach:

"Investing is a two-step process. The first step is to identify situations—managements, products and markets—with which you would like to associate your capital. The second step is to decide what price you are willing to pay to associate your capital with those situations.

"[Individuals should] focus on a small list of superior companies with rapid growth and excellent financial ratios. Then wait for each of them to get knocked down by Wall Street to the point where they are cheap on their price/growth-flow ratio."

The Michael Murphy Approach

Philosophy and Universe

The U.S. is undergoing a major revolution in which technology is the major economic driver. Therefore, technology stocks will be the major area of growth. Investors should focus on a small list of superior companies with rapid growth and excellent financial ratios, then wait for them to become cheap.

Criteria for Initial Consideration

- R&D spending of at least 7% of revenues
- Sales growth of at least 15% per year
- Pretax profit margins of 15% or better
- Return on equity (net income divided by shareholder's equity) of 15% or more

Valuations

Use a company's price-to-growth-flow ratio to determine value:

Per share R&D + EPS = Growth flow

Price ÷ growth flow = Price-to-growth-flow ratio

Guidelines for judging price-to-growth-flow ratio:

Fair: 10 to 14

Cheap: Below 8

Expensive: 16 and above

Other guidelines:

- If price-to-growth-flow ratio is a small fraction of price-earnings ratio, the market is most likely mispricing the stock by placing too much emphasis on current earnings.
- If the price-earnings ratio is below the percentage of sales spent on R&D, the stock is worth a look.
- Pay attention to the actual dollars being spent on R&D. As the sheer dollar amounts get larger, there are few companies that can afford to spend at those levels, which means less competition.

Controlling Risk

Measure the downside risk by taking the average of three worst-case valuation estimates:

- The price-to-sales ratio drops to 1.0
- The price-to-book-value ratio drops to 1.5
- The price-earnings ratio drops to one-third of the growth rate for the last three years

Determine the price to which the stock would fall under each of these scenarios, and take the average of the three. The difference between the current price and the downside price, divided by the current price, produces the percentage risk of the stock—the percentage amount the current price would fall if the worst were to happen. The lower the percentage risk, the better. A downside risk of 50% is common, and a good buying opportunity is when the downside risk is only 25%.

Portfolio Building

Build a portfolio of 10 to 20 stocks, and diversify among the seven major groups of technology stocks:

- Semiconductor equipment producers (companies that make the equipment that makes semiconductors)
- Semiconductor producers
- Large computers
- Personal computers
- Software
- Communications, including data communications (computer-to-computer data) & telecommunications
- Medical technology, including both biotechnology and medical devices

To keep the portfolio to a manageable size, add proportionately to existing holdings when adding new money to your portfolio, rather than buying new stocks. If you feel you must buy a new stock, sell your least attractive stock.

When to Sell

On the upside:

- Sell if the stock's price-to-growth-flow ratio gets as high as the growth rate. In general, however, sell only when there is a better stock to buy.
- If a stock grows so much it represents more than a third of your portfolio, trim it back and reinvest the proceeds in your most attractive other holdings.

On the downside:

- If prices fall and the stock is still attractive on a price-to-growth-flow basis, buy more. However, if fundamentals have changed, or management appears to be failing, sell.

Stock Screens: Applying the Michael Murphy Approach

Michael Murphy believes that today's true growth opportunity is the world of high technology. Our first screening criteria includes only stocks in the technology sector.

Real growth is a critical test for a company. Sales growth, or top-line growth, drives the company's bottom line. Murphy requires that a company exhibit sales growth of at least 15% per year. Growth at this level helps indicate research and development efforts that are proving to be worthwhile. It also indicates that the company is participating in a rapidly expanding market or taking sales away from a competitor.

We screen for companies with annual sales growth of at least 15% over the last three years. Three years was selected as the time frame because it is short enough to reflect a relevant period, yet long enough to identify a significant trend.

As with any screen that deals with a growth rate, it is important to study the sales figures on a year-by-year basis to confirm the strength of the growth rate figure. It is also important to study the passing companies to identify changes that may invalidate historical performance as a predictor of future performance.

Is It Profitable?

Murphy looks for a pretax profit margin of at least 15% to measure the profitability of a firm. The test helps reveal a company that may have a proprietary edge because it is able to deliver its products at a substantial profit.

A high profit margin validates the strength of the sales growth rate. A firm may be able to boost its sales by "giving away" its products, but this can only be sustained for a short period of time. In fact, this strategy can hurt the company in the long run if it does not produce enough profits to reinvest in research and development, provide for expansion as well as reward the shareholders.

Some technology industries have inherently lower margins yet create potentially interesting technology companies for the more sophisticated investor. Hardware manufacturers (original equipment manufacturers) who sell the majority of their goods to computer manufacturers, not consumers, typically have lower pretax margins but offer great growth potential. The lower margins, however, will translate to a higher level of volatility, requiring more diligent quarter-by-quarter tracking.

There are a number of ratios that can be used to measure profitability. For example, the gross profit margin is often used as a top-line representation of profitability. The gross margin (sales less cost of goods sold divided by sales), however, can be very industry-specific and not as useful as a broad screening measure. For some companies, the actual cost of selling their goods (cost of goods sold) is small compared to the sales, marketing and support costs needed for the success of the firm's operation. Pretax profit margin includes the cost of goods sold, marketing and administrative expenses, interest expense, as well as research and development costs, so it is a more universal profitability measure within the technology sector.

Murphy requires a pretax profit margin of at least 15%, which is used as the screen here.

How Is Invested Capital Used?

Murphy looks for a minimum level of 15% for a company's return on equity (net income divided by shareholder's equity) as a measure of a firm's ability to finance its long-term capital requirements internally. He feels that this test is particularly important for companies in capital-intensive industries, such as semiconductor production. Assuming no dividend payout, the return on equity equals the long-term sustainable growth rate. Faster growth has to be financed with additional debt or equity. Taking on debt has absolute limits and must be done carefully by companies in volatile industries. Issuing additional equity dilutes the ownership of existing shareholders, making their stock worthless on a per share basis. Murphy therefore prefers companies with a return on equity that can comfortably fund growth.

The screen here looks for companies with a return on equity of at least 15%. When screening for high return on equity, it is also a good idea to carefully study the level of debt carried by the company. Any final company analysis should include an examination of the financial structure of the company.

Table 1.
Stocks Passing the Murphy Technology Stock Screening*

Company (Exchange: Ticker)	Price ($)	26-Wk Rel. Strgth Rank (%)	52-Wk Rel. Strgth Rank (%)	Ann'l Sales Grth (3-Yr) (%)	Pretax Margin (12 mos.) (%)	Ret. on Equity (12 mos.) (%)	R&D as % of Sales (%)	R&D (12 mos.) ($ mil)	Price-to-Grth-Flow (x)	P/E (x)
Deltek Systems, Inc. (M: DLTK)	13.19	31	34	34.3	29.2	36.5	16.6	16.0	6.9	13.5
Equinox Systems Inc. (M: EQNX)	9.63	20	40	15.7	19.2	16.8	9.9	3.5	6.6	12.0
Indus International, Inc. (M: IINT)	8.36	76	81	24.3	28.6	31.6	16.6	33.7	3.8	7.3
Sunquest Inform. Systems (M: SUNQ)	10.94	11	48	25.2	18.5	17.7	12.0	15.8	5.4	11.0
Timberline Software (M: TMBS)	12.19	51	55	21.3	30.1	35.7	18.7	10.0	7.8	15.6
XOX Corporation (O: XOXC)	2.56	57	na	76.5	36.0	66.7	36.0	0.9	4.6	9.9

na = not available

Exchange Key: N = New York Stock Exchange
A = American Stock Exchange
M = Nasdaq National Market
O = Nasdaq Small Market

*Screening criteria used to produce table results can be found on opposite page.

Statistics are based on figures as of February 25, 2000.
Data Source: AAII's Stock Investor/Market Guide, Inc, and I/B/E/S.

Is It Reinvesting for the Future?

Murphy feels that the success of a technology company depends upon its commitment to research and development (R&D).

If a company is spending a significant portion on research and development, the amount will be listed as a separate line item on the company's income statement. Dividing the company's research and development spending by its sales for the same time period tells you in percentage terms how much the company is spending. As a test of significant research and development spending, Murphy only looks at companies spending at least 7% of sales on R&D. Our screen here requires that a company spend at least 7% of sales on research and development.

Beyond looking at the raw dollars spent on research and development, the company's track record in successfully bringing out new or improved products must be examined. Annual reports will provide some qualitative feel in this regard. Research discussed one year that turns into a product launch the following year and a success the third year is a good indication that the company is able to turn out a steady stream of new products.

The Growth-Flow Model

Identifying a potentially interesting technology stock is the first step, but Murphy does not believe in paying any price for growth. Instead, he prefers to follow the potential companies and purchase them only when valuations reach attractive levels.

To value technology stocks, he uses the "price-to-growth-flow" ratio: per share R&D spending (R&D spending divided by the number of shares outstanding) is added to earnings per share to determine the "growth flow;" dividing the current price of a stock by the growth flow per share provides the price-to-growth-flow ratio. Murphy views technology stocks as fairly priced when price-to-growth-flow ratios are around 10 to 14; anything under 8.0 is cheap and below 5.0 is a real bargain; 16 and over is too expensive.

The screen here specifies 8.0 as an upper limit for a company's price-to-growth-flow ratio. Murphy recommends tracking a small universe of technology stocks closely and taking advantage of price drops when the market pounces on a company's mistake.

Table 1 is a list of stocks passing the screens we used to illustrate how Michael Murphy's technology stock approach could be implemented. It is based on data as of February 25, 2000, using AAII's *Stock Investor Professional*. Screening tips for the Murphy technology stock approach appears on page 157.

Screening Tips: The Michael Murphy Approach

Criteria for Initial Consideration
Technology industry
Most screening programs allow you to screen for a specific industry segment. While the exact list of companies will vary from service to service, it should be easy to obtain a list of technology stocks for further screening.

Sales growth of at least 15% per year
Most screening programs will let you screen for minimum sales growth levels. We selected an annual three-year rate because it is a good balance between a short enough time frame to cover a relevant period, yet long enough to identify a significant trend. You may have to adjust the time period to those supported by your screening program.

Pretax profit margins of 15% or better
There are a number of ratios that can be used to measure profitability. For example, the gross profit margin is often used as a top-line representation of profitability. The gross margin (sales less cost of goods sold divided by sales), however, can be very industry-specific and not as useful as a broad screening measure. For some companies, the actual cost of selling their goods (cost of goods sold) is small compared to the sales, marketing, and support costs needed for the success of the firm's operation. Pretax profit margin includes the cost of goods sold, marketing and administrative expenses, as well as research and development costs, so it is a more universal profitability measure within the technology sector.

Return on equity of 15% or more
Most screening programs report the return on equity (ROE), so it should be easy to specify a minimum ROE level of 15%.

R&D spending of at least 7% of revenues
Not all programs report on research and development spending, so you may have to perform the first four screens and evaluate the R&D spending separately. Companies with significant R&D spending will indicate the annual commitment in their annual reports and 10-Ks.

Valuations
Use a company's price-to-growth-flow ratio to determine value:
The price-to-growth-flow is a unique multiple employed by Murphy. If your screening program supplies R&D figures and allows for the creation of custom fields, then you should be able to construct this multiple and use it for screening. However, if your screening system does not report on R&D or allow for custom fields, you will have to perform the first four screens, and then evaluate the R&D spending and calculate the price-to-growth-flow ratio manually.

C-A-N-S-L-I-M: A GROWTH APPROACH USING TECHNICAL AND FUNDAMENTAL DATA

Investment approaches are often classified as being either fundamentally-based, which focus on company characteristics to determine future prospects, or technically-based, which focus on movements in share price and volume to determine future movements. However, these factors are not mutually exclusive.

One approach that combines both fundamental and technical factors was devised by William J. O'Neil.

O'Neil began his career on Wall Street and eventually founded an investment research firm, William O'Neil & Co., which publishes, among other things, Daily Graphs (a daily chart service), and Investor's Business Daily (a daily financial newspaper). The latter publication was started in 1983 and was designed by O'Neil to provide more investment information than was then contained in daily financial newspapers. As a result, Investor's Business Daily includes in its daily stock price tables information that pertains to O'Neil's investment approach.

C-A-N-S-L-I-M: The Philosophy

William O'Neil is a strong believer in the sustained long-term growth of the American economy due to the freedoms and opportunities available in this country, which he says have made the U.S. a "prime success model" worldwide and a leader in high-growth, innovative entrepreneurial companies. The ultimate goal of investing in stocks, he believes, is to participate in that long-term growth.

With that basic outlook in mind, O'Neil starts with the entire universe of stocks, but he favors the stocks of smaller firms, since most innovations and new products come from smaller and medium-sized companies. His system can best be described as a growth stock approach that seeks companies whose stock prices are poised to rise due to favorable fundamental factors within the firm and industry, such as increased earnings due to new products and services, as well as favorable technical factors regarding price trends and the supply and demand for the stock.

O'Neil says that his approach to investing stems from an analysis covering 40 years of market data, which examined each year's stocks with the largest percentage price increase to find the common characteristics of the "most successful stocks." These common characteristics include both fundamental factors, inherent in the nature of the firm and industry, and technical factors from observing the price patterns of the stocks.

He refers to the approach he ultimately devised by the acronym C-A-N-S-L-I-M, which is supposed to help investors remember the seven key factors of these successful stocks (see Table 1).

Increasing Earnings Currently and Historically

O'Neil believes that increases in earnings per share are the single most important elements of stock selection. In fact, he devotes two letters of his acronym to earnings—C (current earnings growth) and A (annual earnings growth for the past five years). It is the presence of both factors, indicating both past and current growth, that he feels is significant.

In terms of current (most recently reported) earnings per share, O'Neil suggests that investors seek firms showing a major percentage increase of at least 18% to 20% over the same quarter's earnings one year prior. Comparing same-quarter earnings is important to eliminate seasonal earnings fluctuations. O'Neil also warns against meaningless mathematical increases, such as those produced by comparing current earnings with non-existent earnings for the prior year, which would produce a large percentage increase, and those produced by one-time extraordinary gains such as the profit from the sale of a plant (such gains should be omitted from earnings per share figures).

Other positive indicators include quarterly earnings per share that have accelerated over the past 2½ years (in other words, the earnings growth rates are increasing each quarter). On the other hand, decelerating quarterly earnings (declining growth rates) are a bad sign.

In terms of annual earnings per share, O'Neil looks for "meaningful" growth rates of between 25% to 50% annually for the last five years. He also prefers firms that show stability and consistency in annual earnings per share, with annual figures that don't deviate significantly from the five-year average.

What about price-earnings ratios?

O'Neil says that markets are seldom wrong, and thus most stocks are correctly priced, with low price-earnings ratios indicating (correctly) low growth prospects. The best investments, according to O'Neil, are growth stocks in which one must be willing to pay for earnings growth.

Growth Prospects

Earnings growth is one important indicator of a growth company. Also important, according to O'Neil, is the timing factor, indicating whether a stock's price is poised to advance. For that, O'Neil suggests investors seek "new" factors: firms that are developing new products or services, or that have new managements that are able to provide innovations or changes that can lead to sustained earnings growth. Equally favorable would be new changes within the entire industry that could lead earnings to accelerate.

New highs in stock prices are also important. While these firms are often viewed as too high-priced and risky, O'Neil says that these stocks are the ones whose prices advance. Thus, stocks that are reaching new highs after undergoing a price correction, and particularly those that are accompanied by a big increase in trading volume, usually go higher—what O'Neil characterizes as the "stock market's great paradox."

Other Fundamental Factors

There are several other fundamental factors O'Neil suggests investors examine, including:

- **Firms that are in growing industries**, since these provide stronger growth prospects. O'Neil also suggests seeking the top two or three firms in a strong industry. Finding several key stocks within a growing industry group additionally serves as a confirmation that you are looking in the "right" area (in terms of growth); conversely, if you can't find more than one strong company within an industry group, you may have made an error.
- **Companies that are buying back their own stock in the open market.** Not only does this reduce the number of shares outstanding (a plus, since it increases demand and reduces supply), but more importantly it implies that management most likely expects improved sales and earnings.
- **Firms that have a low amount of long-term corporate debt relative to equity outstanding** are preferable to firms with larger amounts of debt to equity. Firms that are more highly leveraged have a much greater risk of suffering from problems in their earnings during periods of high interest rates.

Technical Factors

Supply and demand considerations for the outstanding shares of a stock are important considerations for O'Neil. These factors directly impact the price of a stock, with greater demand and limited supply helping to drive up share prices, according to O'Neil.

O'Neil favors the stocks of smaller firms not only for their growth prospects, but also because of the smaller number of shares outstanding. For these firms, a "reasonable" amount of buying can push up the stock price. On the other hand, he warns that those very same characteristics make these stocks less liquid and more volatile, which are extra risks that investors must consider.

For similar reasons, O'Neil suggests investors examine the "float"—the number of common shares left for possible purchase after subtracting the shares that are closely held by management. Needless to say, stocks with a large percentage of stock held by top management are favorable.

While O'Neil likes a limited number of shares outstanding, he is uncomfortable at the extremes, with little or no liquidity. He warns against owning low-priced stocks with a very low number of shares outstanding and no institutional ownership due to a lack of liquidity and marketability. Thus, O'Neil prefers to see at least some institutional ownership to create

Table 1.
The William O'Neil Approach: C-A-N-S-L-I-M

Factors	Interpretation
C = Current Quarterly Earnings Per Share	
Primary Factors: Should show a major percentage increase (18% or 20% minimum) in the current quarterly earnings per share.	High quarterly growth signals strong recent performance that company is still in uptrend. Watch out for calculations based upon nearly nonexistent earnings, such as a penny or two.
Look at the current quarter's earnings per share vs. the same quarter the year before.	Seasonal pattern for most companies makes it important to compare quarters in the same part of the fiscal year.
Omit a company's one-time extraordinary gains.	Use earnings from continuing operations if available. Otherwise look at companies passing initial screen.
Secondary Factors: Look for accelerating quarterly earnings growth.	A slowing rate of quarter-on-quarter growth may signal a slowing trend for a company.
Find at least one other stock in the same group showing strong quarterly earnings growth.	If you cannot locate another company in the same industry with strong earnings growth, then the chance is greater that the stock may not perform well.
A = Annual Earnings Increases	
Primary Factors: Each year's annual earnings per share for the last five years should show an increase over the prior year's earnings.	Strong steady growth is most desirable. If screening by hand, you may accept a company if it has one down year and quickly recovers; otherwise accept only strong performance.
Annual compounded growth rate should be at least 25% over the last four or five years.	Past winners had strong earnings. While you may pay more for top companies, they will show strongest price appreciation.
Secondary Factors: Earnings estimates should show a healthy increase.	Strong earnings estimates help to confirm the expectation of continued growth, but earnings estimates are not as dependable as past, proven growth.
Earnings should be stable and consistent from year to year.	The more stable the earnings from year to year, the better the chance for continued strong performance.
N = New Products, New Management, New Highs	
Primary Factors: Look for companies with a major new product or service, new management, or a positive change for the industry.	Companies with a catalyst tend to show the best performance as the market jumps on the news and earnings show growth because of the change.
Secondary Factors: Look for stocks close to or making new highs in price after a period of consolidation.	Stocks making new highs often continue to increase in price while those declining often continue to sink.
Strong volume on price move-up.	Volume confirms long-term strength of price move up.
S = Supply and Demand	
Primary Factors: When choosing between two stocks, the stock with the lower number of shares should perform better.	With a few number of outstanding shares, any positive company news should have a greater impact on price.
Stocks with a large percentage of ownership by top management are generally good prospects.	A large percentage of insider ownership reduces the public float, thereby reducing supply.
Secondary Factors: Look for companies buying their own stock in the open market.	The purchase of stock reduces public float and decreases supply. Share repurchase plans should be mentioned in news releases and annual report.
Look for companies reducing their debt as a percent of equity over the last few years.	Lower debt gives company greater flexibility if it should get into trouble or if interest rates increase.
Avoid lower-priced stocks with small capitalization and no instutional sponsorship.	These companies have poor liquidity and are considered lower grade.

Table 1. (cont'd)
The William O'Neil Approach: C-A-N-S-L-I-M

Factors		Interpretation
L = Leaders and Laggards		
Primary Factors:	Buy among the top two or three stocks in a strong industry group.	Buy companies showing strong growth and price appreciation. Stocks without price movements or with prices trending down may be "sleepy losers." Relative strength should help to indicate strong industries and strong stocks.
	Avoid stocks with a relative strength rank below 70.	The market is a good judge of a company's potential relative to other stocks. Stocks outperforming the market tend to do so for some time until a fundamental shift occurs.
Secondary Factors:	Sell your worst-performing stocks first and keep your best performing stocks a little longer.	Don't let your ego dictate your actions. Recognize your mistakes early and pump money into your stronger stocks.
	To upgrade your stock selection, consider companies showing a relative strength rank of 80 or higher with a chart base pattern.	To be more restrictive, consider only the strongest performers after a period of consolidation.
	Don't buy weak performance after a price drop greater than the market.	Losing stocks often continue in their down patterns.
I = Institutional Sponsorship		
Primary Factors:	Look for a stock that has three to 10 institutional owners.	Big demand is required for big price moves and institutional buying has the biggest impact. Examine the number of institutions owning stock or percentage of shares held by institutions.
	Look for institutional owners with a good track record.	It is better to follow the buying habits of institutions with good track records. Follow the holdings of mutual funds with good track records with a growth style.
	Look for stocks with an increasing, not decreasing, number of sponsors.	Look for an increasing number of institutions or percentage of shares held by institutions.
Secondary Factors	Avoid stocks that are over-owned—excessive institutional ownership.	Once a stock is owned by a very large number of institutions, the risk is that a mass exodus can slam the price down on bad news.
M = Market Direction		
Primary Factors:	It is difficult to fight the trend, so try to determine if you are in a bull or bear market.	Lack of profit on the last four to five trades may signal a negative shift in the general market.
	Follow and understand what the general market averages are doing every day.	Read business papers or use technical analysis program to track market performance.
	Try to go 25% into cash when the market peaks and begins a major reversal.	Do not wait to sell if real market weakness develops. Quick action is especially important if stocks are purchased on margin.
	Lack of profit on the last 4 to 5 trades may signal a negative shift in the general market.	If you are buying good companies and stocks but they are not progressing, then it may be sign of a changing market.
	Divergence of key averages may signal major changes in trend.	Market may have topped when original quality bull market leaders falter and a group of lower-quality, low-priced stocks dominate the most active group on up market days.
	Heavy volume without significant price progress may signal a top, but initial market decline may be on lower volume.	Heavy volume when market is at top indicates the first wave of sell-off by market-savvy investors. As market starts to slide down, it may take some time for general market to believe bear market has started.
Secondary Factors:	The change in the discount rate is a valuable indicator to watch as a confirmation of market moves.	Increases in the discount rate often lead to economic and market slowdowns.

demand and thus liquidity and marketability in a stock, and he suggests three to 10 institutional owners as a reasonable number. He also views it as a confirmation of a good purchase. However, if institutional ownership is to be considered as a sign of a good purchase, O'Neil says the institution should have a good performance record. As an example, he suggests that ownership by one or two top-performing mutual funds is a positive sign.

On the other hand, stocks that are "overowned" by institutions should be avoided, since it can create too much liquidity and the possibility of large volumes of sales should something go wrong in the short term.

O'Neil also prefers stocks that are market leaders within an industry. By some measures, this could be considered a fundamental criteria, but one way of measuring a leader, according to O'Neil, is by examining a stock's relative strength, which compares a stock's price performance relative to the price action of the market. A leader is identified as one whose price has outperformed 70% or more of the stocks in the comparison group. In addition, O'Neil suggests that a stock's relative strength should not be trending down.

Lastly, O'Neil is a strong believer in monitoring the overall direction of the stock market. He says it is difficult to fight the trend, so it is important to determine if you are in a bull or bear market. When the market peaks and begins a major reversal, O'Neil suggests putting 25% of your portfolio into cash. Signs of a market peak and reversal downward include:

- A lack of profit in your last four or five trades.
- Heavy volume without significant price progress.
- Divergence of key averages.
- Faltering market leaders.
- Poor-quality stocks showing on the most active lists.

Stock Monitoring and When to Sell

O'Neil suggests that investors monitor stock holdings quarterly by computing the percentage change in price from the prior quarter, and then listing the holdings in order of their relative price performance. This places the attention on the relative performance of stock holdings rather than how much a stock has gained or lost from its original purchase price.

O'Neil also suggests that when a stock is purchased, a "profit and loss plan" should be established—one that sets an absolute loss level on the downside, as well as a goal for the upside. He recommends that investors sell if a stock drops to 7% or 8% below the purchase price. This level is established to limit an investor's absolute loss, and the level therefore need not be raised as the stock price increases.

O'Neil notes that investors must have patience when holding stock with the expectations of price increases, and he suggests that investors wait at least 13 weeks before concluding that a stock is not advancing properly. He recommends taking profits when a stock has gained 20% unless it is a particularly powerful stock with the possibility for stronger gains, both for the stock itself and during a bull market. "Giant profits" in stocks, he notes, take one to three years.

O'Neil in Summary

O'Neil's approach has a growth focus, but is nonetheless difficult to categorize since it uses both fundamental and technical factors. The best summary of the approach comes from O'Neil himself:

"We're buying companies with strong fundamentals, large sales and earnings increases resulting from unique new products or services, and trying to time the purchases at a correct point as the company emerges from consolidation periods and before the stock runs up dramatically in price."

The William O'Neil Approach in Brief

Philosophy and style

Investment in companies whose stock prices are poised to rise due to favorable fundamental factors within the firm and industry, such as increased earnings due to new products and services, as well as favorable technical factors regarding price trends and the supply and demand for the stock.

Universe of stocks

No restrictions—the entire universe of stocks. However, stocks of smaller firms are favored, since most innovations and new products come from smaller and medium-sized companies.

Criteria for initial consideration

- Current quarterly earnings per share that are 18% to 20% above earnings per share for the same quarter one year prior.
- Meaningful growth in annual earnings per share over the last five years (25% to 50% annually).
- New products or services, or new management offering innovation; and share prices that are reaching new highs.
- Small or reasonable number of shares outstanding to create buying pressure; and there should be volume increases when a stock begins to move up.
- Stock should show high price strength relative to other stocks.
- Stock should have a small number of institutional owners with good performance records.

Secondary characteristics

- Quarterly earnings per share that are accelerating. Conversely, decelerating quarterly earnings per share are a bad sign.
- Consistency and stability in annual earnings per share, with few deviations from the long-term average trend.
- Two or three other top stocks within the same industry to serve as confirmation of industry growth.
- Companies that are buying back their own stock in the open market implies expectations by management of improved sales and earnings.
- Low amount of long-term debt to equity.
- A large percentage of stock held by top management.
- Avoid companies that are "overowned" by institutions.
- Avoid companies with no institutional ownership and with low capitalization because of lack of liquidity.

Stock monitoring and when to sell

Monitor stocks quarterly by examining the percentage price increase over the prior quarter, focusing on relative price performance among stocks. When selling, sell worst-performing stocks and let the better-performing stocks 'run.'
To limit losses, sell if a stock's price drops 7% to 8% below the purchase price. Take profits when a stock has a 20% gain, unless the outlook is particularly favorable for further growth, both for the stock itself and the overall stock market.

Stock Screens: Applying the C-A-N-S-L-I-M Approach

C = Current Quarterly Earnings per Share: How Much Is Enough?

The C-A-N-S-L-I-M approach focuses on companies with proven records of earnings growth while still in a stage of earnings acceleration. O'Neil's study of winning stocks highlights the strong quarterly earnings per share of the securities prior to their significant price run-ups.

O'Neil recommends looking for stocks with a minimum increase in quarterly earnings of 18% to 20% over the same quarterly period one year ago. When screening for quarterly earnings increases, it is important to compare a quarter to its equivalent quarter last year—in other words, this year's second quarter compared to last year's second quarter. Many firms have seasonal earnings patterns and comparing similar quarters takes this into account.

Another item to watch out for when screening for percentage changes are figures that are essentially meaningless because they start from a very small base. For example, an increase from one penny to 10 cents is a 900% earnings increase. While it is possible to exclude companies with just a few cents of earnings from the base period when establishing the screening criteria, you may prefer to examine the raw numbers of the companies passing the screen. This allows you to gauge the overall trend and stability in earnings and other items such as sales and cash flow.

It is also important to check if any of the numbers in the calculation are negative. A change in sign, such as earnings going from a negative to a positive, requires special consideration and may result in misleading screening results. When screening on user-defined fields such as custom growth rates, you may find it useful to include some secondary or qualifying criterion to help ensure proper screening results. In our version of the C-A-N-S-L-I-M screen, positive earnings for the current quarter are required to help make the results of the growth rate calculation more meaningful.

Whenever you are working with earnings, the issue of how to handle extraordinary earnings comes into play. One-time events can distort the actual trend in earnings and make company performance look better or worse than a comparison against a firm without special events. O'Neil recommends excluding these non-recurring items from the analysis. With our screen, we examine growth in earnings from continuing operations only. The first two screens are:
- quarterly growth rate greater than or equal to 20% and
- positive earnings per share from continuing operations for the current quarter.

Beyond looking for strong quarterly growth, O'Neil likes to see an increasing rate of growth. An increasing growth rate in quarterly earnings per share is so important in the

C-A-N-S-L-I-M system that O'Neil warns shareholders to consider selling holdings of those companies that show a slowing rate of growth two quarters in a row. Our next screen specifies that the growth rate from the quarter one year ago compared to the latest quarter be higher than the previous quarter's increase from its counterpart one year earlier.

A = Annual Earnings Increases: Look for Meaningful Growth

The C-A-N-S-L-I-M system tries to identify the strong companies leading the current market cycle. The primary screen for annual earning increases that O'Neil uses is increasing earnings per share in each of the last five years. In applying this screen, we specify that earnings per share from continuing operations be higher for each year when compared against the previous year. To help guard against any recent reversal in trend, a criterion is included requiring that the earnings over the last 12 months be greater than earnings one year ago.

O'Neil also recommends screening for companies showing a strong annual growth rate of 25% or 50% over the last five years. Our version of the O'Neil screen specifies a minimum annual growth rate of 25% in earnings per share from continuing operations over the last five years.

N = New Products, New Management, New Highs: Buying at the Right Time

O'Neil feels that a stock needs a catalyst to start a strong price advance. This catalyst can be a new product or service, a new management team after a period of lackluster performance or even a structural change in a company's industry, such as a new technology. These are qualitative factors that do not lend themselves to easy screening. However, it is possible to study the companies passing the preliminary screens to see if any catalysts exist.

A second consideration that O'Neil emphasizes is to pursue stocks showing strong upward price movements. Stocks that are making the new high list while accompanied by a big increase in volume might be prospects worth checking. A stock making a new high after undergoing a period of price correction and consolidation is especially interesting. O'Neil feels that decisive investors should have sold a stock long before it hits the new low list.

O'Neil's newspaper, Investor's Business Daily, highlights stocks within 10% of their 52-week high and this is the criterion we established for our version of the O'Neil screen. The number of companies passing will vary over the course of the market cycle. One would expect many companies to pass during a strong market expansion, while a smaller number of companies would pass during the early stage of a bear market.

S = Supply and Demand: Small Capitalization Plus Volume Demand

As the catalyst starts pushing the price of a company's stock up, those firms with a smaller number of shares outstanding should increase more quickly than those with a large number of outstanding shares.

O'Neil suggests that investors consider looking at the actual "float" of the stock. The float is the number of shares in the hands of the public—determined by subtracting the number of shares held by management from the number of shares outstanding. In our version of the O'Neil approach, we required stock with fewer than 20 million shares available through the float. [The 20 million share figure used was based on academic studies that examined the effect of float on stock prices.]

L = Leader or Laggard: Which Is Your Stock?

O'Neil is not a patient value investor, looking for out-of-favor companies and willing to wait for the market to come around to his viewpoint. Rather, he prefers to scan for rapidly growing companies that are market leaders in rapidly expanding industries. O'Neil advocates buying among the best two or three stocks in a group. You should be compensated for any premium you pay for these leaders with significantly higher rates of return.

After identifying a strong industry, O'Neil warns against avoiding the market leaders by purchasing "sympathy" stocks that are similar but significantly cheaper when examined by factors such as price-earnings ratios and weaker price performance. He says these stocks often continue to languish while the actual market leaders continue their strong rise.

O'Neil suggests using relative strength to identify market leaders. Relative strength compares the performance of a stock relative to the market as a whole. Relative strength is typically reported with a base level of zero or one, in which the base level represents stock performance equal to the market index. Numbers above the base level reflect performance above the market index, while below-market performance can be seen with figures below the base.

Companies are also ranked by their relative strength performance and their percentage ranking among all stocks is calculated to show the relative position against other securities. Investor's Business Daily presents the percentage ranking of stocks and O'Neil recommends only looking for stocks with a percentage rank of 70% or better—stocks that have performed better than 70% of all stocks. For our O'Neil screen we used the percentage rank for 52-week relative strength.

If you wish to make the market leader screen more stringent, O'Neil suggests only considering stocks that have relative strength rankings of 80% or 90% with a chart base pattern.

Screening Criteria for William O'Neil's C-A-N-S-L-I-M Approach
Definitions for screens and terms can be found in the glossary starting on page 191.

Screening Criteria:
- EPS (from continuing operations) growth (latest fiscal quarter over same quarter one year prior) greater than or equal to 20%
- Positive EPS (from continuing operations) for the most recent fiscal quarter *
- EPS (from continuing operations) growth (latest fiscal quarter compared to one year prior) greater than the previous EPS growth compared to its counterpart one year prior
- Positive increase in EPS (from continuing operations) for last 12 months and for each of the last five fiscal years
- 5-year EPS growth rate (from continuing operations) greater than or equal to 25%
- Price within 10% of its 52-week high
- Float (number of shares outstanding less insider shares) less than 20 million shares
- Relative strength rank (52-week) among the top 30%
- Institutional shareholders numbering greater than 3

*Data not shown in table. Also note that the table shows additional data columns that may be of interest to those using this approach.

I = Institutional Sponsorship: A Little Goes a Long Way

O'Neil warns against selecting low-priced stocks with small capitalization and no institutional ownership, because these stocks have poor liquidity and often carry a lower-grade quality rating. Instead, O'Neil feels that a stock needs a few institutional sponsors for it to show above-market performance. Three to 10 institutional owners are suggested as a reasonable minimum number. This number refers to actual institutional owners of the common stock, not institutional analysts tracking and providing earnings estimates on stocks.

We established a screen requiring stocks to have at least three institutional owners.

It is difficult to strike a balance between looking for stocks with room to expand further and stocks that may be over-owned. O'Neil warns that while some institutional sponsorship is required, once everyone has jumped on the stock it may be too late to buy into it.

M = Market Direction: How to Determine It?

The final aspect of the C-A-N-S-L-I-M system looks at the overall market direction. While it does not impact the selection of specific stocks, the trend of the overall market has a

Table 2.
Stocks Passing the C-A-N-S-L-I-M Screening*

Company (Exchange: Ticker)	EPS Grth Last Qtr vs Yr Ago (%)	EPS Grth Prior Qtr vs Yr Ago (%)	Long-Term EPS Grth Est. (%)	Annual EPS Grth Rate (5-Yr) (%)	Float (Mil)	No. of Shares Out-standing (Mil)	52-Wk Rel Strgth Rank (%)	Price as % of 52-Wk High (%)	Inst'l Share-holders (No.)	Percent of Shares Held by Institutions (%)
Amphenol Corporation (N: APH)	41.3	0.0	17.6	29.0	5.4	17.86	80	90	137	30.3
Cunningham Graphics Intl. (M: CGII)	60.0	5.6	25.0	25.2	2.5	5.70	72	90	34	27.7
MYR Group, Inc. (N: MYR)	65.9	56.8	18.0	37.2	1.6	5.98	86	99	41	55.9
Richton International (A: RHT)	85.2	47.6	na	44.8	1.3	3.02	72	91	11	1.3
Techne Corporation (M: TECH)	55.6	33.3	27.5	25.2	10.3	20.18	87	93	170	63.7
TREEV, Inc. (M: TREV)	104.2	74.0	na	42.6	10.6	12.85	77	95	14	1.8

na = not available

Exchange Key: N = New York Stock Exchange
A = American Stock Exchange
M = Nasdaq

*Screening criteria used to produce table results can be found on opposite page.

Statistics are based on figures as of February 25, 2000.
Data Source: AAII's Stock Investor/Market Guide, Inc, and I/B/E/S.

tremendous impact on the performance of your portfolio. O'Neil focuses on technical measures when determining the overall direction of the marketplace. Any good technical program or even a study of the Investor's Business Daily or the Wall Street Journal should provide you with the necessary tools to study market movement.

Conclusion

The C-A-N-S-L-I-M system has great appeal to the active investor looking for growth stocks. While the approach is specific, it also stresses the art of investing when analyzing companies highlighted by the approach and interpreting the direction of the market. Table 2 is a list of stocks passing the screens we used to illustrate how William O'Neil's C-A-N-S-L-I-M approach can be implemented. It is based on data as of February 25, 2000, using AAII's *Stock Investor Professional*. Screening tips for the O'Neil C-A-N-S-L-I-M approach appear on page 172.

Screening Tips: The William O'Neil C-A-N-S-L-I-M Approach

Primary Factors

High Quarterly Earnings Increases

Stocks must show a 20% or more percentage increase between last quarter and the same quarter one year ago. To avoid distorted figures, it is also useful to require positive earnings per share.

Accelerating Quarterly Earnings Growth

Stocks must show a greater percentage increase in earnings between last quarter and the same quarter one year ago compared to the increase from the prior quarter and the same quarter one year prior.

Annual Earnings Increases

To look for consistent growth, specify that earnings per share increase from year to year over the last five years.

High Annual Compound Growth in Earnings

The five-year annual compound growth rate in earnings per share must be 25% or higher to include stocks with meaningful growth.

New Price Highs

Looking for companies with new products or services cannot be translated into a numerical figure for a screen. However, new highs can be screened to guide you in timing your purchase. Require that the price be 90% or higher than the stock's 52-week high price.

Supply of Shares

Specifying a maximum float of 20 million shares keeps the focus on smaller companies with a limited float. O'Neil believes these stocks tend to react more positively on any good news.

Leader Among Stocks

Strong stocks in strong industries can be filtered using a relative strength figure. O'Neil recommends avoiding stocks with a relative strength rank below 70%, so screen for companies whose 52-week relative strength is in the top 30% of companies. If your screening program does not indicate the relative strength percentile rank, it can be found by testing different values for one-year price change until 30% of the companies in your database pass the screen.

Institutional Sponsorship

O'Neil likes prospective stocks with at least three to 10 institutional investors, which helps create demand for the stock and, therefore, liquidity and marketability. A similar screen would be to specify that at least 10% of shares outstanding are owned by institutions.

Investment Characteristics of Stock Screening Strategies

There's more than one way to skin a cat, and more than one way to build a stock portfolio. The previous chapters in this book have presented the investment approaches of many well-known and successful investment professionals, and they showed how a series of primary computer screens could be devised to help capture some of the major elements of each approach.

These approaches run the full spectrum, from those that are value-based to those that focus primarily on growth. Some approaches are geared toward large-company stocks, while others uncover micro-sized firms. Most fall somewhere in the middle. Nonetheless, the investment characteristics of these investment approaches vary widely.

It is important to understand the investment characteristics of any approach you are using. By examining the characteristics of the stocks passing the screens, you can get a better idea of the diversification of your portfolio and how your portfolio may react in various market environments. You also need to make sure that the screens you are using are successful in capturing the kinds of stocks your approach is seeking. Reviewing portfolio characteristics can also reveal practical concerns that may not be obvious when you are developing your approach.

For these reasons, AAII tracks the results of the screens we devised. Every month we perform each primary screen on that month's updated database. Thus, a stock is "sold" (no longer included in the portfolio) if it no longer meets the initial criteria, and new stocks are added if they qualify. The stocks that pass the primary screens are then posted on our Web site.

In terms of overall performance, it is much too early to make any judgment concerning which approach appears to work best—that requires several complete market cycles at a minimum. In addition, stock screening is only a first step in developing a real investment portfolio. These portfolios are merely computer-generated lists, based on our own interpretation of the investment approach--no further fundamental analysis has been performed on the companies. The portfolios are also revised monthly based only on the purchase criteria, a mechanical approach that does not leave room for comparison judgements with existing holdings. With some strategies, this can lead to too-frequent trading, which is expensive in terms of both tax consequences and transaction costs; it also is likely to cause you to sell

Table 1.
Selected Investment Characteristics of Stock Screening Strategies

	Risk			Portfolio Turnover		Portfolio Characteristics (as of 2/25/00)					
	Monthly Gains*		Std.	Avg.	Hold-		Div.	EPS	Mkt	Rel. Strgth vs.	% Held by
Strategy	High (%)	Low (%)	Dev. (%)	Hold'gs (No.)	overs (%)	P/E (X)	Yield (%)	Grth (%)	Cap. ($ mil)	S&P (%)	Inst. (%)
Value											
David Dreman	12.6	−15.4	5.6	21	66	9.6	4.0	15.6	1,330.1	−27.7	51.8
Dogs of the Dow	16.1	−13.1	5.7	10	92	14.6	3.6	9.6	61,467.9	−21.8	61.7
Benjamin Graham—Defensive	15.7	−11.3	6.4	24	85	9.7	3.1	17.3	644.8	−22.6	58.0
Benjamin Graham—Enterprising	23.4	−18.7	6.8	8	73	5.5	3.0	15.6	379.9	−36.2	55.3
O'Shaughnessy—Value	13.9	−14.0	5.9	50	79	14.4	4.4	12.7	17,620.6	−35.9	59.6
Geraldine Weiss Blue Chip	10.1	−10.3	5.2	12	76	12.8	2.3	16.0	1,817.0	18.6	53.0
Growth & Value											
Warren Buffett—EPS Growth	10.7	−20.4	6.7	36	87	20.2	0.5	34.7	17,798.6	1.3	52.6
Warren Buffett—Sustain. Grth.	9.7	−17.5	6.3	21	83	17.9	0.4	32.8	20,918.9	−15.5	55.1
Philip Fisher	23.9	−26.7	9.8	43	70	8.8	0.0	45.4	294.1	−33.0	43.9
Peter Lynch	10.5	−17.4	5.1	25	76	7.9	1.9	26.6	41.6	−15.8	10.4
O'Shaughnessy—Growth	11.6	−17.9	6.3	50	62	35.8	0.2	0.5	1,770.3	139.0	42.8
T. Rowe Price	12.5	−18.0	6.6	21	71	10.0	0.5	30.0	1,820.2	−11.8	48.1
Ralph Wanger	10.3	−18.7	6.4	11	77	13.0	0.6	33.8	232.8	3.9	12.0
Growth											
William O'Neil's CANSLIM	20.5	−23.1	8.7	13	43	31.0	0.1	34.0	584.3	98.0	30.1
Sector/Specialty											
Benjamin Graham—Utility	11.8	−6.6	4.6	20	82	11.1	6.7	4.5	1,687.9	−27.7	40.4
Michael Murphy Technology	43.3	−18.4	12.6	18	77	11.6	0.2	33.1	146.6	9.4	28.7
Indexes											
S&P 500	9.8	−14.5	5.1	na	na	27.6	1.3	13.8	23,080.0	0.0	na
S&P 500/BARRA Value	10.4	−16.1	5.4	na	na	19.0	2.0	7.9	13,467.0	−16.3	na
S&P 500/BARRA Growth	9.3	−13.0	5.3	na	na	44.1	0.7	18.8	57,160.0	24.2	na
S&P MidCap 400	12.1	−18.6	6.3	na	na	20.6	1.1	12.7	2,361.0	−1.9	na
S&P MidCap/BARRA Value	15.3	−16.4	6.0	na	na	13.2	2.3	11.1	1,446.0	−24.2	na
S&P MidCap/BARRA Growth	19.6	−20.8	7.8	na	na	39.6	0.2	13.8	4,448.0	23.7	na
S&P SmallCap 600	13.4	−19.3	6.4	na	na	19.9	0.6	13.0	696.0	−28.1	na
S&P SmallCap/BARRA Value	8.7	−18.0	5.7	na	na	13.0	1.2	10.7	433.0	−26.3	na
S&P SmallCap/BARRA Growth	20.9	−20.5	7.7	na	na	33.7	0.3	14.6	1,226.0	−21.5	na

* The highest and lowest monthly gain or loss; figures are unannualized and do not include dividends or transactions costs.

Source: AAII's Stock Investor Professional. Risk and portfolio turnover statistics are based on data from 9/30/97 through 2/25/00. Portfolio characteristics are based on our 2/25/00 portfolios.

winners too early. However, if you want to examine the numbers, complete performance statistics, including up-to-date total return figures, are available on our Web site at www.aaii.com in the Stock Screen's section.

In terms of investment characteristics, however, the screen-tracking results are revealing. Table 1 presents a summary for all of the approaches. Statistics for several market indexes are presented at the bottom for comparison.

The investment characteristics are divided into three major sections:

Risk: The "monthly gains" column reports the highest and lowest monthly gain or loss as an indication of the volatility that has occurred since we started tracking the portfolios. Also included is the monthly standard deviation over the full period. Standard deviation is a measure of total risk that indicates the degree of variation in the actual returns relative to the average return over the period; the higher the standard deviation, the greater the total risk.

Portfolio Turnover: The "average holdings" column indicates the number of stocks that have been held in the portfolio on average each month since the beginning. The "holdovers" column reports the average holdover percentage from month-to-month; the higher the holdover percentage, the more often companies stay in a portfolio each month.

Portfolio Characteristics: Several statistics are provided based on the most recent screens for all of the approaches, and serve as an indication of the types of stocks held in the portfolios. The current price-earnings ratio (price divided by trailing 12-month earnings per share) provides an indication of the valuation levels emphasized by the approach. Dividend yield (annual dividend divided by price) is an indication of the amount of dividend income generated by the approach, as well as valuation levels emphasized. The annual earnings per share growth rate (last five years) provides a historical earnings growth picture. Market captialization is provided as a gauge of the size of the firms passing each screen. While market cap levels change with market advances and declines, some basic size guidelines are helpful in defining portfolios characteristics. Market cap breakdowns: large cap, greater than $5 billion; mid cap, $1 billion to $5 billion; small cap, $200 million to $1 billion; micro cap, below $200 million. The relative strength index is a momentum indicator that reports whether the selected stocks have prices that are moving up more quickly than the overall market in the recent past. It is calculated against the performance of the S&P 500; stocks with price moves equal to the S&P 500 over the last 52 weeks have a relative strength index of 0, while negative numbers indicate their prices have not moved up as much as the index. Lastly, the percentage of shares held by institutions is an indication of institutional interest as well as liquidity.

The Value Approaches

As a general rule of thumb, approaches that focus primarily on value tend to be less volatile than the pure growth approaches, and they tend to have less portfolio turnover. Typically, they do not invest in smaller firms, preferring to focus on companies that are mid-sized or larger in terms of market capitalization. Historical earnings growth rates are rarely much above the market average, and the prices of the selected stocks do not tend to have momentum relative to the market. Value approaches tend to outperform other approaches during bear markets, but they can fall behind during bull markets, particularly during the strongest portion.

By and large, the approaches here have fulfilled that description. The Dreman screen is a classic value approach. Like most value approaches, its volatility (in the form of a low standard deviation) has been low and for its most recent portfolio, the average price-earnings ratio was among the lowest, the dividend yield was high, and the average size of the firms were in the mid-cap range. On the other hand, it has one of the lowest percentages of holdovers month-to-month, indicating high portfolio turnover relative to the other approaches.

The O'Shaughnessy Value, Weiss, and Dogs of the Dow approaches focus on dividend yields as a measure of value rather than price-earnings ratios, so their price-earnings ratios may seem high for value-based strategies, although the ratios are still below market averages. The Dogs of the Dow and O'Shaughnessy Value screens both have high market capitalization floors (this is implicit rather than explicit in the Dogs of Dow approach, since it is limited to only Dow 30 stocks) that focus the portfolios on large-capitalization stocks. The Weiss screen does not have a market capitalization floor, but it does require a minimum number of shares outstanding and a high level of institutional ownership; the screening criteria has turned up stocks that have averaged closer to the mid-cap range. The Graham Defensive screen has a market capitalization floor, but it is low, ruling out only the smallest companies. Nonetheless, the companies that turned up as a result of the other Graham criteria were smaller on average than any of the other value strategies.

The Graham Enterprising portfolio has a higher volatility than the other value approaches and illustrates some of the pitfalls of stock screening. With a 1.2 maximum acceptable price-to-book-value ratio, the Graham Enterprising screen has effectively been out of the market for the period of the study. The few stocks passing the screen have typically been special situations that do not necessarily capture the spirit of the screen. The most recent portfolio had a price-earnings ratio of 5.5 compared to the S&P 500's 27.6. While a very strict valuation rule may prevent you from buying in overheated markets, it may also leave you with an undiversified group of holdings that have more portfolio volatility than you might have expected.

Interestingly, the Graham Defensive portfolio has a higher price-earnings ratio than the Enterprising portfolio. The defensive portfolio makes an adjustment to the price-earnings multiplier based on current interest rates, which at current levels allowed for an upward adjustment in the acceptable price-earnings ratio.

Growth and Value Approaches

The growth and value portfolios vary considerably, reflecting different emphasis on growth and value.

The Buffett screens first attempt to identify "consumer monopolies"—companies exhibiting high margins, conservative financing, strong and increasing earnings growth, and consistently high return on equity—and then purchase those companies that are priced attractively considering factors such as the normal price-earnings level, historical earnings growth, and the sustainable growth rate. The screens have led to mid- and large-cap portfolios filled with well-known firms, although there are no screens for size. In keeping with the buy-and-hold emphasis of Warren Buffett, the screens have exhibited relatively low turnover as measured by the high monthly retention rates. However, the price-earnings ratios for the two Buffett screens are among the highest for the growth and value portfolios, as are their annual earnings per share growth rates.

The Philip Fisher screen has produced some curious results. The approach attempts to find companies with a competitive advantage that positions them for long-term growth. The screen looks at factors such as above-average profit margins, strong and consistent sales growth, as well as a low forward PEG ratio (price-earnings ratio based on expected earnings divided by expected earnings per share growth).

The Fisher screen has been more volatile than the typical screen or the S&P 500, normally rising higher during bullish periods and falling lower during bearish periods. The most recent screen produced a portfolio with a very low average price-earnings ratio coupled with a high average earnings growth rate. The screen's emphasis on growth, which excluded companies paying dividends, coupled with a focus on reasonably priced growth, tended to turn up smaller-capitalization companies, well below the average for the small-cap index, represented here by the S&P SmallCap 600. It may be more appropriate to judge this approach against a small-cap index, rather than the S&P 500.

The Lynch portfolio sports the lowest average market capitalization, a tiny $41 million. Although there is no screen for market capitalization, the percentage of shares held by institutions serves as a proxy—the Lynch screen does not allow an institutional shareholder percentage above that of the median for all companies, and currently only the small-cap universe has a large group of stocks with low institutional ownership. Despite its small-cap emphasis, the portfolio has had very low volatility--its standard deviation is among the lowest of all the approaches.

The O'Shaughnessy Growth portfolio is also hard to categorize. The approach emphasizes price strength, but it also has a value component in the form of a low price-to-sales ratio screen. It is among the least volatile, with one of the lowest standard deviation of this group. Its portfolio turnover is among the highest, with an average holdover percentage of only 62%. This higher turnover is most likely a result of the relative strength criteria, a momentum screen that seeks stocks whose prices are rising faster than the overall market; the selected stocks had the highest relative strength among all the strategies. The approach also appears to be capturing many turnaround situations where long-term earnings growth is barely existent. More recent earnings growth in the firms (over the most recent 12 months) in the most recent screen is exceptionally high, but not reflected in statistics shown. Although there is no market capitalization limitation, the O'Shaughnessy screen has tended to turn up companies that are in the mid-cap range.

The T. Rowe Price screen is a classic "growth at a reasonable price" approach, screening for above-average growth, below-average price-earnings ratio, above-average margins, high return on assets, and a significant level of insider ownership. Its average price-earnings ratio is relatively low, while its historical average earnings growth is similar to the other growth and value screens. The companies turned up by the screen tend to be in the small-cap to mid-cap range, although there are no market capitalization restrictions.

The Wanger portfolio is also a classic small-cap "growth at a reasonable price" approach, although reaching a bit more for growth—it requires a low price-earnings ratio but one that is adjusted to allow for higher ratios at higher rates of earnings growth. The most recent screen produced a portfolio with a price-earnings ratio roughly below the S&P Small Cap 600, but with a higher long-term earnings growth rate. The Wanger screen does have a market cap restriction, and the stocks therefore are well within the small-cap range. Its volatility has been about average.

Growth Approaches

Growth strategies want to buy growth, period. Their focus is on companies that are rapidly expanding their sales and earnings. Often, these stocks are already on the move, with prices typically moving up faster than the market. The approach tends to be more volatile—prices can move up or down substantially, with small changes in expectations—and it tends to perform better on a relative basis late in the bull market or when the economy is slightly down. For these reasons, it requires close monitoring.

William O'Neil's C-A-N-S-L-I-M approach is the most pure-growth strategy of the group. It has had a high level of volatililty, indicated by a high standard deviation, and it has extremely high portfolio turnover—less than half of all stocks are held over, on average, each month. The screen looks for strong and increasing quarterly earnings growth, strong and stable annual earnings, a limited float (shares available for trading), minimum institutional sponsorship, and strong price strength. As a momentum approach, it is not surprising to see in its most recent portfolio a high average price-earnings ratio, high historical earnings growth rates, and an average firm size that is in the small-cap range.

Sector Strategies

The two sector strategies are at opposite ends of the risk-reward spectrum.

The Graham Utility screen is very similar to the Graham Defensive screen, with only minor financial strength adjustments to accommodate unique industry characteristics. The Graham Utility screen looks for attractively priced stocks using factors such as price-earnings ratio and price-to-book-value ratio, but adjusts the acceptable levels based upon current interest rates, which in the most recent screen produced an average price-earnings ratio that is low, but not as low as the other two Graham screens. The utilities portfolio has a low historical average earnings growth rate, reflecting the maturity of the utility industry. Utilities are interest-rate sensitive, typically rising as rates fall. They also are viewed as a safe harbor during volatile markets. The volatility, as measured by standard deviation, was the lowest of the screening strategies, in great contrast to the Murphy Technology screen, which has had the highest volatility.

The Michael Murphy screen looks for stocks with high sales growth, pretax margins, return on equity, and research & development spending as a percent of sales, coupled with low price-to-growth-flow ratio (price divided by the sum of earnings per share and R&D per share). The screen tries to capture fundamentally sound technology stocks that have been knocked down too far because of a company stumble. The most recent portfolio had a low average price-earnings ratio, which is particularly low considering the lofty values of many technology stocks. The most recent portfolio also held stocks with above-average historical growth rates and a small average market capitalization.

Conclusion

You should keep in mind that the screens here are our own interpretations of the investment approaches advocated by these winning investment strategists. While we have attempted to illustrate a practical set of rules for each approach, the screens are only the first step, generating an initial list of potential investments that merit further research. In addition, the monthly updates do not replicate a buy-and-hold strategy, which is the optimal approach for an individual investor.

A review of the stock portfolios generated by a series of screens, however, does reveal important characteristics about the approach and helps uncover many of the practical problems that you may run into when you are trying to develop your own disciplined approach to investing. Here are some important questions to ask that will help you evaluate any series of screens that seek to capture an investment approach:

- How is the portfolio reacting relative to the current market environment? If it is deviating substantially, what is the cause of that deviation—is it the individual stock picks, or is it overconcentration in an area that is a result of the particular set of screens you have chosen?

- Are the portfolio's characteristics more similar to a value-based or growth-based approach? That may give you a better idea of how the portfolio is likely to behave in the future. Your own approach should match your individual needs, abilities, and risk tolerance.
- What is the proper benchmark to measure the performance of your portfolio? It is important to look at the characteristics of your portfolio (market capitalization, industry concentration, growth vs. value) so that you can properly evaluate the performance of your approach.
- Are the screens actually capturing the kinds of firms you want to invest in based on your chosen investment approach, or are they producing unintentional biases in your portfolio?
- How frequently do your screens cause your portfolio to substantially change? If trading is frequent, you need to consider developing "hold" criteria; selling whenever initial criteria is no longer met may cause you to sell winners too soon.
- Most importantly, remember that screening is just a first step. There are qualitative elements that cannot be captured effectively by the very quantitative screening process. Detailed fundamental analysis of any stock you are considering for purchase is necessary for successful investing.

THE COMMON TRAITS OF SUCCESSFUL INVESTMENT STRATEGIES

The stock market "winners" featured in this book all have very different styles. Yet there are many elements these approaches have in common. A look at these shared traits may give you some useful guidelines when developing your own investment approach. Table 1 presents a summary.

Philosophies & Universe

The philosophies underlying the various approaches vary greatly, but they share one obvious characteristic: They are well-articulated and they define clear objectives. For instance, Benjamin Graham and Geraldine Weiss both strongly emphasize value, but for different reasons. Benjamin Graham believes that investing in companies that are selling below their "intrinsic" value provides a margin of protection on the downside because the risk of the stock dropping further is lower. Geraldine Weiss likes high-quality, dividend-paying companies because of their stability and the extra boost that dividends provide; buying them when they are undervalued provides added return in the form of capital gains once they become overvalued.

The philosophies that place more emphasis on value aim to buy cheap and sell dear, with the notion that investors do not always act rationally and often assess information emotionally, creating price distortions that can be exploited. Most of the value-focused strategies favor the companies of larger firms.

The philosophies that place more emphasis on growth tend to focus on areas of the economy that are in the stage of rapid and expanding growth, with earnings momentum. Most of the growth-focused strategies favor smaller-capitalization stocks.

Very few of the strategies could be regarded as "pure value" or "pure growth." Instead, most use a combination—those that focus on value also seek some growth, while those that focus on growth will not pay any price for it.

Quantitative Criteria

Stock selection criteria, both qualitative and quantitative, stem from the investment philoso-

Table 1.
A Summary of Approaches

Focus	Philosophy	Universe	Quantitative Criteria
Warren Buffett	Invest in "excellent" companies based on their intrinsic value, where value is measured by their ability to generate earnings and dividends over the long term.	No limitation on stock size, but analysis requires that the company has been in existence for a considerable period of time.	**Valuations:** Attractive relative to bonds (EPS for the year ÷ the long-term gov't bond rate). Attractive based on 10-year price projection using estimated earnings growth and sustainable growth models. **Earnings:** Strong and consistent upward trend. **Financial Position:** Conservative financing; little or no debt; strong cash flow. **Performance:** Consistently high ROE, strong operating and profit margins.
David Dreman	Psychological biases can affect investment decisions, but investors can profit from others' over- and under-reactions.	Large and medium-sized companies.	**Valuations:** Low P/Es—(bottom 40%); P/Es below S&P 500. Also high dividend yields. **Earnings:** Higher rate of earnings growth than the S&P 500 recently and projected. **Financial Position:** High current assets/current liabilities; low debt/equity; low payout ratios. **Profitability:** High ROE, high pretax profit margins.
Dogs of the Dow	Annually invest equal amounts in the 10 Dow Jones industrial stocks—high-quality firms with strong financial positions and a long-term history of positive returns—with the highest dividend yields, an indication that they are temporarily out-of-favor and underpriced.	The 30 Dow Jones industrial average stocks.	**Valuations:** Among the 10 Dow Jones industrial stocks with the highest dividend yields.
Philip Fisher	Invest in outstanding companies that over the years can grow in sales and profits more than the market as a whole.	No restrictions.	**Valuations:** Low P/E relative to expected growth. **Financial Position:** Sufficient capital to take care of needs for next several years. **Profitability:** Above average profit margins; strong and consistent sales growth.
Benjamin Graham	Invest in companies whose share prices are below their intrinsic value, which provides a margin of "protection" that can help absorb unfavorable developments.	"Defensive": High-grade dividend-paying stocks. "Enterprising": Unpopular large companies & secondary companies. For both types: Exclude small firms.	**Valuations:** Low P/Es; low P/Books; adjust valuations to interest rates. **Earnings:** Positive and stable earnings for 5 yrs ("enterprising") and 10 yrs ("defensive"). **Dividends:** Dividends for 20 years; "enterprising" investors, some current dividend. **Financial Position:** Current assets 1½ to 2 times current liabilities, LT debt less than 110% current assets.

Table 1. *(cont'd)*
A Summary of Approaches

Focus	Qualitative Criteria	When to Sell
Warren Buffett	• Buy consumer monopolies. • Buy businesses easy to understand and analyze. • Buy quality management.	• Hold for long term. • Sell if company no longer retains features that made it attractive.
David Dreman	To assess earnings growth, make sure to understand a company's main line of business, its components, and which components add the most to earnings.	• Hold for long term. • Sell when P/Es approach overall market's P/E, unless solely due to an earnings decline. • Use a 2-year rule and sell if stock is not moving.
Dogs of the Dow	No qualitative criteria—the purely mechanical nature of the approach forces strict investor discipline.	• At the same time each year, sell all current holdings that are no longer among the 10 Dow stocks with the highest dividend yields; replace them with new additions. • Rebalance other holdings so that each of the 10 stocks represents 10% of the value of the portfolio.
Philip Fisher	Buy firms with: • product or service with strong market potential; • strong marketing; • good R&D efforts; • management depth; • good personnel & investor relations	• Hold until there is a fundamental change, or the company is no longer growing. • Use a three-year rule for judging results if a stock is not moving.
Benjamin Graham	Skeptical of subjective judgments—good management indicated by a good long-term track record.	• Buy and hold for the long term. • Sell if issues rise "excessively" above their intrinsic value and can be replaced by issues much more reasonably priced.

(cont'd on next page)

Table 1. *(cont'd)*
A Summary of Approaches

Focus	Philosophy	Universe	Quantitative Criteria
Peter Lynch	Invest in companies in which there is a well-grounded expectation concerning the firm's growth prospects, and in which stock can be purchased at reasonable price.	All listed stocks—no restrictions.	**Valuations:** Low P/E relative to firm's growth rate (P/E of half level of historical earnings growth), low P/E relative to its historical average. **Dividends:** For dividend investors: low payout ratios and 20 to 30 years of dividend increases. **Earnings:** Year-by-year earnings consistency and growth (but not excessive growth). **Financial Position:** Low levels of debt/equity; be wary of high bank debt; high net cash per share rel. to share price. **Wall St. Coverage:** Low institutional ownership and few analysts cover the stock.
Michael Murphy	Invest in the leading growth area of the U.S. economy—technology—choosing superior stocks when they become cheap relative to other technology stocks.	All major categories of technology	**Valuations:** Low price/growth flow ratios [price divided by (EPS+R&D per share)]. **Research & Development:** R&D spending at least 7% of revenues **Profitability:** ROE, pretax profit margins and sales growth of 15% or more.
William O'Neil (C-A-N-S-L-I-M)	Invest in companies whose stock prices are poised to rise due to favorable fundamental factors within the firm and industry, as well as favorable technical factors.	No restrictions, but stocks of smaller firms are favored.	**Earnings:** High & accelerating quarterly earnings; high & consistent annual earnings growth. **Technical Indicators:** Share price reaching new highs, high relative price strength. Limited number of shares outstanding. **Financial Position:** Low long-term debt/equity. **Wall St. Coverage:** Some, but not excessive, institutional ownership.
James O'Shaughnessy	There is no single strategy that always works best, but any strategy must be disciplined and use rules proven successful (risk-adjusted) over long time periods.	For value-based strategies: Large market-cap companies. For growth-based strategies: All stocks greater than $150 million (adjusted for inflation).	**Value Approach:** Market leaders; above average common shares outstanding; above average sales; higher-than-average cash flows per share; high dividend yields. **Growth Approach:** Market capitalization of $150 million or greater; positive earnings growth for one year; low P/S; high relative price strength.
T. Rowe Price	Invest in companies with long-term earnings growth prospects, and are in the early stages of their life cycle before they have become "glamorized."	No restrictions, but smaller-cap stocks offer greater potential.	**Valuations:** P/E not high relative to historical avg. **Earnings:** Strong earnings grth, & EPS increasing at peak of each succeeding business cycle. **Financial Position:** Increases in capital from retained earnings; availability of add'l financing. **Performance:** Above avg & improving margins.

Table 1. (cont'd)
A Summary of Approaches

Focus	Qualitative Criteria	When to Sell
Peter Lynch	Select from industries and firms with which you are familiar. Other positives: • company is boring; • is a spin-off or in a no-growth industry; • is in a niche; • produces a product bought during good times and bad; • can take advantage of technological advances, but is not a direct producer.	• Hold for the long term. • Sell if the reason you purchased the stock no longer exists.
Michael Murphy	Buy firms that produce a steady stream of new, successful products. Research discussed one year should result in a successful product launch in the following 3 years. At least 50% of revenues should be from products introduced in last 3 years.	• Sell only if there is a better stock to buy • Sell if the stock's price-to-growth-flow ratio is as high as the growth rate. • Sell if fundamentals have changed, or management appears to be failing. • Trim if a stock grows so much it is more than one-third of your portfolio.
William O'Neil (C-A-N-S-L-I-M)	Look for firms with new products or services, or with new managements offering innovation. Also look for firms that are in growing industries, and focus on the top few. The general direction of the market should be positive.	• Monitor stocks quarterly. • Sell worst-performing stocks and let the better performers "run." • Sell if a stock's price drops 8% below the purchase price; take gains when a stock has a 20% gain, unless outlook is particularly favorable.
James O'Shaughnessy	Emphasizes the importance of following a relatively simple, but disciplined and emotion-free approach; skeptical of subjective judgments.	• Do not trade frequently. • Sell stocks that no longer meet the criteria.
T. Rowe Price	Management owns substantial interest and plans intelligently. The company is in a growing industry; little gov't interference & absence of cut-throat competition. Good labor relations; total payroll not large relative to revenues.	• Invest for the long term. • Sell when company no longer fits definition of a growth company. • Trim when stocks reach excessively high relative price-earnings ratios.

(cont'd on next page)

Table 1. *(cont'd)*
A Summary of Approaches

Focus	Philosophy	Universe	Quantitative Criteria
Ralph Wanger	Invest in companies that show evidence of growth potential, financial strength, and fundamental value.	Smaller-capitalization companies that are seasoned; no start-ups or initial public offerings.	**Valuations:** Share price low relative to growth prospects as indicated by earnings, sales or cash flow (depending on the type of company). Also price should be cheap relative to company's asset value; book value is not a useful measure. **Financial Position:** Low debt relative to its industry, adequate working capital, conservative accounting practices. **Wall St. Coverage:** Low institutional ownership.
Geraldine Weiss	Invest in high-quality, dividend-paying companies when they are undervalued.	High-quality stocks: frequent DPS and EPS increases in12 years (5 yrs. for DPS; 7 yrs. for EPS); large no. shares outstanding, large instutional ownership; no div interruptions past 25 years; S&P quality no lower than A–.	**Valuations:** Buy when div. yields are within 10% of their historical highs. Secondary valuations: historically low P/Es and P/Book close to 1.0. **Dividends and Earnings:** Consistent earnings and dividend growth. **Financial Position:** Current assets/current liabilities of at least 2; debt/equity less than 50%. **Dividend Protection:** Be wary of payout ratios approaching 100%.

phy. Quantitative criteria use financial data to sort through and screen for stocks with appealing investment characteristics.

Valuations: Approaches that are concerned with value emphasize companies and industries whose share prices are low relative to share value measures based on factors such as earnings, dividends, and assets. Among these investment professionals, the price-earnings ratio (current price divided by earnings per share for the most recent 12 months) is the most widely used valuation measure, but it is used in a variety of ways: Stocks are sought with low absolute P/Es, low P/Es relative to the market or industry, low P/Es considering interest rates, and low P/Es relative to a firm's historical average.

Among the professionals who also emphasize growth, PEG ratios (P/E divided by EPS growth, with ratios lower than 1.0 indicating value) are used, since they relate P/Es to growth rates, allowing firms that are rapidly growing to have higher price-earnings ratios.

Geraldine Weiss and James O'Shaughnessy's value approaches favor dividend yields as a valuation measure because of problems they see with the use of earnings to measure value. The dividend yield relates dividends per share to share price. Dividend payments, in contrast to earnings, tend to be more predictable and not subject to differing accounting interpretations, and are therefore a more stable measure to relate to share price. Prices, on the other

Table 1. *(cont'd)*
A Summary of Approaches

Focus	Qualitative Criteria	When to Sell
Ralph Wanger	Identify strong social, economic or technological trends that will last five years or longer; select companies that will benefit from them. Firm should have a niche not easily entered by competitors, and a good management team.	• Hold stocks for the long term. • Sell when the reason for purchasing the stock is no longer valid.
Geraldine Weiss	Examine product performance, research and development efforts, and ability to market products or services.	• Sell stocks when they are within 10% of their historically low dividend yield, indicating overvaluation.

hand, go to extremes, causing dividend yields to fluctuate. Of course, a dividend yield approach requires that dividends be paid, which tends to limit the investment universe to larger firms. Weiss does use price-earnings ratios as a secondary measure of value, and in fact many of the approaches use several different valuation measures as a double-check.

Earnings and Dividends: Consistent year-to-year growth is the most common requirement for earnings and dividends among all of the investment professionals. Even the value-focused professionals do not find firms attractive if they are undervalued but have no ability to grow and prosper in the future.

Financial Position: Almost every investment professional requires a strong financial position, which enables a company to work through any period of operating difficulty.

A common requirement is current assets twice current liabilities, and low debt-equity ratios (long-term debt divided by shareholder's equity, which indicates how much of the company has been financed by debt rather than equity).

Several approaches also require sufficient capital to cover current operating needs. And not surprisingly, approaches that are concerned with dividends require low payout ratios (dividends per share divided by earnings per share, indicating the amount of earnings that is paid out in the form of dividends).

Profitability: Another common feature among the investment professionals concerns corporate profitability measures—how well the company is using its assets to generate revenues and earnings.

High returns on equity are required under several approaches. Return on equity (net income after all expenses and taxes divided by stockholder's equity) is an indication of how well the firm used reinvested earnings to generate additional earnings.

High profit margins and consistent sales growth are also required by a number of the professionals. Profit margin is net income divided by revenue, and measures the ability of a firm to generate earnings from revenue. Comparing profit margin to that of an industry average provides an indication of the competitive advantage a firm has against its peers. Favorable profit margins and increasing sales are an indication that a firm has found some kind of market niche or monopoly that it can exploit, a common theme among the growth-focused professionals.

Technical Indicators: Technical indicators are not popular among the value-focused approaches, but are used by two of the growth-focused approaches (James O'Shaughnessy's growth approach and William O'Neil). The technical indicators used are those that focus on price momentum, particularly relative strength. Relative strength measures the price performance of a stock relative to the price performance of the overall market; high relative strength indicates that the price is moving up more quickly than the market as a whole.

Wall Street Coverage: Among the investment professionals, there are two camps concerning Wall Street coverage—those that favor institutional ownership for liquidity (Geraldine Weiss) and those that favor little institutional ownership and low analyst coverage for stocks because they are more likely to be undiscovered, and therefore possibly underpriced (Peter Lynch and Ralph Wanger). William O'Neil has a foot in both camps—he favors some institutional ownership for liquidity purposes, but prefers companies with a smaller number of shares outstanding in order to put demand pressure on the share price.

Qualitative Criteria

Pure numbers don't reveal everything about a firm, and most of the investment professionals also rely on subjective judgments—qualitative criteria. (The exceptions—Benjamin Graham, James O'Shaughnessy and the purely mechanical Dogs of the Dow approach).

A basic understanding of the individual company—its main product or service and market potential, its marketing efforts and ability to expand the business—is a common theme. For that reason, several of the investment professionals prefer to focus on companies and industries that are easier to understand.

Finding companies that operate in market niches, with little or no competition, is also mentioned by many of the investment professionals, both growth- and value-oriented.

Many of the growth-focused professionals tend to use some top-down analyses—identifying themes or economic sectors that are likely to expand in the future, and selecting firms that would likely benefit from these expansions.

When to Sell

The common trait among the investment professionals concerning when to sell is that a stock should be sold if it no longer meets the selection criteria, whether that is because the stock did what was expected, because there has been a fundamental change in outlook for the stock, or because of a misjudgment originally.

Almost all of the investment professionals recommend holding for the long term, and several suggest a two- to three-year holding period rule for stocks that don't appear to be going anywhere but that have not had any fundamental changes.

Common Elements

Here's a summary of the common elements, which you can use to help develop your own stock-picking strategy:

- Make sure you adopt a disciplined investment approach, with a well-articulated philosophy and investment rules that reflect and refine your philosophy.
- Make sure you understand the firm you are investing in—its business and what drives its earnings and revenues, the market in which it is operating, and its prospects.
- Seek stocks with reasonable value: low price-earnings, price-to-sales, and price-to-book-value ratios and/or high yield if you are value-focused; low price-earnings relative to growth if you are growth-focused.
- Seek stocks with consistent growth—that is, consistent growth in earnings, dividend, and sales.
- Invest in firms with strong financial positions: current assets twice current liabilities and low debt-equity ratios.
- Try to find firms that operate in a unique niche, with little competitive pressure.
- Small-capitalization stocks offer growth potential and may be overlooked—and undervalued—by Wall Street.
- Value investing is well-suited for reasonably sound, larger-capitalization stocks.
- Growth investing should be tempered with some value investing rules.
- Adopt a long-term outlook, ignore market "predictions," and concentrate on the fundamental condition of a firm rather than short-term temporary or speculative developments.

Glossary

Book Value: Total stockholder's equity minus preferred stock and redeemable preferred stock. Also known as common stock equity. Tangible book value subtracts goodwill and intangible assets from book value.

Capital (Total): Long-term corporate financing. Equals the sum of long-term debt, preferred equity, and equity.

Capital (Working): Net short-term company assets; it is calculated as current assets minus current liabilities.

Cash Flow Per Share: Earnings per share adjusted for non-cash expenses; the sum of income after taxes minus preferred dividends and general partner distributions plus depreciation, depletion, and amortization divided by the average number of common shares outstanding.

Cash Per Share: Total cash and marketable securities divided by the number of shares outstanding.

Continuing Operations: When used in the context of financial statements, figures from continuing operations exclude the financial impact of extraordinary items and gains or losses of discontinued operating segments.

Current Assets: Short-term assets having a life of one year or less, or the normal operating cycle of the company. Made up of cash, marketable securities, accounts receivable, inventory, and other assets such as inventory that are likely to be converted into cash, sold, or exchanged in the normal course of business.

Current Liabilities: Debt or any other obligations coming due within a year. Made up of items such as accounts payable, short-term notes payable, accrued expense payable, etc.

Curr Ratio (%): See Current Ratio.

Current Ratio: Short-term assets divided by short-term liabilities for the same period. An indication of a company's ability to pay its current obligations from current assets.

Debt-to-Equity Ratio: Long-term debt divided by stockholder's equity.

Div Grth Rate (5-Yr); (7-Yr): See Dividend Growth Rate.

Dividend Growth Rate: Compound annual increase or decrease in dividends per share. An indication of past company strength and dividend payment policy.

Dividend Yield: Annual indicated dividend divided per share by price. The percentage rate of return paid in dividends on a security. Provides a relative valuation measure when compared against a firm's historical average dividend yields or other benchmark dividend yields—a high relative dividend yield may indicate an attractively priced security.

Div Yld (%): See Dividend Yield.

Div Yld 1 Yr Ago (%): Dividend yield from one year ago. Computed by dividing the indicated annual dividend one year ago by the price per share one year ago.

Div Yld (5-Yr Avg); (7-Yr Avg) (%): The average dividend yield over the last five years and seven years. Computed by taking the average high and low yield for each of the included years.

Div Yld (7-Yr Avg) High: The average high dividend yield over the last seven years. Computed by taking the average high yield (annual dividend divided by low price during given years) from each of the included years.

Div Yld (7-Yr Avg) Low: The average low dividend yield over the last seven years. Computed by taking the average low yield (annual dividend divided by high price during given years) from each of the included years.

Div Inc-Last 6 Yrs (No. of): Number of years out of the last six years in which the dividend payout was increased. Provides an indication of the company's dividend payment policy, with an emphasis on the frequency of dividend increases.

Earnings Per Share: Net income divided by number of shares outstanding.

Earnings Per Share Growth Rate: Compound annual increase or decrease of total earnings per share. A measure of how successful the company has been in generating the bottom line, net profit.

Earnings Yield: Annual earnings per share divided by price. The inverse of a price-earnings ratio.

Earn Yld (%): See Earnings Yield.

EPS: See Earnings Per Share.

EPS Cont: Earnings per share from continuing operations.

EPS Grth Rate (3 Yr); (5 Yr); (7 Yr) (%): See Earnings Per Share Growth Rate.

EPS Cont Grth (3 Yr); (5 Yr); (7 Yr): Compound annual increase or decrease of earnings per share from continuing operations over the last three years, five years and seven years.

EPS Grth Est: Consensus earnings per share growth estimate—the median (midpoint) of analysts' expected long-term (three to five years) growth rate in earnings per share. An indication of earnings growth expectations for the firm among Wall Street analysts.

EPS Cont Grth (Q5 to Q1); (Q6 to Q2) (%): Growth in earnings per share from continuing operations from one quarter in the prior year to the same quarter of the current year. Q5 to Q1 compares the percent increase or decrease in earnings per share from continuing operations from four fiscal quarters prior (Q5, or five quarters from the present) to the last fiscal quarter (Q1); Q6 to Q2 compares the percent increase or decrease from six fiscal quarters prior to the second most recent fiscal quarter (Q2).

EPS Inc-Last 6 Yrs (No. Of): Number of years out of the last six years that earnings per share have increased.

Equity (Common): The total stockholder's equity minus preferred stock and redeemable preferred stock. This is also known as book value.

Estimated Ret. Based on Hist. EPS Grth (%): The projected annual compound rate of return based on the historical earnings growth model used by Warren Buffet. Earnings are first projected out 10 years based upon the historical seven-year earnings growth rate. The projected earnings per share figure is then multiplied by the company's historical average price-earnings ratio to provide an estimate of price. If dividends are paid, an estimate of the amount of dividends paid over the 10-year period are also added to the year 10 price. Once this future price is estimated, projected rates of return are estimated over the 10-year period based on the current selling price of the stock.

Estimated Ret. Based on Sustain. Grth (%): The expected annual return based upon the sustainable growth rate model used by Warren Buffett. Buffett multiplies the average rate of return on equity by the average retention ratio (1 – average payout ratio) to calculate the sustainable growth rate. Book value per share in year 10 is then estimated by compounding the current book value per share by the sustainable growth rate. Earnings per share is then estimated in year 10 by multiplying the average return on equity by the projected book value per share. To estimate the future price, the estimated earnings per share is multiplied by the average price-earnings ratio. If dividends are paid, they are added to the projected price to compute the total return in year 10 based on current prices.

Exchange: The primary stock exchange where a company's shares are listed. (N) indicates that the shares trade on the New York Stock Exchange, (A) indicates that the shares are traded on the American Stock Exchange, (M) indicates that the shares trade on the Nasdaq National Market, or Nasdaq Smallcap Market, and (O) indicates that the shares trade over the counter on the Nasdaq Bulletin Board.

Float: The number of freely tradable shares in the hands of the public. Computed by subtracting shares held by insiders from total shares outstanding.

Free Cash Flow: Cash from operations less capital expenditures less dividends paid.

Goodwill: The excess value of a firm over its value as an operating business. Intangible assets created when a firm buys another firm and pays a premium above the firm's fair market value.

Gross Prof Mrg (%): See Gross Profit Margin.

Gross Profit Margin: Gross income divided by sales for the same time period. Gross income is computed by subtracting cost of goods sold from sales. When compared against industry norms and over time, it provides an indication of the competitive nature of the industry and the company's competitive position.

Growth Flow: The sum of research and development per share and earnings per share over the last 12 months. Used in the Michael Murphy approach to valuing technology stocks.

Indicated Dividend: The anticipated dividend per share payout over the next year. Computed by taking the most recent quarterly dividend and multiplying by four.

Industry: The narrow general industry classification. Each company is listed in a broad classification (a sector) and a narrower classification (an industry).

Inside Own (%): See Insider Ownership.

Insider Ownership: The percentage of common stock held by all officers and directors as a group, plus beneficial owners who own more than 5% of company's stock as disclosed in the most recent proxy statement.

Inst'l Own (%): Institutional ownership as a percentage of shares outstanding.

Inst'l Own (No.): The number of institutions (pension funds, mutual funds, etc.) that currently report an investment position in the company's stock.

Institutional Ownership: The percentage of common stock held by all reporting institutions (pension funds, mutual funds, etc.) as a group; or the number of reporting institutions holding shares. Provides an indication of the level of Wall Street interest in the stock.

Intangible Asset: A right or non-physical asset that is presumed to represent an advantage to the firm's position in the marketplace. Such assets include copyrights, patents, trademarks, etc.

Long-Term Debt: Liabilities due in a year or more. Includes bonds payable, deferred taxes, minority interests, and future policy benefits.

Long-Term Debt Relative to Equity: Long-term debt as a percentage of total common stock equity. Provides an indication of financial leverage.

Long-Term Debt Relative to Working Capital: Long-term debt as a percentage of working capital (current assets minus current liabilities). Provides an indication of financial leverage.

LT Debt/Equity (%): See Long-Term Debt Relative to Equity

LT Debt/Cap (%): Long-term debt as a percentage of total capital (total capital is the sum of long-term debt, preferred equity, and common equity).

LT Debt/Wk Cap (%): Long-term debt as a percentage of working capital (working capital is current assets minus current liabilities).

Market Capitalization: Price per share times the average number of shares outstanding for a company. A measure of firm size.

Mkt Cap ($ Mil): See Market Capitalization.

Mkt Cap (% Rank): A company's percentile ranking based on market capitalization. The higher the ranking, the larger the firm. A percentile rank of 70% means that a firm is larger than 70% of all stocks.

Net Income: Sales less all expenses and taxes.

Net Profit Margin: Net income divided by sales for the same period. When compared against industry norms and over time, it provides an indication of the competitive nature of the industry and the company's competitive position.

Net Prof Mrg (%): See Net Profit Margin.

Operating Profit: Sales less cost of goods sold, selling general and administrative expenses, depreciation, research and development, interest expense and other unusual operating expenses.

Operating Profit Margin: Operating profit divided by sales for the same period. When compared against industry norms and over time, it provides an indication of the competitive nature of the industry and the company's competitive position.

Payout Ratio: Dividend payments per share divided by the earnings per share for the same time period. Measures quantity of earnings being paid to shareholders in the form of dividends. Provides an indication of the safety of the dividend; the lower the ratio, the more secure the dividend.

Pay Ratio (%): Payout ratio.

Pay Ratio (7-Yr Avg): The average payout ratio over the last seven fiscal years.

P/Bk (X): See Price-to-Book-Value Ratio.

P/Bk (5-Yr Avg) (X): The average price-to-book-value ratio over the last five years. Computed by averaging the high and low price-to-book-value ratios for each of the last five years.

P/Csh Flow: See Price-to-Cash-Flow Ratio.

P/E (X): See Price-Earnings Ratio.

P/E (3-Yr EPS) (X): Price-earnings ratio using the average earnings per share for the last three years as the denominator. Used in the Graham Defensive screen.

P/E (3-Yr Avg; 5-Yr Avg; 7-Yr Avg) (X): Average price-earnings ratio over the last three years, five years and seven years. Computed by averaging the high and low price-earnings ratio each year for the stated number of years.

P/E Rank (%): Percentile ranking of stock compared to all stocks in database ranked by price-earnings ratio. The higher the ranking, the higher the price-earnings ratio. A percentile rank of 40% indicates that 40% of all stocks with price-earnings ratio have lower ratios, while 60% have higher ratios.

PEG Ratio: Price-earnings ratio divided by earnings per share growth rate. A ratio that relates the price of a stock to its earnings growth rate. Stocks with higher growth rates can trade with higher price-earnings ratios than stocks with lower earnings growth. As a rule, a PEG ratio of 1.0 is considered fairly priced, while ratios below 1.0 may point to undervalued stocks and ratios above 1.0 are potentially overvalued.

PEG Ratio (EPS Est 5-Yr): Price-earnings ratio divided by the estimated five-year annual earnings growth rate. Stocks with higher growth rates can trade with higher price-earnings than stocks with lower earnings growth.

PEG ratio (EPS Grth 5-Yr): Price-earnings ratio divided by the annual earnings per share growth over the last five years. Computed by dividing the price-earnings ratio by the historical earnings per share growth rate for the most recent five-year period. Stocks with higher growth rates can trade with higher price-earnings ratios than stocks with lower earnings growth.

PEG ratio (Div Adj; 5-Yr): Price-earnings ratio divided by the sum of the five-year annual earnings growth rate and the dividend yield. Used in the Lynch screen.

P/Grth Flow: See Price-to-Growth-Flow Ratio.

P/Sales (X): See Price-to-Sales Ratio.

Pretax Profit Margin: Income before taxes divided by sales. Income before taxes is computed by subtracting operating and interest expenses from sales. When compared against industry norms and over time, it provides an indication of the competitive nature of the industry and the company's competitive position.

Pretax Prof Mrg (%): See Pretax Profit Margin.

Price: Share price of the stock. In the tables of companies passing our screens, the price is the closing price for the stated date for NYSE, Amex, and Nasdaq-traded companies.

Price-52-wk High and Low ($): The highest and lowest share prices for the most recent 52-week period.

Price as % of 52-Wk High (%): Most recent market price relative to the highest market price over the last 52 weeks. An indication of current price strength. Used in the O'Neil C-A-N-S-L-I-M approach.

Price-Earnings Ratio: The price of a stock divided by its earnings per share. A measure of the market's expectations regarding the firm's earnings growth potential and risk. Firms with very high price-earnings ratios are being valued by the market on the basis of high expected growth potential.

Price-to-Book-Value Ratio: Share price divided by book value (common stockholder's equity) per share. A measure of stock valuation relative to net assets. A measure of stock valuation relative to cash generation.

Price-to-Cash-Flow Ratio: Share price divided by cash flow per share. Cash flow is defined as income after taxes, minus preferred dividends, plus depreciation and amortization.

Price-to-Growth-Flow Ratio: Current price per share divided by the sum of research and development per share and earnings per share over the last 12 months. Used in the Michael Murphy technology screen to value stocks. As a rule of thumb, stocks with ratios between 10 and 14 are considered fairly valued; companies with ratios below 8 are considered attractively priced and companies with ratios above 16 are considered expensive.

Price-to-Sales Ratio: Share price divided by sales per share. A measure of stock valuation relative to sales.

Profit Margin: Net income divided by sales. Measures the bottom-line profitability of a firm. A high margin may indicate that a company has a proprietary edge because it can deliver its products at a substantial profit. A high margin also validates the significance of the sales growth rate.

Quick Ratio: The sum of cash, equivalents and receivables, divided by short-term liabilities. Tries to answer the question: If sales stopped, could this firm meet its current obligations with convertible assets on hand?

R&D ($ Mil): Research and development costs in millions of dollars.

Rel Strg (%): See Relative Strength.

Rel Strg Rank (%): Relative strength expressed as a percentile rank versus all U.S.-traded stocks—the higher the rank, the better the performance relative to other stocks. A percentile rank of 90 indicates that a firm outperformed 90% of all stocks over the reported period.

Relative Strength: The performance of a stock's price relative to the S&P 500 or the overall market. Provides a measure of how well a stock has performed compared to the benchmark over a specified time.

Return on Assets: Net income divided by total assets. Provides a measure of management's efficient use of assets.

Return on Equity: Net income divided by common shareholder's equity (book value). Measures the overall return on stockholder's equity, and the ability of a firm to finance its long-term capital requirements internally.

Return on Invested Capital: Earnings before interest, taxes and dividends divided by totoal capital (common equity plus preferred stock and long-term debt).

ROA (%): See Return on Assets.

ROE (%): See Return on Equity.

ROE (7-Yr Avg) (%): The average return on equity over the last seven fiscal years.

Sales ($ Mil): Net sales in millions of dollars. Net sales is sales less allowance for returns and discounts.

Sales Growth Rate: Compound annual increase or decrease in sales. Provides a confirmation of the quality of the historical earnings per share growth rate.

Sales Grth (3-Yr) (%): Sales growth rate over the last three years.

Sector: The broad general industry classification. Each company is listed in a broad and narrow industry.

Shareholder's Equity: See Stockholder's Equity.

Shares Outstanding: Total number of shares held by shareholders. Provides an indication of the trading liquidity of the firm.

Short-Term Debt: Liabilities that are due in less than one year. It also includes that portion of long-term debt that will become due within the next year.

Shrs Out (No. Of): See Shares Outstanding.

Stockholder's Equity: Total assets less total liabilities. See Equity (Common).

Sustain. Grth Rate (%): See Sustainable Growth Rate.

Sustainable Growth Rate: The return on equity multiplied by one minus the average payout ratio [ROE × (1 − payout ratio)]. Used in the Warren Buffett approach as a measure of a firm's ability to finance its long-term capital requirements internally.

Ticker: Stock ticker symbol.

Total Assets: The sum of current assets; investments; property plant & equipment; and tangible assets.

Total Liabilities to Assets: Short-term and long-term liabilities divided by total assets of the firm. A measure of financial risk that indicates how much of the assets have been financed by liabilities.

Total Liabilities: Current liabilities and long-term debt.

Tot Liab/Assets: See Total Liabilities to Assets.

Working Capital: Net short-term assets; it is calculated as current assets minus current liabilities.

AAII's Stock Analysis Resources

AAII has many stock analysis resources available to the individual investor. They are available by calling AAII at (312) 280-0170, (800) 428-2244 or by E-mail at members@aaii.com.

Publications

AAII Journal: Published 10 times a year. Each issue includes articles on stock analysis or stock screening. Included with AAII membership, which is $49/year.

Computerized Investing: Published six times a year. Includes articles on the use of computers for stock analysis, as well as reviews and information on software and Web-based screening systems. $30/year for AAII members; $40/year for non-members.

Products

Stock Investing Strategies: A 122-page book teaching the basics of fundamental stock analysis. Using a simple worksheet, various valuation methods are described and illustrated that help you judge how fairly the market is pricing a stock of interest. Appendixes show you how to perform stock screening on a computerized database, using each method to develop a short list of stocks to investigate. $16 for members; $20 for non-members.

Stock Investor and Stock Investor Pro: A CD-ROM-based computer program and screenable database that provides hundreds of financial data items on nearly 8,000 stocks. *Stock Investor:* updated four times a year; $99/year for members; $148/year for non-members. *Stock Investor Pro:* updated monthly and contains deeper data; $198/year for members; $247/year for non-members.

Stock Screening Packet: A selection of past *AAII Journal* and *Computerized Investing* articles that explain how to perform stock screening using various strategies. $20.

The Individual Investor's Guide to Computerized Investing: An investment software guide that includes reviews and information on fundamental stock analysis programs, on-line services and Internet sites. $19 for members; $24.95 for non-members.

AAII.COM

AAII's Web site at www.aaii.com is an excellent resource for further information and study on stock analysis. In the Stock Screens area, located under Tools on the left-hand side of the home page, all of the screens discussed in this book are updated monthly; a performance chart enables you to see how each strategy has fared over time.

In addition, AAII members have access to the *AAII Journal* archives, which include stock analysis and screening articles. *Computerized Investing* members have access to the *Computerized Investing* archives, that contain reviews and information on stock analysis and screening programs. A stock screens message board allows members to share opinions on the strategies. Delayed stock quotes and reports from a variety of sources provide company information as well as fundamental data and analysts' opinions. A portfolio tracker is also available to serve as a stock watch utility.

AAII Seminars

AAII offers comprehensive investment seminars in a variety of areas, including stock analysis:

- *Selecting a Stock Investment Approach:* Walks you through strategy choices and teaches you how to implement them—active vs. passive approaches, growth vs. value, and fundamental vs. technical analysis. Includes case studies of some well-known investors, including those discussed in this book.
- *How to Analyze a Stock:* Teaches how to use fundamental tools, such as a company's dividends, earnings and cash flow, to value a stock.

Our seminars are held throughout the year in major cities nationwide. Seminar schedules are published in the *AAII Journal,* and can be found on our Web site at www.aaii.com (events button>National Programs). To learn more about our seminars, call AAII Member Services (800/428-2244 or 312/280-0170).